AND OUR VILLAGE REMAINED SILENT

A MOTHER'S STORY OF INCEST AND DOMESTIC
VIOLENCE AMID COMMUNITY INDIFFERENCE

AND OUR VILLAGE REMAINED SILENT

CATE SCHENK

And Our Village Remained Silent

Copyright © 2024 by Cate Schenk

All rights reserved

No part of this book may be reproduced, stored in a retrieval system, or transmitted by any means, electronic, mechanical, photocopying, recording or otherwise, without written permission from the author. There is one exception. Brief passages may be quoted in articles or reviews.

Library and Archives Canada Cataloguing in Publication

CIP data on file with the National Library and Archives

ISBN (trade paperback) 978-1-0690175-0-5

ISBN (ebook) 978-1-0690175-1-2

Cover art © Delight Rogers, www.delightrogers.com
Author photo © Susan MacDonald, instagram@suemac7373

DEDICATION
To my forever friend Lennie,
for having a voice when it mattered.

All names, characters, places, and incidents in this book are either the product of the author's imagination or used in a fictitious manner. Opinions and views expressed are those of the characters and not necessarily those of the author.

Although this novel is a work of fiction, it occurs during the 1980s and 1990s, a time when awareness of childhood sexual abuse and domestic violence was emerging into social consciousness. The crisis was real then and continues. Even now, "The most common response to child sexual abuse is silence."[1]

Sensitive Content Warning: This book contains scenes of domestic violence and sexual abuse including that of children. This novel may be disturbing, and anyone unduly distressed by the subject matter is urged to seek support. In the event of a crisis, seek out emergency services within your own community immediately. For a listening ear, you may reach out to this author at cateschenk.ca.

---

[1] Canadian Centre for Child Protection. https://protectchildren.ca

WISHING MY HUSBAND DEAD

I have a secret. In my daily devotions, I plead that my husband will meet a premature death. I go so far as to pray for a fatal car crash during one of his weekly out-of-town business trips. For me, his death would serve two purposes: as a widow, my church and family would surely treat me with kindness, and with him gone, I would finally be safe. God has not been in the habit of answering my prayers, but on the off chance He grants this particular request, I always ensure my husband's life insurance policy premiums are paid up.

Obviously, divorce is a less drastic solution than death, but every time I think of leaving, dread stops me at the door. My insular, fundamentalist community prohibits divorce. I do not personally know anyone divorced and have only ever heard gossip about one couple who split up. They were members of our church's sister congregation and it is common knowledge that the wife was excommunicated when, despite consistory intervention, she refused to reconcile. Without knowing details of that woman's story, my family firmly believes she got what she deserved. Their view is that marriage is for life, and there is never any reason to justify divorce. There is no support to help me leave and nowhere to go.

That I fear for my safety is another secret. I have never told anyone that my husband regularly sets up situations wherein he accuses me of violating some concocted rule of his, and then blames me for causing the punishment he has chosen. I have been duly conditioned to know what he means when he says, "*You are forcing my hand.*" Those words signify that the time has come for him to, by whatever means he deems necessary, be awarded custody of our children. My husband also means that it is time for him to orchestrate my murder.

I stay because I dare not leave and pray because I have no way out.

AT THE END OF MY ROPE

Sunday, 21 June 1987, 4 a.m.
I drag myself awake before tonight's nightmare blows away like dandelion fluff. Tiptoeing through the kitchen, I pause at the counter to pick up a stub of pencil and a scrap of paper. With my husband Fred asleep in our bedroom, I lock myself in the bathroom, the only private place in the house when he is home. Sitting on the cool tile floor, I jot down the nightmare and relive the violence and terror of being a sole survivor of a nuclear war.

I do not understand the meaning of tonight's apocalyptic nightmare or my feeling that we will never live in our dream house—the log home we are building in Parry Sound. It is a feeling I have had for a while. I hear myself say, "We are moving this fall, God willing," yet at some deep level, I know we will never live in that house.

Nuclear war is a movement forward in time from my typical Holocaust atrocity-themed dreams. I am not sure this is a welcome development.

My concentration camp nightmares began around the time of our 1972 wedding. They started before I knew two great-uncles survived German extermination camps and before I knew another great-uncle died by a Nazi firing squad for his resistance work. My family seldom spoke of their WWII experiences, which they tried to leave behind in Holland when, in 1953, they boarded a ship to Canada. They arrived in their new country with notions of religious freedom and financial opportunity.

In the nightmare camps, I was starved, beaten, tortured, used for gruesome experiments, had fetuses ripped out, and forced into repulsive sexual acts. Whenever the nightmare captor gave me a choice of my death or my children's, I always volunteered myself. The next day, I would usually feel both disturbed by the savagery in my mind and proud that, even when sleeping, I put my children's lives before my own.

Recently, when I was browsing in the Christian Book Store, I saw some books about understanding dreams. I bought them, hoping for help, because I am at the end of my rope. Already, my quest to understand the awful dreams has given me some vague clues, premonitions that we are an incipient train wreck, heading toward a catastrophe. What I also learned is that the concentration camp nightmares illustrate the state of my relationship with Fred. He is my captor, my Gestapo chief.

Two weeks ago, I had a nightmare in which I discovered Fred in our bed with our daughter Alida. The following Monday, I had to return to EuroMed Importing to finish invoicing for the deliveries going out early the next morning. The promise of a stop at McDonald's was all it took to convince my kids to join me and do their homework in the office. As usual, salesman Fred was out of town.

I had a notion that the bedroom nightmare symbolized Fred's relationship with our children. That was why, in between bites of chicken nuggets and sips of chocolate milkshake, I asked them, "How do you feel about your dad?"

Kevin told me he was quite upset that his daddy was often angry with him.

Kevin added, "Daddy treats Alida nicer."

Alida simply said, "It's different for me." Then she went into the front office to do homework and refused to re-join us. She was quiet for the rest of the evening. At bedtime, when I tucked her in and asked what was bothering her, all she said was, "Nothing."

That Monday evening in the office, I stepped outside my comfort zone to encourage my kids to talk about their father, but we did not badmouth him. Fred is wrong to accuse me of saying unkind things about him to my sisters and friends. Only my sister Dorothy is somewhat aware that my marriage is not good, but even she knows nothing about specifics such as kicked in windows and doors, porn, affairs, or threats of murder. We discuss marriage only in abstracts such as our church's view that marital success is a woman's godly responsibility, or that a difficult marriage is a wife's cross to bear.

Before our talk in the office two weeks ago, I always stuck up for Fred. I told the kids things like, "Your daddy is just tired."

"Your daddy loves you a lot, but he's just in a bad mood."

"Work didn't go good for Daddy today, so why don't you let him rest a while."

I find it embarrassing that I made so many excuses for Fred's poor behaviour, inadvertently setting my kids up to deny their own feelings.

Since talking to my children and taking an honest look at how Fred's relationship with Alida is different, I can see it is not only by giving her birthday flowers and calling her *"Princess"* that Fred favours Alida. At every opportunity, he aligns with Alida against me.

Fred has a very different relationship with Kevin. He uses our son to manipulate me. When he wants me to do something that I do not agree with, including if sex is too infrequent or not kinky enough for his liking, then Fred takes his frustrations out on Kevin by yelling, berating him, and refusing to keep promises. That Fred uses Kevin to manipulate me is a recent insight, but now that I am aware, I wonder what I can do to ensure both of my children are treated decently.

I get up from the bathroom floor to rip up the paper with the nightmare and flush it down the toilet. When I wash my hands, the mirror reflects my brown eyes rolling in exasperation. Should I laugh or cry about the extent to which Fred sees sexual innuendos in the most ordinary of situations? Yesterday evening, after stopping at the grocery store for snacks, Fred arrived home all fired up. He told me the cashier wanted to have sex with him. I asked how he knew that.

"*Well, yeah.*" He said, "*It was pretty obvious. She smiled. Then she said that she hoped to see me again.*"

Fred sulked all evening because I suggested the woman was simply being a friendly cashier and not putting out an invitation to go to bed with him.

I flush the scribbled dream because the danger of Fred finding it would be enormous. There is no safe place for me to keep anything within my own home. Fred searches my purse, and he rummages through my dresser, and then creates scenarios to berate me for what he finds. A few years ago, he became very angry because a pair of sheer black underwear, a gag birthday gift from a girlfriend, was in a different spot in my lingerie drawer. He calls all female undies *panties* and says it with a sexually suggestive drawl that makes my skin crawl. *Panties.*

The children and I were spending a few days at my family's dairy farm on outskirts of the village of Oregon while Fred was supposedly out of town for work. He knew I was away, came home early, checked out my dresser, and who knows what else.

At 10 p.m., Fred left our home and drove an hour to the farm. He spent another hour standing in the driveway, yelling at me for the black *panties* being on top of the others, not on the bottom of the drawer where they had been before. The fact he knew they were in a different spot made it obvious this was not the first time he snooped.

That night Fred was so angry he was shaking. He insisted, *"I know you wore them for a lover. You are leaving me no choice."*

I spent an hour trying to placate him, but it was impossible to calm him or convince him he was wrong. At midnight, I packed our bags and got the kids out of bed to follow him home. My parents thought it was ridiculous to drive so late at night. I told them I wanted to be home with Fred. That was a lie, but they believed me. I did not know how to tell them I had to go home to beg and plead for my life.

He hounded me until dawn. The later it got, the more unreasonable he became. All his irrational arguments begin late at night. I think he plans them to occur when I am exhausted, so that his whispered words will twist me into webs of confusion. He is an expert at making the irrational seem logical, and he is too clever at being illogical for me to defend myself.

Oh, how I wish I had tossed those black undies when I got them. However, if they were gone, he would have noticed and accused me of wearing them for someone else anyway. If I moved them, it would have inadvertently happened when I packed. Before that time, I never folded lingerie. I now take fanatical care to keep everything in my dresser folded as tight as origami.

Fred's twisted logic was that the black *panties* being moved was proof he red-handedly caught me cheating. For this infraction, I needed to be punished.

"Carlyn, it's your own fault. You are forcing my hand. If only you would be honest with me. I should've done this years ago. You just don't learn."

I had heard this threat enough times to know he meant it was time to hire a killer. For most of our marriage, Fred has not let me forget that he has the expertise and connections to have me killed when he chooses. He holds my life in his hands.

After a night of trying to defend myself against his irrationality and anger, when the morning light finally crept into the kitchen, I was relieved to avoid death once again when he said, *"Okay. I won't do it this time. But if you push me again I will get a divorce and custody of the kids. I will win because I will tell the judge about all of your affairs. I'll have an obligation to bring out all the dirt on you because you would be forcing my hand. Don't blame me."*

Fred was convinced he would have a significant advantage in court because his friend was, and still is, a lawyer. Fred is smart enough to gain custody, and mean enough to pursue it out of spite. I have never been inside a courtroom and only know about court procedures from books and TV. That was not the only time Fred spoke about murder, divorce, and custody. Until now, I have been able to dissuade him with begging and promises. Grovelling for the right to live and parent my kids is a problem, and I am at a loss of what to do about it.

I wish I was smarter so that he could not constantly outfox me when we argue. When I was a teen, my dream was to go to university and study psychology. I did not want marriage or motherhood. I dearly loved my little sisters, but was tired of being a mini-mom. Dad had a clear position on education. The highest calling for a female was to be a wife and mother; therefore, educating girls was a waste of time and money. My father's idea was that I should quit school to provide them full-time help in the house. Mom was also utterly opposed to education beyond grade eight in the Christian School. She thought secular high school teachers and university professors led people astray from the truths of the Bible. That I managed to finish grade twelve in spite of persistent parental opposition was a feat in itself.

Although my parents are well-off now, back then, even if they had agreed to further education, they were financially strapped with a house full of kids to feed and a farm to build up. When I finished high school, our family had nine children and the tenth was born the year I married. In Dutch Reformed families, it is common to have many children and for generations to merge. I have brothers and uncles who are the same age.

In my family, the first two children were boys, born in Holland before they immigrated to Canada. Their names are Albert and Bartus, named after our paternal and maternal grandfathers. We call them "the boys," or Bert and Bart. They are dairy farmers just like our father, and the boys married twin sisters.

I was conceived in Holland, immigrated in utero, and was born in Canada in 1953. My parents named me Carlyn. My distinction is that I am the oldest girl, a position that gave me extra responsibility for those who came after. Child number four who arrived eleven months after me, was Dorothy. She is my first sister. By the third girl, Ellie, born in 1956, it became apparent my parents were using an alphabetical pattern to name their offspring, and at their rate of reproduction, it seemed they were aiming to get to z. We are called "the older girls," and all three of us were married by age eighteen.

The sixth child, baby Frances, arrived in 1959 and died of crib death two months later. I hardly remember ethereal Frances, but have the sense it was a time when the house felt grim. It was as if Frances became an angel.

After a break, which was puzzling because my mother opposed contraception, my parents continued their efforts and had the next set of three, "the little girls." In 1962 Grace was born and moved up to the position of daughter number four; the fifth girl born was Helen in 1963, and Irene was sister number six born in 1965. Our parents' rules relaxed, and the three little girls all went to college or university before they married.

Juliana, named after the Dutch queen, was the *nakomertje* (afterthought) conceived when my mother thought she was too old for more children. Juliana, the baby, was the seventh living daughter. My mother delivered Juliana into our estrogen-rich family a few months before my 1972 wedding. Juliana marches to her own drum, and no one ever stops her from doing as she pleases. With only a three-year age difference, my daughter Alida and her aunt Juliana are good friends.

As a teen, I worked hard and yet had no money of my own and no way to earn any to support myself in post-secondary education. Throughout my high school years, my parents required me to give them at least twenty unpaid hours of work a week, and about sixty hours weekly during summer vacations. The hours seem an exaggeration, but I probably worked even more if I add up the time helping with the kids, babysitting, cleaning the house, chores in the barn, and going with my parents to clean offices in London five times a week. I had no transportation to get from the farm to town and no time for other employment to earn money for tuition. University was an unattainable dream.

While we were dating, my boyfriend Fred gave many reasons to veto my dream. He could and would not wait that long to get married. On his income, we could not afford my education. We had to live in Abingville because of his work, and it was a town without a university. I think of all the reasons he gave me, the most honest was that he thought it wrong if I was more educated than him. Fred says he completed high school, but I have seen no proof in the form of a report card, class photo or graduation diploma.

Abingville does have a college, and when I registered for an evening class in accounting about four years ago, Fred's opposition was sneaky. He did things like promise me he would be home to watch the kids and bail at the last minute, or "accidentally" spill coffee on my finished homework. He consistently sabotaged my dream. I worked hard and passed the class with an A. He signed up for the same class the next semester and said he got an A+ without studying. Again, I never saw his report card.

Fred suggested something to me yesterday that really threw me for a loop. He said that once we settle into our new house in Parry Sound, I may move to Toronto during the week to attend university, and he will look after the kids. That he now offers this opportunity feels devious. I am certain this seemingly kind and generous offer means he is up to something, and I think he wants me out of the house. No matter how tempting university might be, I am suspicious of his idea, mainly because I do not trust him with our children.

Sunday, 21 June 1987, 9:30 a.m.
I pour myself a strong cup of coffee and take it to the deck to enjoy the early morning breeze before I prepare for Alida's birthday party. Waking up late for church makes me feel guilty. Our lives, and my guilt about missing church, probably make no sense without understanding how deeply steeped I am in the Christian Reformed Church (CRC) and Dutch immigrant community. White skin gives me the outward appearance of belonging to the dominant culture, but my religious and ethnic heritage cause me to feel different on the inside. I am a minority of mindset, not of colour. It is impossible to explain how I see the world without describing where I came from.

My parents have always run their home with a rigid set of rules to be obeyed without questioning. In my childhood home, every day began with morning prayers. Sitting at the breakfast table, we would pray for blessing on the food, eat, read a Bible passage and say a prayer of thanks. At amen, we left the table to clean up.

On Sunday mornings, my sisters and I cleared the table and then put on our pretty dresses. Mom said dressing up was to show respect for God. No matter how tough times were for my immigrant family, we always had nice Sunday clothes. Being the oldest girl meant I needed to help Mom get the younger ones ready. It got a bit hectic, tying baby shoelaces, combing hair, getting bows on the backs of dresses just right, and everything else that needed to happen to get our large family out the door in time for the 10 a.m. service.

Dad was always the first one ready. He preferred to be in church a half-hour before the service to get a good pew. Mom did not share his love of punctuality. Dad sat in the pickup truck and laid on the horn while Mom fussed in the kitchen. The horn continued as she got herself dressed. Then the baby's diaper needed changing. On Sunday mornings, I was torn. I did not know whether to take sides with my mother or father. Sometimes I did one, sometimes the other.

Finally, with our entire family either squeezed into the cab of the pickup or sitting on straw bales in the box, Dad drove to church in fuming silence. The ritual never varied. Mom's dallying gave her some control over her husband. The timing was safe, just before church when there was not enough time for Dad to escalate into one of his blind rages. His temper always cooled down during the service.

Church services lasted an hour and a half. I always felt a sense of community when we prayed for the specific needs of people in the congregation during what we knew as "the long prayer." Then came the sermon, also long. After the service, someone from our church community usually "came for coffee." Every Sunday, lunch was Gouda cheese sandwiches and a pot of Dutch *groenten soep met gehaktballen* (vegetable soup with meatballs) prepared the day before.

Once the dishes were done, there was time for a quick snooze, and then we would get up to do church all over a second time.

The longest stretch of the week was from 4:30 p.m., when we got home from the afternoon service, until bedtime. It was difficult to find things to occupy us since we could not ride our bikes, go to the beach, or do crafts. My family did not have a TV, so we escaped the sin of watching *Lassie* or *Gunsmoke*. My favourite activity was to read. It was a way to stay out of my father's crosshairs and escape the boredom of those long, lazy Sunday afternoons and evenings.

The only driving allowed on Sundays was to and from church or family visits. We could not buy anything or eat in a restaurant, although our large money-strapped family never ate in restaurants any other day, either. We were careful not to behave as a "Canadian" might. We were Canadian, but not "Canadian." It is less confusing than it seems. The different meanings are easy to detect in people's tone of voice. In reference to a citizen, Canadian sounds kind and soft compared to the hard nasal and derogatory tone applied to heathen "Canadians" who did not attend the CRC.

Most CRC children attended the Christian school. That assured parents their children received proper religious instruction and that they did not associate with worldly, heathen "Canadians." With no sex education, vetted Christian books, and teachers who were members of the CRC, children remained adequately naive about the larger community, which was how parents wanted it. In my fundamentalist Reformed community, we were "in the world but not of the world."

Then and now, the CRC has a firm hierarchy. A minister in any Dutch Reformed church is called the *dominee* (pronounced *dow-mi-nay*). Every church has their own consistory, an administrative group made up of the *dominee*, elders, and deacons. Elders do annual *huis bezoek* (home visitation) and deacons manage the finances. In terms of church protocol, catechism classes start around the time of puberty and continue until the later teens when we do

Public Profession of Faith, which admits us to CRC membership. Among other privileges, membership allows participation in the sacrament of communion, permission to vote for consistory candidates from a list of men's names nominated by the all-male consistory, and to have one's children baptized. For boys and girls, the church has Cadets and Calvinettes, and Young People's Society for older teens. Married couples go to Couple's Club, women to Ladies Society, and men to the Men's Society. There are also various Bible studies on weekday mornings or Sunday evenings.

When I was little, we breathed religion from morning to night. My last chore before bedtime was to get on my knees to ask forgiveness for the sins of the day. All that praying should have made me an expert, but it had the opposite effect. I ended up believing I was too bad to say prayers properly and that I was simply a bad girl. Every night, after my mother turned off the lights and went back downstairs, I would lie awake for hours chanting, "Wash me, and I shall be whiter than snow. Wash me. Wash me."[2] God was silent, which I understood to mean that I was too bad, too dirty. All my prayers and attempts to follow the rules were never sufficient to assure me that I was worthy.

Although immersion in the CRC culture has continued unabated throughout our marriage, there was an added layer of complexity when the church officials repeatedly became snarled up with our family. Fred and his parents have been notorious for dragging the ministers and consistory into their business problems with other members of our congregation. Their complaints always garner attention because it is felt that animosity between two members is a blight upon the church. Fred knows how to activate a response from

---

[2] My chanting was based on the hymn, "Whiter Than Snow," composed by James Nicholson in 1872. The hymn was based on Psalm 51:7: "Purge me with hyssop, and I shall be clean; Wash me, and I shall be whiter than snow."

the church, and as Mrs Fred, I am dragged along. It is impossible to be an accepted member of the Smit family and remain neutral.

Fred and his parents' CRC problems have generally related to one of the family businesses and some CRC person who purportedly wronged them. The list of people who have offended Fred and his parents is extensive. I cannot follow it all or know exactly what the truth is. The most controversial issue to date happened when one of Fred's companies had unpaid loans at a bank where another church member was the bank manager. The bank took action to recover their funds. Fred claimed that he got the inside scoop from the bank's accountant that the bank had acted illegally. Fred complained to the church, and I do not know how many times we had ministers, elders, and others over to deal with it. Unfortunately, or perhaps inevitably, it is still not resolved to Fred or his parents' satisfaction.

Initially, I believed Fred's story that the bank had done something illegal. Later, when I collected a pair of Fred's jeans from the bedroom floor where he always left his dirty clothes, and I emptied out his pockets to do laundry, I saw mail from the bank's accountant. It was a stern letter in which the accountant denied ever saying the bank's actions were illegal, and he threatened to file a defamation action against Fred if he did not cease and desist. The letter disappeared, and later I believed Fred had been dishonest all along because he stopped talking about the accountant. All the same, Fred continued to want the CRC to censure the bank manager, preferably by excommunication from the church.

John, a kind and caring man from our church, started visiting us when he was an elder, and he tried to resolve one or another of the family gripes. He still drops by every month or two, and I like him. Sometimes, I want to tell him about things such as the accountant's letter, my suspicions that the family's problems are their own doing, and the pressure Fred exerts on me to stay away from the CRC. To date, I have said nothing. If I did, Fred would cause trouble for John, and I would feel like it was my fault. I know how much trouble Fred can make for people, so I kept his secrets.

Even with opposition from Fred, I have taught Sunday school, young girls in Calvinettes, and am currently a co-advisor of the Young People's Society. Our children attend the Christian School, Cadets, Calvinettes, and they will soon start catechism class. The children and I always say bedtime prayers. I do not know if Fred does.

Fred is quick to ridicule and belittle me if I go to church services. Whether I attend or not creates a lot of stress. I cannot resolve discrepancies in the lessons I have learned. The two teachings most troublesome to me are that church attendance is required for salvation, and that a wife's Christian duty is to submit to her husband's authority. My husband is clear he does not want me to go to church until they excommunicate the bank employee. If I want to do the right thing, do I attend church or not? Either way, someone judges me as being wrong.

Sunday, 21 June 1987, afternoon and evening

It is noon when Dorothy, her husband, and my two young nieces arrive at our house for Alida's birthday party. Since our mother always checks that we have gone to church, Dorothy and I make up a sermon topic with a corresponding Bible passage. A consistent story about our imaginary attendance will keep our mother off our backs.

Our non-traditional Sunday lunch is great. The barbecued T-bone steaks are perfect, and we have baked potatoes, several salads, green beans, corn, dinner rolls, and a good Beaujolais wine. Dessert is an ice cream cake I made yesterday with twelve birthday candles, freshly brewed Douwe Egberts coffee and Amaretto liqueur.

Fred and I have a tiff over whether the children may have wine. He berates me for being too prudish. Then he rants about how kids in Europe drink which, he says, is the reason European alcoholism rates are lower. I find that doubtful. While he can rationalize anything, I do not understand why he insists our kids need to drink. This is not Europe, and supplying children with alcohol is illegal. Despite my protests, Fred pours Alida, Kevin, and my seven-year-old niece Nakita each a glass of wine. During the meal, I catch Alida sliding her glass toward her dad. I glare at him and he smirks while he refills it.

After lunch, our kids go outside to play. It takes no convincing to get the two men to park themselves in the living room. Dorothy and I simply omit the charade of asking for help, not that they would. Fred only ever does dishes at my parents' home to maintain my mother's delusion that he is a catch of a husband. The men confine themselves behind the chatter of Sunday afternoon TV sports, one nodding off on the couch and the other sprawled out on the love seat. Both are holding a beer and are oblivious to their families.

Dorothy and I are thankful for the opportunity to chat without interruption. As Dorothy puts a washed plate into the drying tray, she resumes our ongoing theoretical conversation about marriage.

"I was listening to the Christian Radio Station and a man, I think he was a Christian psychologist, said that even if a couple fights a lot, it is always better for children if parents stay together."

I take the clean plate out of the rack and idly wipe it. "I am not sure I believe that is true. Of course, divorce is hard on kids." Edging a bit closer to my sister, I whisper, "But what if the children are being hurt?"

"What do you mean, being hurt?" Dorothy asks.

The kids interrupt and we give them a tray of drinks and snacks. In hope of stealing a few extra minutes alone, we fill the wading pool, put the kids in bathing suits, and send them outside again with Alida supervising.

With the splashing and laughter of our children as background music, my sister and I keep one eye toward the patio door and one ear tuned to the living room. As long as the kids and men stay put, we will be able to keep talking. I take a deep breath and decide to confide in my sister.

"Well, I had a really embarrassing nightmare and I think it means Fred is hurting our kids. In it, in the dream, I come home to a quiet house. I search for Fred and the kids. There are noises in the bedroom, so I open the door to see what is going on. Fred has Alida pinned down on the bed doing nasty things to her. I send Alida out of the bedroom. Then I yell at Fred and…."

My voice trails off when Dorothy drops a plate into the porcelain sink where it shatters, and her face goes white. She says, "We're all praying that isn't happening."

A quick peek into the living room assures me that the men have not budged.

"What? Why? Who are we?"

"Well, you know, all of us in the Ketel family are praying Fred isn't doing that kind of thing to Alida."

That rattles me. "Why are you all praying that?"

The only reasons Dorothy offers are that Fred favours Alida, gives her flowers on her birthday, and he calls her "*Princess.*"

Other than that, my sister shuts down. I know those reasons are not enough to warrant such specific prayers, and I tell her so.

By the time we finish the dishes, she admits, "There is more, but I promised not to talk about it to you."

While the two husbands nap, we take our four kids for a walk to Centennial Park. On the surface, we appear as two sisters who are playing with their children on a sunny Sunday afternoon. In reality, every time the kids are out of earshot, I try to poke holes through my sister's barricade of silence.

"Who did you promise not to talk to me?"

"What is going on?"

I try to guilt her into telling me. "You aren't being fair."

Then I bully, "You owe it to me."

Nothing breaks her silence, so I resort to religious badgering. "As a Christian, should you not tell the truth?"

It is almost time for dinner when I give up. We head back home.

While I prepare a charcuterie platter for our Sunday evening meal, Dorothy goes to bathe her youngest daughter. About ten minutes later she asks me for help in the bathroom.

Dorothy locks the bathroom door behind me and I notice her red eyes. She sniffles, and then whispers, "Grace, Helen, and Irene all said Fred did things to them when they were teenagers." She is referring to our three little sisters who are now young adult women.

It occurs to me that the wife is always the last to know.

Our visitors stay until well after dark. Feeling detached and outside of myself, I watch us play euchre. As my partner, Dorothy covers up my distraction while Fred talks non-stop about the business, the log house, our upcoming move, and how he believes he was wronged by the Christian Reformed Church. He is unaware of my preoccupation. For once, his egocentric jabbering is a blessing. The men win five out of five rounds. I pretend that losing the game matters.

Sunday, 21 June 1987, 11 p.m.

Fred naps on the couch after Dorothy and her family leave. He will not work on the Sabbath, so he sleeps until midnight. Then he gets up to go to the office to finish preparations for EuroMed Importing's trade show that will be starting at 9 a.m.

When I hear Fred's car drive away, I shake off my numbness to phone Helen. I have to hear the truth from her. With the one-hour time difference, I am thankful she is home and still awake. I keep idle chitchat to a minimum. Never mind trivia. I need to know what happened.

"Helen, Dorothy was here today. She told me Fred tried some things with you. Is that true?"

She sighs and pauses. Then I hear a timid, "Yes, it's true."

A nuclear bomb explodes in the pit of my stomach. I had hoped it was all a big mistake.

Then I become desperate for details to give Helen's "yes" substance. "When? And what did he do?"

"It was in 1977 when Fred opened the store in Windsor. He asked our parents if he could hire me for a week, and they were fine with it. We had separate but adjoining motel rooms, but he kept coming into my room. It started with him giving me a back rub."

She goes on to describe convincing details. I also recall back rubs when we began dating, and how his hands roamed downward, pushing against my boundaries. Helen's description of the incident started out the same way, although what Fred did next took on a disgusting twist.

"I'm so sorry. I'm sorry Helen." I am unsure if I am apologizing because Fred is my husband, making what he did somehow my fault, or if I feel badly for her, or both. Probably both.

Helen goes on to tell me, "Grace said Fred did things to her the summer she was a counsellor at that camp in Orillia. Irene also said he hurt her when you were in the hospital after having the car accident. When was that, in 1980?"

"It was 1980. Helen, what about Juliana. Did Fred do anything to her?"

"No. Irene, Grace, and I had a pact to protect Juliana. I guess you didn't notice that we never allowed her to visit your place without one of us coming along. Also, Juliana promised us she would never be alone with Fred. We protected her."

As to why they withheld all this from me, Helen explains that three years ago Grace had been to see a Christian counsellor. To have support in telling our parents what Fred had done, Grace had asked them to attend one appointment with her. It was during this session when they learned what Fred had done to Grace and our sisters. According to Helen, the counsellor told them not to talk to me, but advised them to have a discussion with Fred.

"So, who talked to Fred?" I ask.

"I don't think anyone has."

"Helen, why didn't you tell me?"

"I've thought about it so many times, Carlyn, but I was scared. That time in the motel, Fred told me not to say anything to you because you would be mad at me. He said you already knew, and that you would accuse me of lying. He assured me that you would take his side. Also, I was ashamed to tell you."

"Helen, what he said doesn't make sense. I am not taking his side, and I don't understand how you could stomach living with us the two years you went to college in Abingville."

"Fred pretty much ignored me when I lived with you guys. You two seemed to be getting along quite well, and I didn't want to cause problems."

In spite of the Christian counsellor's advice not to tell me, I am still puzzled by how they could all remain silent.

"Haven't you been worried about my children?"

"Oh, yes," said Helen. "We all worry, and that's why we pray for God to protect Alida."

Monday, 22 June 1987, 12:45 a.m.
After speaking to Helen, it is too late to contact Grace or Irene. I

will call them tomorrow. I sink like a weighted shell onto the side of the bed. Stupefied. Hollow. Staring. I am in a state of shock with no sense of time. Gradually, the detachment subsides and my mindsettles back into my body.

I pan through my memories for clues that I should have known. I assumed that Juliana's less frequent visits were because there is a vast difference between ages twelve and fifteen. It turns out that was not it at all.

It was in 1977, when Helen was fourteen years old, that Fred opened the Windsor store. I was not happy about the store for both practical and financial reasons. I was struggling at home with an active two-year-old and a colicky new baby. Fred often did not bring home pay cheques, so it was tough enough for me to pay the bills without him risking our finances on a venture that had little hope of success.

Once the premises were rented, Fred spent time in Windsor to prepare for the grand opening. When he needed extra help, I heard him ask our parents if Helen could work for him. They agreed and Fred promised to take good care of her. There was nothing to raise suspicion, and I had no inkling that anything awful had happened.

It baffles me that this occurred to my sister without my knowledge. I now question the closeness I believed we had. Could it have been real if for ten years Helen kept me in the dark that my husband had been in bed with her. I believe that she did not consent, but all the same, it happened and I did not know.

During the two years Helen lived with us, Fred was aloof with her and uncharacteristically decent toward me. He had convinced Helen with his loving husband act, and she said nothing. Her silence gave me two years of respite from the worst of Fred's meanness. Those were the two best years of our marriage, and that I received better treatment at her expense makes me feel terrible.

I picture my family sitting at the table after meals, closing their eyes and folding their hands, while my father prays for God to spare Alida. They deceptively omitted those prayers when I ate at their table. In spite of the counsellor's recommendation, none of them confronted Fred. For the past three years, the entire Ketel family knew what Fred had done, and they never said anything to me. I feel betrayed by their silence. What also bewilders me is that there has been no change in how they treat Fred. Mom has not wavered in her view that Fred is a great fellow.

Fred has always said my family was the one of his dreams. I am sure we were, and now I understand why. A family with unworldly parents and seven simple barefooted farm girls was everything he wanted.

That he harmed my little sisters is too much. I have stayed with Fred despite everything, but this time, he went too far. I am done with him.

The Ketel family is praying for Alida.

Not Alida. Oh, God. Please, not Alida.

If Fred was unable to draw the line at my little sisters, is it possible that he stopped when it came to his own daughter? I hope the sick feeling I have that he molested Alida is wrong.

I scroll through my memories to see if there is something I missed that can either prove or disprove my concern. For every birthday, he buys Alida flowers. Flowers only from him with cards signed, "*With love Princess, from your daddy.*" He does not get anything special for Kevin. I always do, and sign a card, "Love, Daddy and Mommy."

Last week, on Father's Day, we took the children to Rondeau Provincial Park. Fred spent hours on the beach looking through the new binoculars we had given him for his previous birthday. I spent most of the afternoon sitting in a lawn chair, reading a book, and enjoying the sun. I glanced up regularly to check on the kids. When I followed the direction of the binoculars, he had them aimed at bikini-clad girls. Fred said he was watching the boats on the lake. He thinks I am stupid.

Part of our Rondeau tradition has always been to go for an ice-cream cone. Fred stayed on the beach with his binoculars while I took the kids to the store near the front gates of the park. Kevin was feeding peanuts to the chipmunks, leaving Alida and me sitting beside each other on the railroad ties that marked off the parking area. I knew my daughter was upset and asked what was going on.

"Mom, how can I ever attract any guys when you are around?" she snapped at me.

I tried to assure Alida that any fellow who might look at a married woman my age was too old for her anyway. I knew I did not convince her. I could not imagine why my daughter felt competitive with me.

The episode at the beach made me realize that I was right about noticing that Alida was interested in much older boys. Whenever she pointed out a fellow she considered hot, I thought they looked more like young men than her classmates did. In her opinion, boys her age were boring.

I sum up what I now know. Today I learned that my husband molested three of my sisters. Alida is interested in older boys, and she is jealous of me. Fred calls Alida his "*Princess*" and buys her flowers. I had a dream about Fred doing nasty things to Alida. My family is praying for Alida, and she says things are different for her. Those things are certainly something, but not proof her father molested her. Faulting Fred without evidence is cruel and low. An accusation of child sexual abuse would be catastrophic. I cannot imagine anything worse. Once made, that accusation is not erasable with a simple sorry.

If I ask Alida, I am afraid of putting ideas in her head. So, what should I do?

I will not tolerate him forcing himself on my little sisters. Needing to leave him brings me full circle. If it were not against our religion, if I thought any semblance of my, and by extension, my children's reputations could remain intact, if I would not lose custody of the children, and if he would not have me killed, I would leave Fred. Since leaving Fred is not an option, all I can do is....

No. Nope. I have given my best and I am done. I no longer choose my marriage. I will take my chances and leave Fred.

This is the final straw.

Leave him? Yes. And yes, he will be mad.

It dawns on me that, in learning about the harm he inflicted upon my sisters and realizing that my daughter is in danger, the risk of staying has outweighed the threats of leaving.

The business will really complicate leaving Fred. Because he went bankrupt in 1981 and still does not have that discharged, all our assets are in my name. So are the extensive debts. We may be doing well financially, but I am not foolish enough to think much is recoverable in a distress sale. He will fight tooth and nail for his share, and if I walk away from it all, he will find a way to leave me stuck with the debt. I have no illusions about how dirty he will fight or how low he is capable of going.

My head is exploding. Taking aspirin will make me feel sick, and this headache will not resolve until I come up with a plan of how to proceed.

I cannot go to my parents. Dad made that clear years ago. My in-laws always support their golden boy and they will take his side. I have no idea how to get out of this ugly mess and there is no one to ask for help. It is entirely up to me alone to figure a way out.

In the dark quiet of 3 a.m., I hear Fred's car a block away. I can tell his temperament by how he drives. I feel like a dog who is ultra-sensitive to her master: always alert, and always anxious to approach him according to his mood to avoid being kicked. Tonight, he does not rev the engine or slam on the brakes. It is a good sign that means I will be able to stay in bed and pretend to be asleep.

He rummages in the kitchen, and I hear the pop of a beer cap. The TV turns on and the channels switch. Our bedroom is close enough for me to hear him grunt to take off his stinky socks. He will throw them on the floor and leave them for me to pick up. About twenty minutes later, the TV goes off, the beer bottle thumps on the table. Then I hear his footsteps go upstairs to the kids' bedrooms.

Learning what he did to my sisters gives me good reason not to trust him alone with our children. I can only imagine what he is doing upstairs in the bedrooms of our sleeping kids. It is far too quiet in the house.

With faked grogginess, I call out, "Fred, is that you?"

He comes down the stairs, strips, and crawls into our bed. I make some guttural noises, hoping he believes I am just stirring. He snuggles up close behind my back and puts his arm over my waist. It takes all my willpower not to push him away. Instead, I force myself to lie still and wait until his breath deepens. Finally, he snores.

Monday, 22 June 1987, 5 a.m.

I am standing on the hill at Calvary, and Jesus is on the cross. I look around and notice I am the only person there.

I look up at Jesus and with puzzlement ask, "Where is the crowd?"

His kind eyes look into mine and Jesus gently says, "There is no one else. I am here for you." A clear, beautiful Light engulfs me in warmth. For the first time in my life, I feel the comfort of being worthy.

When I become aware of being in bed beside Fred, the clock reads 6 a.m. The pure, calming Light continues to surround me. It is the same Light people describe in near-death experiences. The CRC is sceptical of what they would call supernatural claims. The Pentecostals would say it was God speaking to me in a vision or an epiphany. Atheists would attribute it to an overactive imagination, and psychiatrists would say it was a hallucination. Some might think it was a dream, but I know I was not sleeping. The definition does not matter; it was a gift, and the effect is astonishing.

Total clarity replaces all confusion. I know exactly how to go forward.

The CRC rule around divorce cannot apply to this. It simply cannot. I get out my Bible and a Bible concordance to do a bit of research. Whereas I formerly understood the Bible to say God disapproved of a wife leaving her husband, I now see that God recognises sexual immorality as justification for divorce.[3] The church is wrong about divorce, and I will not allow them to dictate this.

Our parents, Fred's and mine, will adjust and support me, or more than likely they will not. Fred will be angry; he will fight for custody, and he may well decide to act on his longstanding threat to kill me. I have no doubt he is smart enough to get away with it.

As to the remainder of my problems, I have a newfound faith that everything will be resolved. Most of Fred's clashes will relate to the business and assets. He will fight skirmishes and battles for money. I will face the danger and fight the war for my children's safety.

---

[3] King James Bible, Matthew 5:32, Matthew 19:9.

The blinding headache has disappeared and it feels as if I just had a long, peaceful sleep. There is no fuzziness that typically comes from being awake all night. I shower, get ready for work, get the children off to school, and then wake Fred.

At work, I get through the day without arousing anyone's suspicion. I laugh and chat as if today is the same as any other. As soon as the last trade show customer leaves, I rush home. With the kids playing outside and one ear cocked for the sound of Fred's car, I quickly make the phone calls necessary to move forward.

I phone Grace in Kenora and then Irene in Moose Jaw. Both confirm what Helen already told me, and each of them gives me heart-wrenching details that I believe. I care deeply, yet cannot allow what they experienced at the hands of my husband to crumble me. My three "little" sisters are safe, having moved halfway across Canada. Now I need to take action to ensure that Alida is also safe.

The next two phone calls are to Mom and Dorothy about taking my kids for a while. Mom will take Kevin, and Dorothy is happy to have Alida visit. I will drive the kids to Oregon on Wednesday afternoon when the school summer holidays begin. The children usually spend some of their vacation with my family, so my request is natural. It surprises me that Dorothy does not even ask me what is going on.

The next phone call is to a CRC counselling agency in Toronto. I schedule a two-hour appointment on Thursday morning with the same counsellor who helped a relative of mine with some religious and emotional issues after his wife died. That he needed help was a secret Mom told me. The family myth is that we do not have problems. The goal for this appointment is to get guidance as to how I can ask Alida if anything happened without putting ideas in her mind.

The last call is to our lawyer, and he can see me Friday after lunch.

Until 24 hours ago, I lived a flat, black and white existence where I accepted everything at face value. All of a sudden, my past bursts forth in blinding, three-dimensional colour, and I re-examine it for deeper truths that I had not seen before.

Irene was a high school student when I had the car accident and landed in the hospital for a week. Should I have known that Fred mistreated her when she came to help him with the kids and chores? How could I have known? What makes me furious is that Fred should have been running the vacuum cleaner instead of running after my sister. At that time, she was only fifteen years old and Fred was thirty-two. The creep was more than twice her age!

About a year after the car accident, in 1981, Irene suddenly broke up with a boy she had been dating for quite a while. Helen and Mom told me Irene stopped seeing the boy when he tried to kiss her. If that was true, her reaction was extreme. Even in the Christian Reformed community, girls and boys usually do kiss each other after they have dated for some time.

I distinctly remember asking Mom and Helen if they thought someone had sexually abused Irene. I can still see myself at Mom's kitchen table, cutting out fabric to sew Irene a new Sunday outfit, broaching the question if one of our uncles was a possible offender. I named our two funny uncles, and not humorous kind of funny. I never considered that one of her brothers-in-law, least of all my husband, might have molested Irene.

Mom and Helen said they were sure there had been no sexual abuse, but Helen agreed to ask Irene. I was relieved because, by then, Irene had pretty much quit talking to me. The whole thing bothered me enough to ask Helen several times afterward if she had checked it out with Irene. The last time I asked, Helen quickly said Irene had told her nothing happened.

It turns out that when I asked, Helen too had already been abused by Fred four years before that. I have no idea if Mom knew then, but that Helen said nothing in spite of my suspicions is disturbing. At the time, I had thought Helen's answer that nothing happened had been too quick. Now I realize that her answer had not been true.

Then there is Grace. I regret that my sister and I are no longer close. She was only ten years old when Fred and I married. In the early years of our marriage, she frequently visited, although that later changed. The summer between grade eleven and twelve, Grace was a counsellor at Camp Couchiching. The camp was outside of Orillia, and I was aware that Fred frequently visited her there. He said he only made a point to see Grace when he did sales calls at a nearby store in Barrie. I had a vague notion he was seeing the Barrie customer more often than usual and always on Grace's day off, but I had no way to prove it. I once asked Mom if she thought it strange that Fred saw Grace so often, brought her presents, and took her out for dinners. Mom thought I was being petty, and it was kind of Fred to take the time to go and see poor Gracie who was so lonely.

Somewhere around the middle of August of 1982, Fred came home from a weekly sales trip and said that the evening before he had taken Grace out to a fancy restaurant for lobster and a drink. Since Fred had gone bankrupt, our limited finances did not allow dining out. At that time, Fred was bringing home no income whatsoever, so I got a job as a pharmacy assistant at Shoppers Drug Mart. While I worked to pay our household bills and childcare for our young children, and while we ate rice and beans, he was being Mr Big Spender, buying expensive meals and booze.

Fred got nasty when I explained to him why I was bothered about him taking my underage sister on a special outing that almost sounded like a date. He said, *"Now you have really gone too far. You are making a big deal out of nothing. Gracie is your little sister, and you know she's all alone there. I'm in the area anyway, so what's wrong with me stopping by? We both have to eat, you know, Carlyn. I had no idea you were such a pervert. If that is what you think about me, maybe I should just take the kids and leave. I cannot have my kids living with a mother who has such perverted ideas."*

He muzzled me by projecting his perversion onto me and I said no more. My instincts had been spot on, and I should have challenged him further. I now feel guilty that I allowed his threats to silence me.

Grace was looking for work the summer after grade twelve, and Fred offered her a job. She was indecisive and reluctantly took it when nothing else came up. Grace stayed at our house and was terribly moody. I knew something was amiss and asked her a number of times what was wrong. Grace always said, "Nothing." Now, I finally understand why Grace quit the job after a few weeks, even though she needed the money for school. I appreciate she did not want to spend more time with Fred, and good for her to get out of the situation, but I wish she had told me what happened. Grace had already enrolled in a nearby college, but at the last minute, she switched to a school in Kenora. It had seemed strange then. It turns out she probably did it because Kenora was far outside of Fred's sales route.

Tuesday, 23 June 1987

Last night, I touched Fred out of necessity. I put my leg over his hip throughout the night, hoping that any movement from him would alert me. It did not matter because I did not sleep. This morning I feel tainted, and a shower does nothing to help me feel clean. We work together all day and I manage to keep my revulsion from showing.

After dinner, Fred wants to take Alida for a drive to the car dealership to see about buying a new work van. I remind him we neither need nor can afford a new vehicle, but he ignores me and tells Alida she can choose the colour. I put up a fuss and make her stay at home to tidy her room. He is put out and she stomps off in a snit. Keeping Fred from being alone with Alida while we live under one roof is not something I can keep up for long. It is difficult enough during the day, and with the strange hours he keeps, I cannot stay awake all night every night to ensure he is not going into her bedroom.

Because I am afraid of what he might do if I fall asleep before him, I keep busy until after he goes to bed and starts snoring. When I finally stop for the day, the house is spotless, the laundry folded, and the kids' suitcases are packed for family visits. I am ready to take the next step. To keep things as normal as possible without arousing suspicion, I am allowing my children to enjoy their last day before school lets out for summer. We will leave town when the final bell rings. My poor dears do not know what difficulties they will face at their Christian school in September when they have to bear the stigma of their parents' separation. The decision I have made will change our lives forever.

Thursday, 25 June 1987

By the time the sun starts to come up, my white car is already on the 401, east of London, heading toward the 9 a.m. counselling appointment. I am relieved to have had a couple hours of decent sleep before the screaming in my head woke me. Driving two hours to see a counsellor may seem excessive, but I would walk ten thousand miles to get the answers I need.

Travel time does allow a quiet space to think. My parents are not happy with me. Last night, I told them Fred and I are, without a doubt, separating. They said that was the reason they never told me what Fred did. They were afraid I would leave him. It is mind-boggling they still want their grandchildren with Fred after what he did to their daughters. I keep forgetting my parents knew for years, and I only just found out. They really do want me to stay with Fred.

My thoughts alternate between worry about Alida and guilt over putting my younger sisters at risk. I brought Fred into our family, so that must make this all my fault. My mind goes back to our courtship and wedding. I always believed I had no choice but to marry Fred; now I feel incredibly guilty that I had been so weak.

The autumn of 1968, when I was fifteen years old, I received parental permission to date, along with strict instructions regarding conduct. Dates could only be with boys from our church. Dating "Canadians" was forbidden. My sister Ellie, bless her rebellious heart, tried once. The boy who came on his motorcycle to pick her up left in a hurry when our dad threatened to chase him off the property. I did not have her courage, but I sure admired her gumption.

All the adults in our constrained world united in giving us the message that sex outside of marriage was an unforgivable sin. We were to go into marriage pure. Boys wanted sex and girls said no. A wife's gift to her husband was her virginity. If she had premarital sex, even with her husband-to-be, he would lose respect for her. A girl from our church who became pregnant at age fifteen was married off quickly and quietly. All the girls I knew shuddered.

Mom told me, "You are de oldest daughter and de standard bearer for de rest of de girls. You are de example. If you von't have sex before you marry, your sisters von't eider."

Being my sisters' protector was a heavy responsibility that I took seriously. I was determined to be a virgin on my wedding day.

All the young people in our church faced the same dilemma of creatively finding time alone during dates. The solution was to "go parking" down a quiet gravel road or in the back of a cemetery to share a kiss or to "make out." The relationship with my first boyfriend lasted only a few weeks. He was nice enough, but I broke up because I felt pressured to do more than just kiss when he took me parking. The only way I knew to say no was to break up. Unaware of why I no longer wanted to date the boy, my father grounded me for three months. At age fifteen, that was a lifetime.

Dad said the reason was, "You can't go out wit a lot of boys. Dat gives nice boys de idea you are easy, like a street-valker, a whore."

It was so frustrating. I had been eager to explore the world of dating and boys. I was mad at my parents, and in passive-aggressive defiance I began calling them "the Kettles," a play on our last name. The Dutch word *ketel* means kettle. The other kids in my family thought it was funny and followed suit. Now we all refer to our father and mother as the Kettles.

A few weeks into the grounding was when I first saw Fred. He came for an event at the Thursday evening Young People's Society meeting at our church in Oregon. Then he attended weekly. One time he gave me a ride home in his canary yellow Dodge Super Bee with bucket seats, and that was enough for him to start showing up at our house uninvited. Before long, he weaselled his way into the Kettles' good graces. The next thing I knew, they invited Fred for dinner before Young People's on Thursday evenings.

The three-month grounding was not over yet when Fred asked their permission to take me out on dates, and they agreed. They thought he was such a respectful young man. I did not choose to date Fred; the Kettles decided it for me.

Early dates with Fred were okay because he was fun and seemed to have money to burn. He was seven years older and a city man, so he stood out as sophisticated compared to our simple farm family. The age difference originally made me susceptible to his flattery. This charming mature man was who my parents saw and quickly became fond of. When Fred was assured he had my parents firmly in his corner, I started to encounter a dark side of him that I could not defend myself against. He had flipped from being a fun guy to a man who managed to chip away at the little self-confidence I had until I felt shamed for being so simple and stupid.

Fred worked with his father in their Abingville business importing and retailing medical equipment and supplies. He went on month-long European buying trips twice a year. It was soon after meeting Fred that my father began to talk about opening a store. Fred assured my father that he could be the main supplier. Shortly after our wedding, the Kettles opened a store in Strathroy. While my father and brothers farmed, my mother took over running the store, and the older kids still living at home took on more responsibility for the little ones.

When Fred started hanging around my family, he brought my mother flowers and chocolates, things my farmer father could not afford and probably never thought of doing. While I was attending high school classes, Fred frequently dropped by for coffee klatches with Mom. It was bizarre that my boyfriend, who was only fifteen years younger than my mother, spent hours alone with her. At the time, I did not dare make a stink about it, but I sure thought it was weird.

Once, during their visits, my mother took Fred to my bedroom. Her reason, she said, was to show Fred what a slob I was. She thought he should know what he was getting into. Later, Fred made much ado of being in my bedroom and seeing my dirty *panties* on the floor. He made sure everyone heard about it. I was mortified.

Fred had my mother firmly enthralled by the time he started his relentless pushing at me to have sex. Once he had permission to date me, he replaced his cool yellow car with an old man beige car that had a bench seat. I was unimpressed when he said he traded cars because the new one was better for necking and making out. When we "went parking," Fred always tried to go further than I wanted. It quickly became a big issue. If I gave in even a little bit, he would go on and on about how experienced I seemed for a girl who claimed she had previously only kissed a boy. If I did not give in, he claimed that the physical pain of his yearning drove him crazy. The ache in his groin from "blue balls" was unbearable. I teased him, he said, and then left him unfulfilled. It baffled Fred that I thought being called a cocktease was insulting, when he meant it as flattery.

We had been dating for almost a year when Fred made a big deal about disclosing to me that he had sex with his former girlfriend. He claimed to feel remorse and guilt. Upon confessing, he cunningly twisted it so that if I broke up with him, I would be punishing him for his honesty. His confession turned into a trap that held me tight.

After Fred's disclosure, he began to put pressure on me to marry him. I was unable to put him off and was still only sixteen years old when this older man marked his territory with a diamond ring. Although I thought I was too young, no one in my church or family voiced any concerns. Looking back, I realize it was not only that I was too young, but that I was too scared to say no or put up a fuss for what I wanted, or did not want. Fred took advantage of my timidity by constantly tearing at my boundaries until he created a gaping hole and walked right through it. That is how he swept me deeper into this relationship, and by the time I was a grade ten student, I could no longer find a way out. I felt like a rabbit in a snare.

Fred thought we should get married as soon as I graduated from high school. I wanted to work for a while first. Dad insisted I owed them a few years of help for feeding, clothing, and housing me. I disagreed and the argument became my excuse to leave home. I quickly got a factory job and a room in a boarding house in Abingville.

When Fred said he could not wait to get married, I knew what he meant. During dates, he would lapse into extremely long silences. I would coax him to talk, and his reason for shutting down was always that I stymied his efforts to go "all the way." I would apologize and agree to alternate ways of alleviating Fred's suffering. For a while, I kept us from having "real sex," yet still managed to semi-satisfy Fred. The longer we dated, the greater Fred's urgency. We had endless, unresolved arguments about my unwillingness to give him what he insisted he needed. By then, I was scared to break up because the Kettles were enamoured with him, and I did not trust Fred to be quiet about the touching we had already done.

About six months after leaving home, I moved from the boarding place to a ten-by-ten space in a rooming house. It was the first and last time I had a room to call my own. Then he violated that space and me. Fred was visiting one night, and his gloomy quietness became severe. I apologized after a few hours. I just wanted him to leave so I could get some much-needed sleep.

That night, in my tiny room, Fred had a new solution for his frustrations. He knew a special way whereby I could stay a virgin and he would be satisfied. I cannot recall asking him to stop. I do know I said it hurt and that I did not like it. Shame had stopped me from screaming. Being face down made it easy to cry into the pillow so the other tenants in the house did not hear us.

Desperately wanting to break up, I spoke to my favourite aunt for support and advice. I suppose it was hard for both of us. Our family uses vague generalities to describe sex. I was unable to figure out what words to use, and she seemed to not understand that there was anything heavy weighing on my mind. Getting her help had been my last hope.

Fred kept on about getting married, the honeymoon, and the great sex he expected to have. When he got tired of my delays, he suggested soliciting the Kettles' assistance. He was sure they would see reason once he told them how far we had gone. I knew what he forced on me in my rented room was not normal, but I did not know how to talk about such an unpleasant, intimate encounter. I was also aware that, if Fred told my parents we had sex, a wedding would be mandatory sooner rather than later and my wedding dress would be other than virginal white. My only choice, if it was a choice, was to make the best it and proceed with marriage.

It was a great relief when Fred agreed I could continue working until we had children. By then, I had left the factory job for a receptionist position at Abingville General Hospital. I hoped we would wait many years before we began having children, if we ever had any at all. The Kettles, with their plentiful offspring, had required me to take on many childcare responsibilities, and I had had my fill of babies. I did worry about the fights we were already having about sex. Fred was confident all would be fantastic once we were married. I hoped he was right.

We were both horribly wrong.

I remember the night before our wedding so well. Instead of sleeping, I sat staring out of the open bedroom window. My wedding dress, and all the girls' dresses that I had sewn, hung beside me in the large plywood wardrobe my dad had built for his daughters when he moved us into an old farmhouse with no closets. By the faint light of the moon, I could see the outlines of trains, and I could hear the haunting whistles as they approached the next crossing. I wanted to board a train to escape, but had no place to go.

Life ahead was so bleak. The situation reminded me of a high school English story I wrote called "No Way Out." That story, a desperate cry for help that went unheeded by the teacher, was about a girl in a similar situation who ended her relationship by suicide. With less than twelve hours to go to walk down the aisle and no way out, I longed to die, but believed suicide was a sin.

I lacked the courage to tell anyone that I wanted to cancel the wedding. Fred would talk to the Kettles and they would force me into marriage, whether I liked it or not. I told myself to have faith that, in doing God's will to marry the man who had had sex with me, things should work out.

My hopes rose the next morning when there was a flurry of phone calls. There was some mistake about the reading of the banns, which meant the marriage certificate was invalid. At one point, the *dominee* threatened to cancel the wedding. I thought God was intervening on my behalf. My stomach lurched when the mistake was determined to be a miscommunication and the wedding was back on. Under the circumstances, I think my portrayal of a happy bride was a stellar performance.

In the required pre-nuptial counselling session, we had discussed our plans for the service and our future as a couple. Yes, I intended to work until we had children, and yes, we planned to live in the way of the Lord. The *dominee* said he had a concern to address before he agreed to perform the ceremony. He was worried that a job would interfere with my ability to be a good wife.

I asked, "How is it that men can work and be good husbands and wives can't?"

I knew the question was defiant, but I asked because the double standard bugged me. I should not have bothered.

The *dominee* chided, "Carlyn, now you are being silly. You know better. Men have to take care of their families. A woman's job is to be a helpmate."

Our wedding took place on a muggy Southwestern Ontario day in June of 1972. It drizzled off-and-on all morning, but as I walked up the steps of my plain childhood church, the sun reappeared.

Inside the sanctuary, everything looked lovely. The custodian had closed the curtains to keep the glare down. The afternoon sun bleeding through the heavy weave of the gold drapes gave an unexpected, serene glow. Because I could not pick one sister over another to be my attendants, I included them all, except for baby Juliana who was born three months earlier. I had quickly sewn her a frothy bubble gum pink dress, and she looked like a little doll.

Fred's sister Allison was my maid of honour, my sisters Dorothy and Ellie were bridesmaids, and Grace, Helen and Irene were my junior bridesmaids. In their innocent youth, the girls were an array of fresh flowers in pink, lilac, blue, yellow, mint and light green. The smiling daisies and yellow roses we carried complemented the cheerful atmosphere. This shimmering scene of heat and light resembled an Impressionist summer garden.

I lifted my white virginal veil, kissed my father, and dropped it back over a sunny smile. Then my father led me, his eighteen-year-old daughter, to the altar.

Standing there at the front of the church in my white dress, thoughts of the pre-nuptial office visit with the *dominee* were far from my mind. I agreed to honour and obey Fred until death do us part. In the CRC tradition, a sermon followed the vows. The *dominee* began preaching by comparing a marriage to the day's weather, and the need to look for silver linings and positives when times become stormy.

The remainder of the hour-long sermon was, perhaps, punishment for my insolent questioning or for taking lightly the vital and serious wrongdoing of married women working. He jabbered on in front of family and friends that my first and only role was to be Fred's wife. He chastised me for wanting a career. It was a ceremony of "shame-on-Carlyn."

Our wedding guests said the sermon seemed long because of the stifling weather, but it was lovely. The *dominee* did such a good job summing up what marriage is all about. Before my mother took her place in the reception line, she slipped the audio cassette of the sermon into her purse. Mom would play it over and over, as she did with all her favourite sermons. I never listened to it again, nor did I ever watch the 8-mm home movie of the service taken by a family friend.

Fred's father gave him some parting words before we left on our honeymoon. As we drove from the reception hall to the motel, Fred told me that my new father-in-law said I might be okay, but he had preferred that his son marry the teenage girl who worked at his store on weekends.

Whenever I shared hurt feelings, Mom said I was too sensitive. I figured I was being too sensitive about my new father-in-law's comment. I was hopeful that once he really knew me, his opinion might change, and I think it did. I worked hard to gain my in-laws approval, and recently they told me I was as close to them as their own children were. When they said that, I felt I had finally earned a place in the Smit family.

My father had given me parting words, too, words I kept from Fred. With his heavy Dutch accent my dad told me, "Now dat you have made your bed, you vil have to lie in it."

In case I did not understand, he added, "You never have to bodder wit trying to come and live at home again. You are not velcome back. If you and Fred fight, ve don't vant to see you."

With that, my father gave me a smile and a hug and sent me on my way. Their door slammed shut behind me.

The best thing I can say about our honeymoon is that it was a tragedy. There was no dreamy closeness. The downward slope began the first night. In his own way, Fred tried to make the start of our honeymoon romantic. While I had a bath, he put champagne on ice and dimmed the lights. The drinking age had just come down to eighteen and this was my first time having a drink. Alcohol, stress of the wedding, and lack of sleep made for an exhausting combination. When we finished doing it, I wiped the tears, just as I had that night in my rented room and just as I would do so many nights to come. It hurt and I felt scared.

Fred loudly expressed annoyance that I had not made sex good for him. He was also concerned I had no bleeding and decided I must have lost my virginity to someone else. I could not explain to him why there was no blood on the sheets.

Our honeymoon spot, a cottage on Smoke Lake in Algonquin Park, was a beautiful and secluded place to spend a first week of wedded bliss. We had no bliss. Within a day of our arrival, my tanning efforts left me red and sore, and the black fly bites left my neck a swollen mess. The photo album shows me either sleeping or reading, and that was pretty much all I did. I did not want to be touched. Fred fished and read. I felt ashamed of my lack of enthusiasm. I am unaware if Fred felt anything other than anger.

We were not prepared to claim defeat, so we went as scheduled to Toronto, Ottawa, and Kingston. In Toronto, we saw the movie *The Godfather*. Like a premonition, the movie was a fitting part of our honeymoon. When we toured Fort Henry in Kingston, it was raining, and Fred slipped on a rampart. If I had not grabbed him, Fred would have slid under the railing. For a split second, I considered not reaching out. Already, before our honeymoon was over, I wished Fred dead.

I spent our entire marriage shoving angry feelings back into the deep recesses of my mind. I thought it was what a good wife did. Look for silver linings. That was what the minister said and exactly what my mother always did. My mother taught me, "Always look for the best in people and focus on that." That attitude allowed Mom to ignore things she should not have ignored, like Fred's treatment of her daughters. Being docile and accepting of mistreatment has gotten me into this mess, and now, regardless of the consequences, I need to change.

The miles fly by as fast as my thoughts. I snap back to the present when a police car flies past me with its lights flashing and siren blaring. I hope again that this counsellor will prove to be helpful. If he tries telling me separation is sinful and I must submit to my husband, I will disregard him.

He leads me into his office, and I tell him what I know so far about what Fred did to my sisters and the reasons for my suspicion about Alida. My agenda is very clear. I need answers to three questions. One, do I have enough evidence to worry about Alida? He says yes. Two, how do I go about asking her? It takes a fair bit of discussion to find words that are not leading but are also not evasive. We finally come up with a script about which I feel okay. The final thing I need to know is, if Alida answers yes, what then? If what I fear is true, I will need to help her. The main things I come away with are that it would be important to tell her that I believe her and to keep her safe.

Dorothy and the Kettles agreed that if Fred phoned, they would support my story of spending the day shopping. In the unlikely event Fred were to come over, my family promised they would not allow him to take the kids. I was not fully convinced they would follow through, so when I drive past Dorothy's house, it is a relief to see Alida playing outside with her cousins. When I turn into the laneway of the Kettle farm, I see Kevin in the pasture trying to saddle up the ornery pony my father boards for one of the neighbours. I feel like a mother hen making sure her chicks are close and safe.

I phone Fred and blatantly lie about buying a little black dress to make the shopping trip sound legitimate. He will never know the difference. Fred wants me to come home right away since he will head to Parry Sound in the morning to check progress on the log house. He says he misses me. I plead a headache and say I will see him when he gets back. Thank goodness, he is unaware of what Saturday will bring.

To avoid suspicion, I even manage the customary, "I love you."

In catechism class, they taught us that saying "the fear of the Lord" was another way of saying "the love of the Lord." I thought fear and love were the same thing. Now I see they are not and it makes me sad to realize that ever since I met Fred, I actually feared him. Although there were some times I liked him, I cannot recall a time that I ever truly loved my husband.

Friday, 26 June 1987, 5:30 a.m.
Sleep evades me again. When I hear Dad get up and leave the house to milk the cows, I quickly get dressed and borrow a bicycle from the garage to take a long ride. I hope the wind in my face will help clear my mind.

My thoughts keep going back to my relationship with Fred. Once upon a time, when I still lived in a fairy tale, I could see Fred's redeeming qualities. Over the years, they have become less obvious to me, but I still keep living as if the good things exist and as if we are happy. Our happy family image is carefully crafted, with us acting out the charade over and over again.

To the outside world, Fred is oh-so charismatic and my smile is oh-so bright.

What everyone sees is a well-to-do couple with two attractive children, a boy and a girl, a banker's family. We live in a charming Victorian house with a wrap-around porch in an affluent section of town, drive new vehicles, dress well, own a business and frequently entertain. Twice a year, Fred goes on business trips to Europe and I have gone with him several times. We are planning a family vacation to Paris next summer. Our new log house on Georgian Bay in Parry Sound is under construction. We often take weekend trips, and the last time we were in Muskoka, we danced at Deerhurst Resort while the audience clapped and cheered.

Fred's artistic skills are exceptional and his penmanship is impeccable. The signs and advertisements that he creates are always little masterpieces. Fred is knowledgeable about current affairs and politics. He ran for City Council once. His intelligence is as sharp as a blade. When Fred is in a good mood, he is absolutely endearing. If I could trust him to be like that all the time, I might actually like him a bit more and even grow to love him.

I have tried my best to make our marriage better. I wanted to love my husband. A few years ago, I persuaded Fred to come with me for marriage counselling, to a CRC approved counsellor, using the clichéd excuse that it was to improve communication. During the sessions, I dared not talk about Fred's leanings toward porn, hookers, strippers, swinging, threesomes or nudist bars. Fred, on the other hand, was not shy about telling the counsellor that, *"Carlyn had at least two affairs."* I was too frightened of Fred's reaction to explain it was two incidents with one man, and it happened because Fred pestered me until I agreed. I also did not say anything because I worried that I would be harshly judged.

As it was, this Christian counsellor thought I was the root of our marriage problems. He told both of us that, "You, Carlyn, have trouble submitting."

Counselling felt too much like our wedding sermon. I quit, more frustrated and less hopeful than before. Fred went a few more times and smugly told me how well the counsellor had been able to help him cope with my affairs. If that were true, why does Fred keep bringing it up as something for which I need punishment?

Counselling did not improve our marriage and might have made it worse.

In addition to marriage counselling, I tried many other things to improve our relationship. These included not arguing, praying, going to church, not going to church, quitting my job to be the stay-at-home wife Fred said he wanted, acting docile, and isolating myself. When Fred is away, I read the Bible to try to find solutions to our marriage problems.

In the church library, I found literature on strengthening marital relationships. I went as far as using the tactics in an evangelical marriage manual wherein the author outlined how a godly wife was to act sweet and meet every desire of her husband. In a desperate effort to improve our marriage, I tried the recommended tactics until I felt like an unpaid prostitute instead of a wife. I decided I would not demean myself for marginally better treatment. The book went into the garbage along with whatever porn Fred had in the house at the time.

In each of these efforts, trying to be someone I was not eroded my sense of self. I have become a mess of bits and pieces, not stitched together into one cohesive person.

My thoughts go back to our honeymoon and what came later. A dismal first year of marriage began when we came home from our disappointing honeymoon on a Sunday evening to find our first apartment burglarized. The police assumed a transient had broken in looking for food, liquor or cash. Very little was missing, but a sense of security in my own home was stolen. Fred left on his weekly sales trip early the next morning and said he should be home Thursday or maybe Friday.

Quite freaked, to say the least, I sought safety at his parents' home while Fred was away. That lasted one night. Fred's mother was having a rather bad day and things got worse as the evening ground on. My mother in-law threatened to kill either herself or her husband. She was upset because she thought the teenage girl who worked in their store on the weekends was flirting with my father-in-law and that he did not discourage the girl. She was the same girl my father-in-law wanted Fred to marry. That night I stayed, too afraid to venture downstairs and too scared to walk back to our apartment in the dark. My new in-laws fought all night while I listened in terror. I had no idea this happened in their home. I had never seen or heard my in-laws fighting before then.

When Fred phoned on Tuesday evening, he assured me, "*Yeah, my mom does strange things sometimes. She's tried gassing herself with her head in the oven a few times. She throws dishes and knives regularly. Once, my sister found her lying on the railroad tracks. She ignored Mom, so she finally got up and went home. It just gets worse if you give her attention for being crazy.*"

The second night Fred was away, two weeks after our wedding, our apartment seemed relatively less frightening than his parents' home. Besides, I reasoned, my husband had a job that took him out of town weekly so despite the break-in, I had to get over the fear of being alone. That evening, I was in bed before dark. Whenever Fred was away, I continued to keep early bedtimes for the two years that we lived in the apartment. In the winter, I would come home from work and go to bed without dinner because I was afraid to be in the main-floor kitchen after dark. I always slept with the light on.

If weekdays were lonely while Fred was away, the weekends were worse. The days he was on the road doing his sales calls, I would look forward to him coming home, which was usually late Thursday evening. On Fridays, he worked in his father's store from 9 a.m. to 9 p.m. or later, and Saturdays from 9 a.m. to 6 p.m. Every Saturday evening, Fred prepared for his Monday morning departure. I am not sure how hard he actually worked because whenever I dropped by, he was drinking coffee and taking cigarette breaks, but he was always devoted to "De Business."

Sunday was Fred's day of rest and boy, could he rest. If he got up in the morning, he came to church with me, but mostly I went alone. After church, we would visit his parents for coffee and *gebakjes* (Dutch pastries). Fred spent the remainder of every Sunday lazing around, which was very different from our dating days.

It was not that I begrudged Fred time to relax, but I was getting cabin fever from being alone so much. Every Monday morning, he left Abingville to visit storekeepers across Ontario in hopes of peddling the merchandise he had loaded into his vehicle. Every week, without a car, without a husband, and with only one friend in Abingville, I felt lonelier and more isolated.

Occasionally, we went to visit my family on Sundays. Aside from that, during the first year of married life, we went out only three other times. The first time we saw a movie with Tessa, my friend, and her new husband. Fred did not like any other date night ideas I suggested.

For our second outing, my husband took me out for a drink on my nineteenth birthday. It was my first time in a bar. I was shocked when I found out this establishment had strippers. It quickly became evident that Fred had experience in strip clubs. He proudly shared his knowledge of the norms, etiquette and lingo, which included terms such as G-strings, pasties, lap and private dances. Fred gave me a glimpse into a dimension of society my sheltered life had not previously admitted. I was disturbed to learn that my newlywed husband frequented these places and was exceedingly comfortable within this subculture.

Fred also arranged our third outing. It was a weekend in Toronto to visit his cousin Jeannie and her boyfriend. Fred thought the four of us should go to a great new bar on King Street called Mynah Bird. He had been there and claimed it was nice. It sounded innocent, but he fooled me again. I was not suspicious when we saw the owner's live mynah bird in a cage at the entrance and not when we sat at a virtually empty bar listening to a terrible band. Fred was vibrating with eagerness as he led the way to a back room. In the dim light, we saw a room full of naked men with their willies wagging. I felt huge relief when Jeannie's boyfriend said, "It's time to leave." To this day, I am not sure if the place was a male nudist bar, a gay bathhouse or something else.

Friday, 26 June 1987, 10:30 a.m.
I get back to the farmhouse just as my father comes in from the barn and I park the bicycle. I firmly hug myself to shake off the past and get my thoughts back into the here-and-now. Alida stayed overnight and when she finishes breakfast, I suggest we go outside to talk. We wipe the farm dust off one side of the picnic table and take a seat. She tells me her plans for the day, and then we sit peacefully for a few minutes. I visualize pulling the veil of Light around us and silently pray for wisdom as well as courage for both of us.

In my thoughts, I go over the question the counsellor and I scripted yesterday, take a breath, and speak. "Alida, is there anything about your relationship with your dad you want to tell me about?"

"I do, Mom, but promise you won't get mad." That she does have something to say and needs assurance gives me a good idea of what is coming. I brace myself.

"I promise I won't be angry with you. You can tell me anything."

"Dad's been doing things with me he should only be doing with you."

Even with her head down, I can see her peer through her hair to gauge my reaction. I ask what those things are and she tells me. Nothing can prepare a mother for this. There are no words sufficient to describe the violence that lands on my heart. Thinking about my twelve-year-old girl being hurt in abstract terms was one thing. Hearing about her shattered innocence in excruciating detail is quite another. I mentally pull the Light tighter to protect my ravaged emotions from spilling onto my daughter and to envelop her with the strength to continue.

Alida tells me it happens every day when he is home. She has no idea how old she was when it started, but thinks it has been happening for a few years. I cannot imagine how this could have gone on right under my nose. I ask her where I would have been. She says it sometimes happened in the living room when I was in the kitchen doing dishes or in the basement doing laundry. Sometimes he did it in other places, like when he took her for a car ride or when she helped him in the warehouse.

Alida says she never told me because her father said I already knew and that I would be mad if she talked about it. He also told her it was their special secret.

I assure Alida that did not know before this and that I believe her.

She is still worried about me being angry with her. I say, "Oh, my dear Alida, of course not. This is not your fault. I know you love your dad a lot, but that doesn't mean you wanted him to do that!"

As soon as the words are out, I realize that I should have stopped while I was ahead. I have no idea if she truly loves him and Fred may very well have used his smooth-talking skills to convince his daughter that she wanted what he did to her. He rewarded her in many ways, by fighting her causes, giving her flowers and attention, and by choosing her to be his special Princess.

Alida tells me she has been considering running away to Toronto. I realize just how close I was to losing her. If she had run away, I might never have known why. It hurts knowing she felt unable to tell me and that she believed she had to handle it on her own. I feel like a terrible mother because she did not trust me, regardless of her father's brainwashing. The only consolation is that she trusts me enough to tell me now. I am so glad I asked. I promise her it will not happen again and that she is safe from here on out.

Alida is eager to go. I am not sure if it is to get on with her day or to be done with our conversation.

I join the Kettles at the kitchen table for mid-morning coffee. I feel too stunned to notice a cup and a piece of *boterkoek* (butter cake) appear in my hands. It surprises neither of the Kettles when I tell them Fred also did things to Alida. However, they are upset that I still intend to leave Fred.

"Is dere no udder way? Leaving Fred is so wrong, de Bible says so."

Before I leave for home, I do what has always been my weekly chore, and put curlers in my mother's hair. As I finish up, Mom cries, "Oh, why did dis have to happen to us?"

I think it is her way of consoling. She is wrong though. It did not happen to us. It happened to my daughter and to hers.

During the drive to the lawyer appointment, I think about Mom's comment. It is an open invitation to sink into a crippling tangle of, "Oh woe, poor me." I do not want to go there. I need to be strong and self-pity will get me nowhere.

A more appropriate question, I think, is, Why would it not happen in our family?

It is as if a light comes on, and for the first time I can see clearly that jamming unpleasant realities behind a nice-family façade allows an optimal environment for incest and sexual abuse. Behind the façade, women silently submit and have no voice. Funny uncles are allowed to mercilessly tickle their nieces. Families keep secrets. Secrets and silence create unobstructed openings for molesters to prance through unfettered.

The Kettles knew for three years that my husband had molested their daughters and they concealed the truth from me. They were aware their granddaughter was at risk. That is more than one thousand days and nights that they knew enough to pray, while I had no clue, and my husband sexually abused our daughter.

That is why this happened. We provided the environment and Fred took advantage.

Back in Abingville, I see my lawyer. He is also our neighbour. I worked with his wife on a volunteer committee and my responsible Alida has been babysitting their children. I hope those things tip his sympathies in my favour. I tell him I need help. That is funny. Boy, do I need help!

For legal advice on the separation and divorce, he refers me to his partner. After ensuring his confidentiality, I ask him to please listen and take notes. I inform him of what Fred did to the girls and my plans for a confrontation with Fred tomorrow. The lawyer agrees to contact the police and show them his notes if anything bad happens to me. I am not explicit in telling him of my fear that I may meet with a premature death and that what I told him will inform the police of a motive for murder.

When I finish with the lawyer, I stop by at my friend Lena's home to let her know what is going on. I tell her that tomorrow afternoon, when Fred returns home, I will be confronting him. She agrees to drive past my house tomorrow at 6 p.m. If the situation is under control, there will be a plant on the windowsill. If there is no plant, she will phone the police and ask them to check on me.

I return to the office of EuroMed Importing after being absent for a few days. My father-in-law is there. As soon as I walk in, he pounces on me to find out why I saw my lawyer. He asks if I plan to leave Fred. It is eerie. I have no idea what makes him suspect anything other than he might have happened to see my car at the lawyer's office or that maybe my mother called to recruit his assistance in persuading me to stay with Fred.

I think I spend more time with the father than with the son. Every workday he comes to the office. Ever since the children were babies, my father-in-law visits our house, sometimes only once, but typically three or four times a day. He does this regardless of whether Fred is home. I often wonder if Fred has co-opted his father's services to keep an eye on me, but since I am doing nothing wrong, I do not care. We still go to my in-laws for coffee and *gebakjes* every Sunday. Although my father-in-law has confided in me about his marital problems, never once did we discuss the troubles between Fred and me.

Without offering Fred's father any details, I admit to considering a separation. He does not understand why and tries his best to convince me I must stay with Fred for the sake of "De Business." Curiously, he does not plead with me to remain for the sake of the children. I try to appease him by saying we are just arguing and I am sure we will work it out. After a while, he leaves the office. I finish the most urgent work and go home.

At 6:15 p.m., my father-in-law is in my kitchen. I pour him a coffee and watch him finish his cigarette. I steer the conversation everywhere but my marriage. Then the headache ruse comes in handy again. He leaves, but an hour later, he is again sitting at my kitchen table, arguing that I cannot leave Fred. He is obviously quite bothered and so, with my fingers crossed, I promise him I will not leave his son. I lie to get through the night without my father-in-law creating a crisis and because I cannot risk Fred being forewarned.

Once Fred's father leaves for the second time, my thoughts zigzag back down memory lane. Before we married, Fred had wanted sex. Once we were married, I learned that he had not been doing without it all the time he was hounding me for it.

I was a newlywed girl who had become bored to tears by my own company. I had become a pro at every variation of solitaire I knew and craved human connection. I thought the girl who worked in the store on weekends seemed nice, and decided my mother-in-law's shoddy opinion and my father-in-law's preference of her for his son would not stop me from making friends with her. Being terribly shy made it difficult to reach out, so I told Fred about wanting to get in touch with her. I was mustering up the courage to alleviate my aching loneliness and was looking to my husband for support.

Lying in the arms of my husband under the mauve bedspread I had carefully chosen for our first bedroom, Fred told me what had happened between him and the girl I wanted to befriend. I was already wearing his diamond ring when he took her to Burlington to help him at the Home Medical Supply Show. He said they had been in bed together, but *"we never went all the way."* He claimed they had come close until he stopped her. The same thing apparently happened the next year when she went with him again. Having to worry about them never occurred to me. Right then, I decided not to strike up a friendship with this girl.

Before our engagement, when Fred told me he had had sex with his former girlfriend, he assured me there had been no one else.

"It was a one-time thing," he had said then.

With the wedding ring firmly on my hand, I suppose he thought it was okay to tell me more. Before he met me, he had done some sexual exploring with his cousin Jeannie, which carried on until just before our wedding. Again, he said he was the one who stopped things from going too far. He brushed it off as child's play, kissing cousins.

Fred further confided to me, his supposedly precious bride, that while we were dating, he had been with prostitutes in the red-light district of Amsterdam. The first time was before he met me.

"The last time," he said, *"was during my last trip to Holland. It was before we were married, so you don't need to make a big deal about it. What I did had nothing to do with you."*

When I asked why he would do that when we were supposedly in a committed relationship, he said, *"What was I to do? You had not been giving me sex, and I was frustrated, so I paid for what I needed. If you hadn't been so prim, proper, and prudish, I would never have needed to do it."*

I seriously considered divorce but had no one to turn to and no place to go. That my husband had been with prostitutes made me feel defeated. Fred's range of experience had been much broader than I had known about. Stepping into his adult world was like trying to manoeuvre in a house of mirrors. I tried my best to forgive, forget and go forward.

Saturday, 27 June 1987, 6:15 a.m.

After another sleepless night, I get dressed at sunrise and leave the house for another long bike ride. I mean to plan the confrontation I will have with Fred when he gets back home mid-afternoon. Instead, my thoughts go right back to the misery of our marriage.

Later in 1972, I was still working as a hospital receptionist and noticed a co-worker noticing me. After Fred turned our mauve bedroom into his confessional, I assumed my experienced husband had all the answers and could help me with my feelings. I was a nineteen-year-old fool to talk to Fred about it.

Our accounts of this conversation are vastly different. Fred claims what happened was all my idea. What I remember is that Fred told me the 1970s was the era of sexual revolution and people all over were into open marriages, wife swapping, and key parties. He knew how the parties worked and named seemingly respectable couples from church who, according to Fred, were into swapping and sharing. He refused to tell me how he knew because, according to him, *"they swore me to secrecy."*

"Experimentation and exploration are good for a marriage," I recall him saying. *"Variety keeps things interesting."*

My recollection is that over the course of a few months, he kept after me to alter our marriage to be open, and he strongly urged and then begged me to *"go for it."*

It was a blustery Wednesday evening when my friend and I went for a drive. Fred was home early from his weekly sales trip when I walked through the door at 7 p.m., and I told the truth when he asked why I was late. I did not consider lying. Fred did not believe that all we did was talk, and he was upset because *"the deal,"* as he put it, was that *"we do it together."* That was a lie. We never made such a deal.

Fred became very insistent and did not relent until I arranged a visit with my friend and his partner. Within a few hours at their home, time spent in small talk with social drinks, Fred and my friend's wife were madly necking and feeling each other up in one corner of the living room, edging toward the bedroom. I do not recall who suggested it, but my friend and I went to our apartment. In the hour we were alone, I did not feel dirty or scared. It was the first time I had enjoyable sex that felt normal.

The following hour was also a new experience, but less pleasant and quite sobering. Fred, without his keys, smashed our basement window, crawled inside, and came after us with a knife. There was lots of noise, and a small crowd of neighbours came to ogle at the door.

After things had calmed down, and my friend and all the spectators left, Fred turned on me. He was livid because I had fooled around on him. First, he came after me with a chair, and then with his fists and feet until I lay whimpering in a little heap in front of the closet on our bedroom floor. He gave me one extra kick before he crawled into bed and was snoring before I got up off the floor.

A week later, I rallied sufficient courage to tell Fred that if he ever hit me again, I would report him to the police.

"*No,*" he hissed, "*I won't. I have something better in mind. During my travels, I have met lots of people who know how to go about hiring a killer, someone from Montreal. These men kill for very little money and yeah, man, they're really good. They won't leave any traces that will lead back to me. If I ever need to, if you force my hand, then that's the route I'll go. No, I'll never dirty my hands by hitting you again."*

Fred acted upset with me much longer than it took the bruises to heal. He said I was a sleaze whom he could no longer trust. His slightest displeasure would result in threats to report to my parents what their skanky daughter had done. He seemed to have forgotten that what we did was his idea. It was at this point that I recognized my husband was psycho.

I meant it when I pled, "Please don't call them. Please forgive me. I'll never do it again."

Fred continued to chastise me for that incident of unfaithfulness, and for one more. About a year after the time he beat me up, less than two years into our marriage, Fred was going to Europe for a month-long business trip. He hounded me for both of us to have sex with someone else while he was away. Looking back, I was young and stupid. Mostly stupid. Very stupid.

With Fred's blessing, a second opportunity for normal sex, and realizing that I was going to be accused if I did it or not, I contacted my friend. When Fred came home from Europe, he acknowledged having a fling, and he gave me a lot of detail about what they had done. When I told him I saw my friend, he claimed to have tricked me into confessing and refuted his story. I think he only recanted so that I was the culprit. Again.

Fred refers to the two incidents as *"your affairs."* It feels like I have begged for his forgiveness a trillion times. Fred makes my head spin. He endlessly berates and threatens me. I am fed up with being called an untrustworthy slut and saying how sorry I am. Initially, I had been sorry about the infidelity. With Fred's repeated use of my actions as a weapon, my bigger regret became admitting to him what I had done.

I guess that because I gave in to him twice, Fred thought that if he pushed hard enough, I would eventually capitulate with another of his psycho ideas. In between calling me names and berating me, he has asked me too many times to count, *"Oh Carlyn, wouldn't you love to do it again? Just imagine what it would feel like. I want to watch. I want to participate. I will set it up. Please do it for me."*

Six years after what he calls *"your second affair,"* Fred surprised me with another outing. That evening I had been working at Shoppers Drug Mart until 10 p.m. and when I walked into a dark parking lot at the end of the shift someone scared the heck out of me. It was Fred, leaning against the passenger door of my car with a lit cigarette dangling from his mouth. He said he was taking me out for a drink. His date idea made me nervous, but I went along with it because it was just easier that way.

It was obvious Fred was fired up. He made quite a commotion to have me seated with a good view of the hotel's stage, and that was when I saw my friend playing the drums. I had not seen him since our last encounter. The only way Fred could have known he was playing in the band was if he had been in the hotel earlier. Fred denied it, saying he had been working.

That was a bad night, and he carried on until dawn. Fred tried every variation of, *"Would you please have sex with him again, and please, please let me watch if you're too much of a prude to let me join in. You are just self-centred and want all the fun for yourself. You always deny me happiness."*

Even if I had agreed, it is unclear where Fred got the notion that the drummer was interested. Nonetheless, Fred was quite disturbed that I refused see my friend for a threesome.

Despite my continued refusal, Fred keeps badgering me to go to bed with him and another man. Any other man would suit him. He has lewdly suggested every new male acquaintance and almost all nonrelated men we ever knew (friends, bank manager, customers, and his lawyer buddy) as potential sex partners for us. I feel sheepish when I see any of these men.

I found out last year that his fantasies are not sex-specific. A woman who said she was selling advertising kept coming into the office, and somehow, she always knew when I was there. Eventually, I talked to Fred about how uncomfortable I had been when this woman told me I was pretty and she wanted to spend time with me. Naively, I thought it was okay to talk to Fred because she was female. He suggested she wanted to have sex with me.

"Go for it. Why not take a day to pamper yourself and meet her? Have a nice cosy lunch somewhere, a few drinks, and then see what happens. Maybe she'll take you back to her place. Wouldn't you love to have a woman touch you in ways that only a woman knows how to do? Imagine her sucking and licking your breasts, and imagine ... and imagine ... and then later, when you are comfortable together, I can join in."

I was irritated to hear my husband talk like that, not because she was a woman, but because he was again, or still, inconsiderate of my feelings. Fred kept on about her since then. I was glad he was not in the office the last time she came in. I hid in the storage room until she left, and the employees must have thought I was strange. Did Fred set the scenario up with a paid escort? That sounds paranoid, but quite possible given Fred's keen fantasy for a threesome.

When we entertain friends or family, he inevitably makes suggestive remarks. He complains about not getting enough. He belittles me by saying he will not be getting sex because I am on my period, he laughs and calls me frigid, and he offers me aspirin so I cannot use the excuse of a headache to turn him down. He does whatever possible to present himself as sex savvy, with no regard to the shame and humiliation I feel. When the company leaves, I know my choices are to either argue about sex all night or let him have his way with me and be done with it. I usually give in because it is just easier that way.

The whole sex thing made me bonkers for another reason. While we were dating, I never saw any of Fred's pornography. The first I realized he liked nude photos was during our honeymoon when he pulled a new Polaroid camera out of his luggage to take pictures of me in the bath. After this I began wearing pajamas with more coverage and locking the bathroom door for privacy from my husband.

Fred first brought his pornography collection into our apartment weeks after we married. He kept accumulating and had a generous stash by the time our children were babies. When we started using babysitters, I needed Fred to get rid of it all. At that point, it was mostly porn magazines that came into our house after his business trips in Europe. According to him, he bought the porn at sex shops in Amsterdam's red-light district because Dutch laws allowed more explicit material than what was available in Canada.

I asked Fred numerous times to get rid of his magazines. He did not, so I waited until he was out of town and packed it all up into five sturdy boxes. I will never forget the day I got up early to lug the entire stash outside to the curb. As I peeked from behind the curtain, watching to make sure they dumped everything into the truck, the garbage collectors opened and rifled through the boxes. Loud hoots of laughter expressed their delight in finding Fred's extensive collection. Now, more than ten years later, I still hide Wednesday mornings when the garbage truck comes by. Curiously, Fred never mentioned his missing porn.

Fred's magazine mania continued beyond my fateful morning with the garbage truck. Every trip to Europe, he returns with a briefcase full. He now also buys pornography in Canada that I doubt is legal. It comes into our home in brown paper bags stuffed into his briefcase and goes out to the road, one piece at a time, buried deep in garbage, double or triple wrapped in newspaper and plastic bags.

The magazines I most dread are those with nude prospective candidates for "swinging" or group sex. Fred typically waits until late in the evening when the kids are asleep and I have had a few drinks. He slaps his briefcase on the kitchen table and opens it with a flourish. Out come the brown paper bags with his naughty swinger magazines. I know when he begins his magician routine that it is time to raise my defences, tune him out, and repeat the word, "No."

Fred never accepts my refusal to have *"a threesome or a gang bang."* He also never appreciates, or cares, that to me pornography and swinging magazines are offensive. I wish he would listen when I tell him what I like. It does not need to be miserable and complicated. What I learned from my *"affairs"* is that my preference is man, woman and respect. Ordinary.

This past March, Fred spent two weeks alone in Europe. Well, without me, but not alone. He came home with a new batch of porn and an infection. Fred claims he contracted a yeast infection from an English woman he met on the train. I am not sure I believe he had a chance encounter on a train or that he contracted a yeast infection. I worry he might have brought home another sexually transmitted disease and I worry it might be the untreatable new HIV/AIDS.

Now Fred insists that this English woman was his first affair since he met me. That is a delusional and blatant lie, but a lie he seems to have convinced himself is true. He knows he needs a clean bill of health before I will consider being intimate with him again. It is three months later, and he has taken no steps to prove he is safe. I think that because for the first time in our marriage I took a stand and said a firm no to sex, Fred is being vindictive toward me by becoming more nasty toward Kevin. Albeit in different ways, both my children have been mistreated by their father.

Saturday, 27 June 1987, 8:30 a.m.
I head home from the bike ride, thinking I still have lots of time for a shower and to plan the confrontation. When I turn the corner, Fred's Chrysler is already in the driveway. Oh, shit. This is not good.

I lean my bike against the fence and go inside to make us both a cup of coffee. We sit at the dining room table, underneath the deflated balloons and drooping crepe streamers from Alida's recent birthday party. Fred is clearly agitated. What if he already talked to my mother or his father?

"What's wrong, Fred?"

He tells me that yesterday, Friday morning, at 10:30 a.m., something happened that is difficult to describe. He was driving on Highway 69 near Parry Sound when he suddenly felt compelled to stop at the side of the road. He got out of his car and walked through a ditch toward a field. He cannot explain why he did that. All of a sudden, out of nowhere, a very dark shadow surrounded him. It was not a dust cloud, storm, or tornado. There was no wind and the sun was shining above the blackness.

Fred said, "It was black and inhuman. It was evil."

This is surreal. Evil darkness overcame him at precisely the same time I was talking to Alida. I encircled us with Light as he walked into Darkness. It sure feels like a larger drama is unfolding. A clash between good and evil. Spiritual warfare.

Struggling to remain calm, I force myself to progress with the confrontation. "Fred, there is something you need to tell me."

Fred recognizes a shift in me, fidgets, and proceeds to tell me how sorry he is about phoning a 1-900-Sex Talk number the other day and for charging it to my business credit card. I wonder how much cash he has dropped into pay phones to do the same. Fred goes through substantial "unaccounted-for" amounts of money.

A few years ago, I took over the bookkeeping for his father's store, and every year I was unable to reconcile the books for $10,000 or more. I know my father-in-law gave Fred hundreds of dollars in spending money each week, and much more when Fred went to Europe. Fred treated this money like his personal allowance. He did not share any with us and he never provided receipts to account for the money. Fred did the income tax paperwork, and it baffled me how he was able to doctor the books to cover that much, and how he got away with it. In May, Fred's cash supply from his daddy dried up when the store sold. Apparently, he has now started using my credit card.

I catch myself from going off track and refocus.

"This is not about making a phone call, Fred. You are going to tell me what has been going on with Alida."

Fred looks at me as if I am a two-headed monster. He uses his most scornful tone, the one that formerly humiliated me into submission. *"You must be crazy. Nothing is going on. Yeah, I'd never do anything to hurt my Princess."*

I continue to challenge him. "Yes, Fred. There is something going on and you will tell me about it."

"What are you talking about?"

I do not know how I know, I am not an experienced interviewer, but I know I cannot allow him to control this conversation, and I cannot let on what I learned from Alida. I hold my tongue and stare him down.

It takes a good ten minutes of my glowering and his fidgeting before he finally breaks the silence. When he starts talking again, I can almost feel that for the first time in our relationship, the balance of power shifts to me.

"Well, yeah. You know, I've been kind of doing things I shouldn't have."

I ask him to explain, and he says the same things Alida said. Then, I bluff and press on.

"And what else?"

"Well, I kinda, you know, yeah, been rubbing myself against her."

I have no mercy. "What part of you?"

"Yeah. Well, you know."

"No, what?"

With tears rolling down his face, Fred says, *"You know, my, you know what I mean. Yeah, but really, honestly, yeah. I got off but never went too far with her. We never made it."*

His tears do not move me. It had already gone too far.

He makes it sound like she was a participant, which she was not. The filthy animal.

I let Fred know I am aware he was also inappropriate with some of my sisters. He wants to know which sisters and what I know, probably to get his story straight and argue with me over details. I do not indulge him.

"Fred, I don't need to tell you. You know because you were the one who did it."

Finally, I drop the bombshell. "You need to leave."

He argues until I agree to consider it a temporary separation. I know that I will be divorcing him, but if he believes he has a chance to come home, he might just leave the house calmly, and I may be safe for the time being.

Fat chance.

"This is my house, too, you know. Where do you expect me to go?"

"You should have thought about that before you molested the girls."

"I learned my lesson, and I will never do it again. Carlyn, can't we work it out?"

I hold my ground. "It will be easier for you to go, and it would look bad on you if you make your children leave their home. What would people say?"

Appealing to his overblown concern for his self-image is effective. To my amazement, he willingly takes my credit card to spend the night in a motel. Thankfully, we can afford alternate accommodations. I do not know how long I could have persevered if he had nowhere to go.

I put the plant in the window and ignore the phone when it rings, and rings, and rings.

QUATERVOIS

(n.) a crossroads; a critical decision or turning point in one's life.

Sunday, 28 June 1987
The plan to take care of my priorities is complete. After years of wanting out of my marriage, I finally did it. There is no turning back now.

If anyone could see inside the kitchen, they would notice my elbows on the table and my head in my hands. It might look as if I am in prayer, and in a sense, I am. How will I ever find forgiveness for staying with Fred at the expense of my little sisters and my daughter?

At noon, I hear tires screech around the corner and skid into our driveway. It sounds like Mr Hyde is home. My life seems to revolve around the coming and going of his Chrysler. I do not want to see anyone, Fred least of all.

Fred unlocks the back door and by the time he enters the kitchen, he has switched to his Dr Jekyll persona. He hangs his head low and his entire demeanor says he is so, so sorry. Even his voice sounds remorseful.

"Carlyn, my love, please forgive me. I know I've done wrong. Please don't throw me out. Please reconsider for my sake. You know how much I love you guys. Oh Carlyn, I can't make it without you. I talked to Herman last night. He prayed with me and asked God to forgive me."

Fred's sorry voice drops to a whisper. I know he is trying to hold my attention and keep me on the edge of my seat, listening. While that always worked before, now it only makes me angry to have to strain to hear him. I am not in the mood to humour him.

"Fred, you have to speak up. I can't hear you."

His voice gets louder for a few minutes and then it fades again. I am so weary of his games. I sit across from him and tune out his whispers. I see the face of the man I once persuaded myself I loved. The father of my children. The man whom I thought I would grow old with. Despite my mistakes, I have invested so much in trying to make our marriage work. How can I give up? I feel myself wavering.

As Fred speaks, his jaw is tight, and his lips barely move below his big nose. I know how to read the twitches of his face, his moods, and his gestures. I recognize the signs of being conned. The whispering is one indicator, and another is how his words squeeze out as if there is a handful of marbles in his mouth.

He says more words. That is all they are, just words. He rambles on.

"*I love you, Carlyn. God loves me even as I am a terrible sinner. What about our family? The kids need a father. You guys are all I have. It was good to talk to Herman, and he helped me see how I had strayed from the Lord. He says he will do all he can to help me, his school chum. I forgive you and now you need to forgive me. I love you so much Carlyn. God...*" and some more about God. "*You can't send me to the klink. Guys who molest kids get killed in the bucket.*"

This startles me. I have heard those words before. Fred often watches TV crime shows. More than once, he has said that a wrongful conviction could happen to anyone. Shows about sex offenders always prompt Fred's speculations on how long they will stay alive in jail. Fred told me that child molesters are prison scum.

He has prepared me so I would feel sorry for him if, or when, this confrontation came.

It works. While I still believe the girls, I also feel sorry for Fred. I doubt he realizes he just told me I could go to the police. It had not dawned on me that I could report him. I know I will not. His preparation of me for this situation is effective.

My thoughts do not interrupt Fred and his voice drones on.

When I tune back in, I hear him tell me how messed up he became after he was sexually abused by a prominent man in the Dutch community. That supposedly happened when Fred was a teen. He said his mother had also done something terribly inappropriate to him and his baby sister Allison when he was nine years old. Why is he telling me this now? No doubt about it, I would feel for him if it was all true, but I am wary of his so-called honesty. He may very well be accusing his mother to get my sympathy. If I tell Fred that I am sceptical of his stories, we will have a big fight because I believe my sisters and not him. If he is telling the truth, he does have a right to be heard. His claims are messing with my emotions.

I decide to give the impression of taking him at his word. "Well, since you know how much you hated what happened to you, I expect you'll have a good idea of how distressing this is for the girls."

That shakes him up, and quite badly. Fred stops talking about abuse and gasps for breath. His hands rub his chest as he hunches over. He stumbles outside to the deck for some fresh air. I follow him with a cold drink and a damp washcloth. His face is pained and drawn.

"*Oh*," he complains, "*this stress is going to kill me. I think I'm having a heart attack. This is all too much. I can't handle it. Oh, my heart.*"

Fred goes overboard on dramatics. He moans and groans with

too much vigour for a dying man and he talks way too much. He had me going for a few minutes and now it takes everything I have not to bust out laughing. Next, I expect he will clutch his chest, look heavenward and, like Red Foxx on the sitcom *Sanford and Son*, call out, "I'm having the big one, Carlyn. I'm going home."

I play along with his farce and suggest he rest. He goes back inside the house to the couch and quickly starts snoring. I am thankful for a break to get my bearings. It is taxing to keep up with him.

After a few minutes of peace, I realize for the first time how his manipulation techniques follow an entirely predictable trajectory. He has used flattery and solicited pity. Next, he will move on to berating and name-calling, and then he will resort to anger. Anger scares me. An angry Fred is a mean man.

I am alone with him. If I voluntarily leave the house now, it will only delay the inevitable faceoff. If I let on that I am afraid, he will be relentless in using my fear against me. Besides, I have nowhere to go with my kids. Although there is a newly built women's shelter in town, I am not a battered woman, as I do not have any broken bones or cuts and bruises. The only time Fred was physically violent was years ago, and the bruises on the outside have long since healed. All I can think to do is plow on without showing a glimmer of how terrified I really am. I am taking control to protect my children. He has no idea how determined I am.

Just in case I need to escape the house tonight, I hide the second set of car keys outside and bury our ID and all the cash I have in the trunk of my car. Once dinner is ready, I wake Fred. I wait until his plate is empty to tell him it is time for him to leave. That does it. I have poked the bear. It is showtime.

"How dare you kick me out? Who do you think you are, eh? What right do you have to give me the boot? Who do you think I am, anyway, some creep who hurts his daughter?"

I keep my opinion to myself. He is a creep.

His tirade gains momentum. *"What is this, some trick to get rid of me? I can't believe what a cold-hearted bitch you are."*

I am sure he does think I am a bitch. Provoking him further will not help this situation, so I do not respond. Fred continues as I expected he would. One of his favourite rants is about bra-burning, ball-breaking women and he carries on about that for a while.

"The more you talk to your women libber friends, the more you get stupid ideas in your bird brain. You goddamned women think everything is about you. I can't believe how much you changed from the nice girl you were when we met. Now it's women this, women that. You would as soon castrate a man as save him if he was dying."

Over many years of fighting, we have perfected our routine. Before he gets angry, I usually start apologizing and backtracking. Because I am not responding according to the script, he finds my silence provocative. At this rate, our argument will soon be physical and I cannot match his strength. I know he will intimidate me until I buckle. I have conditioned him to believe that, with his unrelenting persistence, I will cave. I have to somehow calm him down and still hold my ground.

Just then, an idea pops into my little bird brain. I know exactly how I can be safe tonight.

On Wednesday, when I dropped Alida off, Dorothy thought I was too uptight. She gave me a handful of Valium tablets: "mother's little helpers." She was right. They will help, but not the way she envisioned. There should be enough pills to calm Fred, but I hope there are not so many that they will kill him. Murder is very tempting, but I do not want to go to jail and leave my children orphaned.

I have to get the pills into his stomach without his knowledge. He will never take them willingly. I ask if he wants a coffee before he leaves and he smirks. He thinks he is winning.

"Oh, sure Carlyn, that'd be nice. I always like having coffee with

you. You are so good to talk to. I really treasure the time we have together."

While I realize I have outgrown his flattery, I also recognize that it works in my favour that Fred believes it is still an effective technique to control me.

I put the kettle on and spoon instant coffee and three teaspoons of sugar into his mug. Then I shiver and claim a chill. The pills are in my purse so I nonchalantly take it off the back of Fred's chair and go to the bedroom. I pull on a sweater to keep my story consistent, open the medication bottle, and tip all the pills into my left hand.

Back in the kitchen, with Fred sitting a few feet away on my right side, I shield the mug from his sight and empty the pills from my fist into his mug. I add boiling water and pretend fascination with him while I over-stir to dissolve the pills. By the time he tips the mug back to empty it, I am a wreck, worrying about floaters and dregs. He notices nothing. Within an hour he is back on the couch and fast asleep. I keep watch over him all night, making sure he neither dies nor wakes up and catches me off guard.

This is all so weird. Here I am, hardly sleeping in the middle of the biggest crisis of my life, scared half to death, and I feel stronger than ever before. The adrenaline is pumping. It is the same good feeling I had yelling at Fred in the bedroom dream, only this is real. The energy coming from a higher power, whether that is God or Light, is uncovering inner reserves I never knew I had.

Monday, 29 June 1987, 7 a.m.

My invigoration is short lived; I am as depleted as Alida's birthday balloons that hang flaccid above the dining room table. Fred says his sleep was the best he had had in a long time. I bet!

I watch him go through his morning routine as if nothing has changed. He has his coffee, reads the *London Free Press*, shaves, and showers. After fastidiously styling his hair, he leaves for the office wearing one of his three-piece suits with the silk square tucked neatly into his breast pocket. I woke him early to allow him time to pack his clothes, which he did not do. He leaves for work still believing he won. He thinks I capitulated and that he will return home tonight. That will be one problem to deal with today.

I dread what will undoubtedly become huge issues relating to the business. Fred will turn our separation into another chapter in his very long saga of financial and business battles. This will become ugly if not illegal. Fred does not have a moral compass to worry about criminal actions, and he is nonchalant about consequences, as evidenced by how he conducts himself as a businessman.

The history of Fred's employment is ridiculously complicated. The businesses he worked in with his father, owned or partly owned, had a variety of different company names and were located in four different Southwestern Ontario towns.

When I met Fred, he and his father jointly owned a store where they sold medical supplies for home use, and much of their stock came from Holland. By the time of our 1972 wedding, they had divided the business in two; the father got the store and Fred got the import/wholesale company. The one arm, the store, went through a few names, and is currently known as Abingville Home Health Solutions. With our plan to move to Parry Sound and my father-in-law's retirement, the men decided to sell the store. The sale went through in May, six weeks ago, shutting down his father's retail arm of "De Business." A consequence of the sale was that Fred's petty cash supply, his allowance, dried up.

The second arm, the import/wholesale business, was held by Fred. For this company, he went to Europe twice a year to buy stock in Holland (and visit Amsterdam's red-light district), and he began to sell his wares to stores across Ontario. His import/wholesale ventures went through several incorporated companies and names, with the second being a company that went bankrupt. The third incorporated company, the current one, is EuroMed Importing.

In 1973, Fred started scheming about expanding his empire to include a large chain of stores across Ontario. He opened three. The first store was in Chatham. Within a year after the grand opening, it failed, and Fred evacuated in a fly-by-night operation so the landlord could not seize stock in lieu of outstanding rent. In 1975, Fred opened the second store in Windsor, and a year later he opened a store in Sarnia. The last two became part of a newly incorporated company that never turned a profit. When it collapsed a few years later, we lost our investment. I never once set foot in any of those three out-of-town stores.

Not only did those stores fail, but also during the late 1970s, the import/wholesale company had serious financial difficulties. By the early 1980s, it appeared the only option was to declare bankruptcy, and that happened in 1981. Another investor, a nice man from our church, had lent Fred his family's savings. Fred squandered the money and showed no remorse. He said the man took a chance, lost, and that was that.

Fred, the eternal optimist, always had another idea up his sleeve, and he came through with a solution. He would start a new import/wholesale company using another name. Before the bankruptcy occurred, Fred persuaded my father, in name only, to incorporate EuroMed Importing. Fred's lawyer buddy drew up the paperwork. Fred thought of the company as his, since he planned to operate it and my father only held the shares. I never understood why my father agreed to this plan other than that Fred had used charisma, charm, and coercion to convince the Kettles only he could supply their store. If Dad did it to help me, he did so without asking my opinion.

Back in 1981, when EuroMed Importing was established and the other company's bankruptcy became inevitable, Fred spent weeks working into the nights later than usual. He said he was getting the books in order. I did not realize he might be doctoring books, rather than updating them, until he was done. I clued in when Fred told me he was moving merchandise from the warehouse and that the Kettles had agreed to store the goods in their basement. My father, my brothers Bert and Bart, my father-in-law, and my husband worked throughout the night.

I wavered about calling the Abingville City Police to report a theft-in-progress. What stopped me was that Fred had involved my brothers for the heavy lifting, and they did not realize they were accomplices to a theft. I did not want my brothers criminally charged, and in honesty, I was also worried about what Fred might do to me if I got him into trouble with the police. Fred came home when it was almost morning, and a few hours later, he took the business keys to Lawyer Buddy's office and declared bankruptcy. Fred was not bothered about the loss of his company because EuroMed Importing was all set up and ready to go.

An insurance company had awarded me a decent settlement for injuries I sustained in the 1980 car accident (which I now know was when Fred molested Irene while I was in the hospital). Although I secretly hoped to save the money for university tuition one day, I caved soon after I got the settlement when Fred again needed money, this time for the new EuroMed Importing.

Fred was still an undischarged bankrupt when he determined EuroMed Importing required operating loans and lines of credit. My credit score was great, so he elected me to be the official borrower. I agreed under the condition that my father transfer the company shares to me. I encouraged this transfer thinking that the sooner my father distanced himself from Fred's messes, the better it was for him.

Fred felt he contributed to the new company too because he found a way to turn the stolen goods into cash. He sold the stock from my parents' basement and, rather than itemize everything, he invoiced it all as Lot #s. Thus, he avoided leaving a paper trail. That sounded like money laundering to me.

Dad's transfer of all the shares to me was how it came about that I acquired 100 percent ownership of EuroMed Importing. With my name and my credit score at stake, I started taking an active role. I made sure I understood anything I signed and learned as much as I could about how the company operated. EuroMed Importing had a lot of potential, and Fred had no choice but to accept my restraints on his overbuying tendencies and his constant push to engage in business ventures that risked everything. Not to brag, but with my involvement, in a few years, we went from broke to prosperous.

On a Thursday morning five years ago, our situation became harrowing. The kids were at school and Fred had been out of town since the beginning of the week. There was a knock on the door, and I groaned at the sight of two men dressed in dark suits. Two by two, they came regularly because I usually spent time discussing the differences between our religious views.

I opened the door and said, "Sorry gentlemen, I don't have time today."

The two men did not give courteous Jehovah's Witness smiles and they did not politely turn around to leave. Both men put their hands inside their jackets and I could see their holsters before they produced badges. It was then I comprehended they carried guns, not Bibles.

As they shoved the door open and elbowed past me, they said, "Royal Canadian Mounted Police, ma'am. Let us in. We have a warrant to search your home."

The RCMP warrant was for all company and personal records between December 1977 and 1981. The grounds for the search was that Fred, "between 1979 and 1981, did by deceit, falsehood or other fraudulent means, defraud his creditors of $240,000, more or less, by means of a Fraudulent Assignment in bankruptcy, contrary to Section 338(1) of the Criminal Code of Canada."

Two armed detectives raiding our home was a personalized remake of a Godfather scene. They were uncommunicative, and I was disappointed they did not ask me any questions so that I could explain the relevance of the Lot #s on the invoices they were carting away. The first time I did not rat on Fred was the night he stole the stock. The day of the RCMP raid was the second time I chickened out.

That Thursday, Fred had come home from his sales trip earlier than usual, and he turned up at his father's Abingville Home Health Solutions store just as two RCMP detectives arrived. Fred stayed to support his father and left me to contend with the detectives at our house. Another pair searched his parents' home, and the men left Fred's mother to deal with them. My father phoned to tell me two detectives were raiding their farmhouse and another two were going through their Strathroy store. I guess the RCMP had no inkling where the stock in the Kettles' basement came from. I was not the only one who remained silent. During the raid, Dorothy was working in the Kettles' store. She did the store books, and she had to have known the merchandise stored in the farmhouse basement was illegal. Dorothy, Fred, his parents and mine did not share what they knew with the RCMP. Two entire families keep the secret of Fred's theft, including me.

Throughout the day, many of our customers let us know of searches at their businesses. This all happened at precisely 10:30 a.m. on January 21, 1982. I counted sixty-two RCMP detectives involved in raids at thirty-one locations across Ontario.

What astonished me is that not one customer stopped being loyal to Fred. Not one. They all carried on as if nothing had happened.

Perhaps they all wanted the good prices he offered, or they believed his stories about what he supposedly had or had not done. These successful storeowners subsequently wrote Fred cheques for tens of thousands of dollars, often weeks before they got their deliveries. They trusted him. That is an indication of Fred's salesman skills, and how effectively he targets people's vulnerabilities, naivety, and greed to get what he wants.

The evening of the raid was an accurate snapshot of our bizarre life. We took the children to Oregon to see my sister Ellie and her baby girl born that day. The Kettles were also there. We all pretended our day had been uneventful and like any other.

I knew the Abingville Dutch community had gossiped about the bankruptcy. When word about Fred getting criminal charges made the rounds, they must have had a heyday. Who could fault them? It was juicy news. Fred kept fuelling the gossip by complaining about being wrongly accused. He had no shame. It was my impression he enjoyed the notoriety one receives in a tight community when things happened. I wanted to hide under a rock. I suppose I did in a way, when I buried myself deeper into denial behind the façade that all was well.

When the RCMP completed examining our papers, Fred said it was my job to retrieve the confiscated records, so I did. The lead investigator told me he would meet me at the Abingville RCMP detachment. I went there determined to tell him what I knew about the stolen merchandise. I was sick of being sick about the whole thing. Fred told me they could not ask me questions since I was his wife and I could not testify against him. I figured I could still talk. I cannot recall exactly what I said. However, the investigator did not seem to understand I wanted to tell him something important.

I was in distress, and he patted me on the shoulder and told me it would be fine. I drove away with the secret still burning a hole inside of me. It was my third chance to say something and I blew that opportunity, too.

Fred was criminally charged and, looking back, I realize we did not talk about it, not really. He went to criminal court in London a few times that I know about, and by 1985, Fred said the court dropped the charges for lack of evidence and closed the case. I appreciate that it is incomprehensible, and likely unbelievable, that to this day I do not know how Fred altered the records, when formal charges were laid, how many charges there were, if the RCMP arrested him, if he had a bail hearing, or if his name really was cleared.

Other people's willingness to trust Fred enough to write him large cheques may astonish me, but it blows my mind even more how I lived in a bubble of "speak no evil." I am not sure if it is a reasonable defence to say that my cup had overflowed by years of his escalating skullduggery and nefarious dealings. By that point, I had pretty much closed myself into a cage of my own making. I just wanted him to take his bullshit elsewhere. All the same, the price of shame for not telling the authorities what I knew leaked out into an array of physical symptoms: nightmares, bellyaches, and headaches. Those unpleasant symptoms were partially instrumental in forcing me to take a closer look at what was happening in my life.

That I have 100 percent ownership of EuroMed Importing assures me that this divorce will centre on the business and become dreadfully malicious. Fred and his father believe I am simply a placeholder for ownership until Fred gets his legal troubles and bankruptcy sorted out. They will go to extreme lengths to protect "De Business" that, regardless of ownership, they consider belongs to them. I agree that I would never have been in this business without them, but I hold 100 percent of the outstanding debt.

I alone owe the bank for our house mortgage, loans for the Parry Sound warehouse and log house properties, four vehicle loans, operating loans, and lines of credit that total more than $500,000. To come through this divorce financially intact, I will need to be on the ball, bold, and brave.

Monday, 29 June 1987, 9:30 a.m.
When I dare not dally at home any longer, I join Fred at the office. We do little work and a lot of arguing about him being banned from his own home. Today, he sees me as his oppressor. He takes no responsibility whatsoever for why I needed to make the decision necessary for our daughter's safety.

Late this afternoon, Fred gathers some moving blankets from the back room and makes a bed on the cement floor. It is just another ploy to solicit my pity. The man who spent an average of three or more nights per week for twenty years sleeping in motel rooms without complaint now claims it is unbearable to stay in a motel one more night. A motel room is too lonely during this stressful and terrible time. He says he will be living in the office until he comes back home. I sarcastically suggest he might need a shower sooner than that.

I go to the bank to make a deposit and stop at a pay phone to arrange for the house locks to be changed. It is not that I think locks will keep Fred out, but if he decides to break in, I might hear him.

The first time Fred smashed a window to get into our home was early on in our marriage, in 1973, with the first *"affair"* fiasco. The second time he broke into our house was the summer of 1984. He had been active in an Abingville service club, and one of their main fundraising events was the local fair. Fred liked dealing blackjack at the fair casino. He was dealing one Saturday evening when he phoned to inform me that he would be home late. He insisted I was to leave the back door unlocked for him.

I said I would rather not because I was scared. The break-in of our first apartment still affected me. I asked Fred to just telephone before coming home and I would get up. I knew he was mad when he slammed the phone down. Five hours later, at 3 a.m., I woke from a crash and a clatter. The fence was leaning into the front fender of his car, and for two days the back door of the house hung broken off its hinges. Our Sunday plans to go to the beach also crashed as Fred slept off his alcoholic stupor.

By Sunday evening, he had concocted a story that he had no choice but to break down the door because he knew I had boyfriends in the house. That is his typical way of justifying what he does: he adds in a bit of truth to make his lies sound reasonable. The truth in that case was that I had a man in the house once, eleven years before. Anytime I argue about his lie, he focuses on the little bit of truth and I feel helpless.

Tuesday, 30 June 1987

Being at the office is an exercise in standing firm on my decision to separate. We pay Fred's father a stipend. We say it is to do odd jobs, but this seventy-year-old senior citizen appears primarily to visit, smoke, and drink coffee. This morning, he comes to the office while Fred is out and we have quite an argument. He demands an explanation as to why I refuse to let Fred come home. I fully expect him to understand once I explain what Fred did. Instead, he accuses me of giving Fred no choice. He thinks I made Alida into a sex symbol, and his evidence is a lovely picture taken of her at my sister Irene's wedding when Alida was eleven years old. Turns out, my father-in-law is also a creep.

I get another lecture about the need to keep our marriage intact for the sake of "De Business." The darn business means more to him than the safety of his granddaughter. My father-in-law traps me against the desk, nose to nose, with his bulky body shaking in fury and frustration. Being just as loud and stubborn, I forget I am less than half his age and size. People going by peer into the windows and still, neither of us budge from our position. I finally tell my father-in-law to calm down or leave. Much to my surprise and relief, he leaves.

I have no doubt my mother-in-law will side with her husband and son. One set of parents object to this separation for the sake of religion, and the second set for the sake of "De Business." None of them argues for the sake of the children. Two sets of parents down and none to go. This is going to be tough, but no tougher than I anticipated.

Canada Day, 1987
I take advantage of the holiday to take my children on an outing. It is too cold for the beach so we see some sights and eat pizza. I tell them their father and I have separated. The reason, I say, is that we are having too many fights. Alida's look rips my heart out. I tell them leaving is my decision. Alida needs to know that I am standing behind my promise to her. I need her to know I am in control and that I will make the necessary decisions that will protect her going forward.

Thursday, 2 July 1987
Fred vacates the makeshift bed on the office floor to move in with his childhood friend Herman, Herman's wife, and their children. I use the word "friend" liberally, since Fred only calls people friends when he has a personal use for them. In all the years I have known Fred, he has never talked about Herman or visited him. This family has three daughters around the same age as my kids. I hope this couple is aware of what they are risking. For Fred, it is good he has

people who care. The poor bugger needs all the support he can get and I cannot help him. I have my hands full with the three of us.

As quickly as he finds a new home, Fred also finds what he calls *"full forgiveness."* It causes a terrible argument that I am nowhere near ready to forgive him for what he did to Alida and my sisters. He is adamant I must absolve him so we can go back to how we were. I will never go back there. Fred says he forgave those who sexually abused him, and since he never abused me, I should find forgiveness easier. He reasons that my refusal to grant him forgiveness means I am pushing for a divorce, and since God opposes divorce, Fred has no choice but to fight me.

Friday, 3 July 1987

I wonder if Herman's influence or true remorse helps Fred see reason. Waiting on my desk is a beautifully handwritten poem in his calligraphic script. It starts with *"Words are empty, and have no meaning anymore."* In the poem he says that even while he knew he was causing pain, he continued to love us all.

His words might be empty and meaningless, but he sure uses a lot of them. In an attached letter he says sorry in about as many ways as a sorry man can. Page after page, he goes on along in the same vein. I wonder if he intends to make me feel sympathetic toward him. During all our years together, whenever he said a sorry that sounded somewhat sincere, I convinced myself that our future would improve. It never did. I believe he is only apologizing now to elicit my submission. This time, he leaves me cold.

> *Carlyn, you always will be my love. I want us to be able to make it. I hope you understand that I can't go through a separation, not knowing what will happen. Sorry, but my faith is too frail and my hurt too great.*

How dare he talk about his hurt when he hurt so many? He is not the victim.

Early afternoon Fred appears at the office to crow about his confessions. He apparently visited the man from our church who lost money in Fred's bankruptcy. I am unclear what Fred admitted to, but he said the man forgave him. Fred tells me he went to see friends, acquaintances, and the parents of our children's friends. He claims to have told everyone what he did to Alida. Then he refuses to explain to me what, exactly, his confessions were.

Fred supposedly also went to Price Waterhouse Bankruptcy Trustee to tell them that he stole merchandise from his company before it went bankrupt. He suggests he may have to go to jail for theft, which does not make sense because in 1985, he told me the criminal case was dropped. He tries to get me to write him a cheque for $20,000 because that was the amount he apparently said that he stole. I ask him to get it in writing from Price Waterhouse that I owe them money and then we can discuss it.

Going around telling everyone what he did is certainly getting him attention, and it seems to me that Fred believes negative attention is better than no attention. This forgiveness thing is out of hand. He needs to get off his Jesus drugs.

Fred is so narcissistic that he cannot, or will not understand that his profuse confessions unnecessarily expose our children to shame and stigma. Whatever his motivation, his divulgences are treacherous. It is good fodder for the Dutch community gossip mill. I worry that other parents will consider my children damaged and from a bad family. With Fred's loose lips flapping nine miles in the wind, protecting my children's reputation and mental health just became infinitely more difficult.

Saturday, 4 July 1987

I go from being a zombie to a raving lunatic. I wake from a nightmare in which Fred ejaculates all over the school desks and belongings of both our children. In the dream, I gag while I clean it up. I wake up retching. This dream gives me a graphic depiction of my disgust and repulsion. I will need to keep those feelings to myself so the girls he molested will never think I regard them as disgusting. It is not them. It is what happened to them, and the man who did it, that sickens me.

Fred does not ask to visit Alida nor does she want to see him. He does want a visit with Kevin, so I arrange for pick up at the Kettle farm. Mid-afternoon, once the visit is over, Fred phones to let me know they had a nice time.

I check with Kevin and he says his daddy took him shopping and got him the new Light and Sound XT Starship Lego set. He bought Alida a Papa Smurf and a heart necklace with a real diamond in it, but Alida does not like the gifts. She gave the Smurf to her cousin Nakita and the necklace to Aunt Juliana. Daddy bought himself a new Bible and a pair of sandals like those Jesus wore.

Kevin says the visit was good, but why can Daddy not come home? Daddy said he did some bad things and although he is sorry, Mommy will not forgive him. Kevin says he is supposed to ask me if they may visit again tomorrow. I tell Kevin not tomorrow and that his Daddy is right. Mommy will not let him move home. We talk about how, if someone hurts you and says sorry, it still takes time to earn back trust. Sometimes trust never comes back. Kevin says he understands.

I am angry that Fred is putting Kevin in the middle of our dispute and pitting him against me. Rather than provoke Fred by calling to tear a strip off him, I decide to simmer down first. I go out to buy a notebook and start writing. When I finish, I have several pages filled with an outpouring of feelings that rehash old beefs. Writing helps me recognize how I allowed Fred's anger, threats and criticism to influence me into being passive when I should have spoken out. I see how I distanced myself from my friends and the church community. I dutifully followed my husband. I was such an idiot for supporting him all these years. My guilt and shame are overwhelming.

So is the anger. I hate Fred for what he did to the girls. It makes me want to puke. In time, I might be able forgive him for all the things he did to me and that includes cheating on me with my sisters and daughter, though I am not sure sexual assault is considered cheating. I am not sure what it is, but I do know that it shatters me.

Fred is still making the rounds and he is suffocating me. This morning, he went to see Tessa, my first friend in Abingville. He kind of told Tessa he had done something to Alida and that I was having a bad time with it, and he suggested she visit me. Tessa tells me all this when she drops by late this afternoon. It is okay she comes over, but I wish he would let me contact my friends at my own pace. I assume that he is trying to get to everyone first so he can control the story and indirectly control me.

When we start talking, I am convinced Fred must be lurking outside since he asked Tessa to visit. I keep getting up to check and finally just lock the doors and close the windows, even though it is stifling hot. Tessa thinks I need professional help and she offers to find someone with whom I can talk.

Sunday, 5 July 1987

I dream of being tossed back and forth between heaven and hell; I wake up in hell. Sleeping on the couch with one hand on a butcher knife does not help, but I cannot tolerate being in "our bed."

I call Fred to tell him there will be no visit with Kevin. He is none too happy, and I end up sucked into a long-drawn-out exchange. He wants to come home and put this all behind us. I tell him it is not possible because I still feel angry and sick about what he did to the girls. He does not understand why I have such unladylike feelings. When I ask, he says he is not responsible for the "Mr Nobody" phone calls. I have been getting several a day and they go on late into the night.

Waking up in hell awakens a level of anger I have never felt before. It gets worse when, by mid-afternoon, I have seen Fred drive by five times, his father twice, and I answered the phone to the heavy breathing of a Mr Nobody seven times. With him mouthing off to everyone, I feel like a goldfish in a bowl, and with the incessant drive-bys, I feel like a sitting duck. Nothing feels safe. Vulnerability overload.

I try to write but have to quit after two pages. My rage scares me. Fred will never see or hear of what I am writing in my new journal. I know better than to ever give him another word written by me. Without a doubt, he will twist the meaning of everything and use it against me. I am sure we will end up in court. The man is lawsuit happy.

I do not recall how many suits he has filed, threatened, and been involved with, excluding the RCMP investigation. He even sued for my 1980 car accident. Within weeks after the accident, Fred said he would like to run for a position on Abingville City Council. I opposed based on needing help at home since I had a cast from ankle to groin, two kids, two boarders (my sister Helen and another college student), and a large dog.

Fred put his name in the hat anyway and used our household funds to cover his campaign costs. He would be off shaking hands and kissing babies while I would bum scoot down the stairs to do laundry and up the stairs to put the kids to bed. I would pop 222s (prescription pain medication) to dull the pain. When he did come home, Fred would be frustrated that I was too dopey and in too much pain to give him the sex and attention he thought he deserved. Fred sued the insurance company for loss of companionship and got a financial settlement. I could have slapped him silly for humiliating me just to get a little cash, but humiliation was his area of specialty, so why was I surprised?

Monday, 6 July 1987, workday
There is another letter from Fred on my desk when I arrive at work. I guess three days of remorse was enough for him and all he could tolerate. This is the Fred I know best. Even his handwriting is different than the previous letter. In this one, his sentences are choppy and his penmanship is messy. His mood is evident by the slashes in the paper where he pressed too hard.

In today's letter, he writes exactly how he has always argued. He talks a lot, kind of admits what he did, spins reality and timelines to suit his story, and then pins blame on someone else. In this situation, it is entirely predictable that I am the one he blames.

> *Your turn lady. Yeah, bullshit. I was just looking at what I thought was "goodie goodie" you. Well, I think I understand. You're as full of it as you try to make me feel.*
>
> *Good ol' Carlyn. She's just protecting her kids 'cause she loves them so much. Crap.*
>
> *Yeah, I've been a really BAD s.o.b. You know it and I know it. Yeah, I hurt you many times. Well, I got it back plenty of times too. And yeah, I've been a lousy father to my kids. You're no prize either.*
>
> *So, I did something really stupid. Yeah, I admit I got a problem. And it probably did hurt Alida pretty bad. But not half as bad as you're trying to make it. You just got something so you could grab me by the you-know-what's by.*
>
> *Okay perfect mother, have fun. But they'll be over 18 someday, then your turn will be over.*
>
> *Hey, I was just trying to make you feel better, taking all the blame, believing all the things you said I did. Well, it's a load of crap.*

Yeah, once you started talking about that guy being interested in you, I got on the bandwagon and went all the way along. Yeah, and then I even started instigating the filth. But just remember baby, you're the one that brought it into our marriage. I ain't perfect. But you sure as heck aren't either.

But all the times you never wanted sex with me, from day one, that was all my fault. It was cause I pressured you, tried to get too much before we were married. Yeah, I did and yeah, I wasn't too nice about it when you didn't want it.

Sorry lady, don't push that one all on me. What I did was your own doing. You are a flirt and don't even know it.

Well, maybe with a little love & understanding on your side I wouldn't have done anything with Alida either. I know, I know. It's my fault for being so stupid, but you sure helped me look elsewhere.

He was stupid and I made him look elsewhere? Really? He blames me for making him turn to our daughter? Fred has always been on the prowl and looking elsewhere did not need to mean Alida. Since we were married, I saw him making out with my friend's wife, he had a fling in Europe, a different time he came home with chlamydia, and this spring he came home with some other kind of infection. There were times he said he was at the office working late, when he was actually at one of Abingville's stripper clubs. Only he knows what he did during all his nights out of town and during his month-long European trips twice a year when he visited Amsterdam's red-light district to cater to his porn and sex obsessions.

While we were dating, Fred found opportunities for sex with prostitutes and he made out in a Burlington hotel with the teen girl who worked in the store. It reminds me of the motel scenario with my sister Helen, and it makes me suspect that what happened at the Home Medical Supply Show with the teen employee might not have been mutual. Had it really stopped because he ended it?

Perhaps what transpired with his cousin Jeannie was not mutual either. Now that I think it through, he is eleven years older than Jeannie. If he started before he met me, she was not yet a teen, and there is no way that would have been legal.

Monday, 6 July 1987, evening
I have a serious work problem. This afternoon, Fred stormed out of the office. He said he quit. He left his briefcase and the papers for the shipment arriving in Abingville tomorrow morning. I open the briefcase and pitch out another porn magazine. More smut.

I see that he has not yet begun the customs brokerage work, a job he always said was difficult and very complex. I have never before done this paperwork and have no idea where to start. The transport truck with the container is already underway from the harbour, and it is too late to hire a customs broker, even if I knew where to find one. I might not be able to do it, but I will give it my best try. I have fifteen hours to get it together.

If I work at home, Fred and his father will see the lights on all night when they drive by and that will freak me too much to concentrate. With Fred's mood, working at the office alone after dark is dangerous. I call my friend Lena, who says I may use her home office. If Fred finds out where I am, he will not dare tangle with Lena's strong husband. I am thankful that the kids are still in Oregon, unaffected by this situation.

After arranging for staff to unload the shipment tomorrow, throwing all papers I might need into a box, and schlepping the typewriter to the car, I drive to their farm and hide my car behind the hog barn. It feels good to get out of town and to be safe for a little while.

After dinner, Lena's rough-around-the-edges husband asks, "You left Fred. What's up, anyway?"

When I tell him Fred has been after my sisters and Alida, he gruffly questions, "What the hell. Weren't you giving him enough?"

"Really? If you don't get enough from your wife, do you force yourself on your daughters?"

"Of course not. That wouldn't be right. I'd just find some woman who did want it."

Lena cringes for me and I for her.

"It was not just girls. I know for a fact that Fred has also been with other women."

He thinks, then nods. With that slight movement, I know he understands and that he has my back.

Tuesday, 7 July 1987

It takes me twelve hours of concentrated effort to finish the brokerage papers. It was time consuming, but not really all that difficult.

Standing in my friend's shower at 7:15 a.m., I shudder. Was Fred initially attracted to me because I was skinny? Was he always after me to shave down there like the females in his porn magazines because it would make me look young? It occurs to me that, at one hundred and twenty pounds, I outgrew his preferences for little girls and tiny young women. It is beyond sick that he has turned to our daughter who is four feet, nine inches (145 cm) tall and weighs a mere seventy pounds (32 kg).

Canada Customs approves the brokerage clearance papers and they release the shipment. Just as the transport backs up to the unloading dock, my father-in-law's car comes screeching into the parking lot. It burns him up that I will not say who completed the paperwork. My employees are kind enough to pretend they do not notice the scene. He shouts that he quits his job and throws his car keys at me. They land in the dirt, so I pick them up and hand them back to him. My father-in-law drives away in a furious cloud of dust and I hear his tires squeal when he reaches the pavement.

While we were emptying the container at the back of the premises, Fred came into the front office and left another note on my desk. He offered to do the customs paperwork. I am sure Fred thinks I need him. Ha. These two men, father and son, cannot seem to make up their minds if they are working here or not.

As soon as the container is empty and the customs official and his sniffer dog finish their final check, I go home to crash. Two Mr Nobody calls are enough to warrant taking the phone off the hook. I have a solid two-hour nap. Exhaustion has benefits.

Wednesday, 8 July 1987

This morning, Fred appears at the office again, acting as if he never quit two days ago. It is entertaining to watch him try to figure out how I got the shipment customs cleared. It gives me great pleasure to know that I accomplished it on my own and even greater pleasure to let him stew.

Fred needs money, and when we agree on a fair amount, I write him a cheque. He wants to see Kevin on the weekend and needs me to answer immediately so he can make plans.

Everything he does sends me in a dozen different emotional directions. I am relieved that he arranges the visit with me and not Kevin. I am curious why he only wants to see his son. It is so unfair that he is the cause of my problems and yet he is the one with the luxury of making weekend plans.

A big thing helping me through is my notebook. Writing allows me to release some of my pent up feelings. In case of a lawsuit, it is wise to keep a record of events. With facts and feelings so tightly intertwined, I find it easier to write everything in one notebook. A diary and a journal. Given Fred's tendency to twist reality and timelines to suit his stories, I am betting on minimally needing the facts for divorce court and if Fred carries on true to form, he will likely find other alleged infractions of mine to justify filing more lawsuits.

When I write, I let my pen follow my mind's ramblings without censoring. Writing clarifies things. Putting my thoughts into words gives me strength to hold firm on not allowing him back home. Already, I can see that in a matter of days, my thinking is less jumbled and I am growing stronger.

Thursday, 9 July 1987

Tessa came through with help by arranging an appointment for me with the Abingville Task Force on Domestic Violence. I meet with the Task Force counsellor and tell her what my three sisters and Alida disclosed. She wants to know if I ever saw Fred touch Alida. The question stumps me, so I tell her I saw Fred hug Alida around the waist. This happened after I suspected something was going on, but before Alida confirmed it. It made me feel yucky but was not really anything sexual. Fathers hug their children. I am not sure why I even tell her that.

The counsellor says she can also talk to Fred, so I give him her card. I hear him make a phone call and he leaves the office for a few hours. When he returns, he tells me he met with the counsellor. He told her everything, and cried like a baby. His impression is that she thinks he is okay. He likes her.

He has conned me for so many years, it is easy to imagine that she believes he is a good guy. I wish I had not given Fred her card. She probably thinks she can see him for who he is, but I have seen Fred convince too many people of things that defy logic.

When the counsellor phones me, it comes as a shock. Apparently, she thinks what Fred did was not okay. She will be making a report to the Children's Aid Society (CAS). I struggle to understand why, since Fred is no longer at home. She explains she is not picking on me, but the law requires her to report any incident of child abuse. Another piece of my world crumbles.

Friday, 10 July 1987
In my dream, I wake up from noises and see Fred banging a stick against the foundation of our house. I recognize the dream as a metaphor for Fred smashing the footings of our life and the walls of our family crumbling like old masonry.

I sit at the kitchen table with my morning coffee, paging through a glossy woman's magazine. I thought I had read it from cover to cover before, but somehow, I must have skipped this article. I am a voracious reader and have never before read anything about sexual abuse in any woman's magazines.

Reading the details of the article through three times makes me feel lightheaded. It is as if the author looked into my family and described us to the world. It makes me feel exposed and vulnerable, but also validates that it happens in other homes, too. My sisters and my daughter are not alone. I have a sense that in my home and in the world around me, we are on the cusp of recognizing that child sexual abuse is a much greater problem than most of us ever acknowledged.

I am still woozy from the dream and the article, and am working on pumping caffeine into my bloodstream to get me moving when the telephone rings. It is Maggie, a CAS intake worker, with instructions to bring my children to her office. Immediately. She cautions me not to say anything to the kids about why they must go. I do exactly as she directs.

I pick the kids up in Oregon. All I say is that we have an appointment because some people have questions, and it is important that they answer honestly. The incongruence in urging my children to speak the truth and my years of living a lie does not escape me. I vow in the future to practice what I preach.

The calm I present is only skin deep as we traipse into a small, windowless waiting room crammed with ugly vinyl seating. The cold 1960s orange furniture is hardly suitable for a basement rec room. Wrecked like our lives. Scummy furniture. Bad scummy Mummy who had no idea what her husband was doing. Cranked up air conditioning amplifies the chill of anxiety, bringing to mind a morgue.

Maggie introduces herself and a police officer, Detective Kingston. They do not allow me to stay with the children during their interviews. Their concern is that the children might find it difficult to talk in my presence or they may feel pressured to repeat what they think I want them to say. I am unsuccessful in assuring Maggie or the detective that I want my kids to tell the truth, whatever that is. I get the impression these professionals doubt me. Scummy Mummy might be lying.

One by one, my children go into the interview room. I have quickly become rather low in the trust department, and entrusting them to strangers is quite a heavy burden. It is ironic that I taught my kids to beware of people we do not know. Something bad happens, and I am boxed into a position where I must hand them over to strangers. It makes no sense to me.

By my watch, each child is gone for about forty-five minutes. Time distorts and it seems two lifetimes before they finish. I leaf through old *Reader's Digest* magazines. Then a brochure called *Child Sexual Abuse*[4] catches my attention. I read it and inhale the information.

---

[4] Ministry of the Solicitor General, *Child Sexual Abuse,* Ontario, n.d.

- **Child sexual abuse is any incident of sexual contact between a child and an adult who is in a position of authority, including rape, fondling, molestation, exhibitionism, sodomy and/or incest, with or without force.**

This definition describes exactly what happened to Alida, and maybe Irene and Helen too, because they were both minors and he was their caregiver when he molested them.

- **Surveys of previous victims indicate that a girl born today has a one-in-four chance of being sexually abused before the age of eighteen, the risk for boys is one-in-eight.**

I had no idea sexual abuse was so common. Before this, I only knew of one grade school friend who had sworn me to secrecy when she told me a neighbour had locked her in his garage, tied her to a table, touched her, and took naked pictures. I felt terrible for her, but being in a culture that did not speak of such things resulted in me having no idea who to tell or how to help her. The only molested boy I ever heard about was Fred, assuming what he said was true.

I use a list of information and instructions for parents to evaluate how I am doing.

- **Your reaction will have a major effect on your child's response to the sexual abuse. Make it clear to your child that your anger is directed at the offender. NOT YOUR CHILD.**

I am angry with Fred and not the girls. I guess that is a pass for me.

- **Let your child know you believe what he or she tells you.**

Pass.

- **Your child is not responsible for the abuse, regardless of the circumstances.**

Pass. I believe Alida and my little sisters and I told them so.

- **Say that you will protect him or her from further abuse by the offender.**

Pass with Alida. So far, it seems my reactions have been okay. This no longer applies to my sisters who protected themselves by moving halfway across the country.

- **It is not limited to any social, economic, or ethnic class.**

This means we are not freaks.

- **Most offenders are male, 85% are known to the child, and child sexual abuse most often happens in the home. It may eventually involve intercourse, but typically begins with touching.**

I know I had done a good job warning my children about stranger danger. Now I can see that was not nearly enough.

- **Children rarely tell because they are frightened, afraid they won't be believed, or afraid they won't be protected.**

This is a horror for the girls and a strange kind of relief to me. I hope it means that those people interviewing my kids will have some understanding as to why I did not know sooner. They do not say anything in the pamphlet about offenders brainwashing to insure silence. However, if we are somewhat typical in this bizarre situation, we may still be a little bit normal.

The brochure goes on to say that if you know or suspect a child is being sexually abused, you must contact your local police or the CAS. I did not know I had a requirement to report. I hope these people will forgive my ignorance. The irony of our situation is that Fred's disclosure to the Task Force counsellor is what made her report to the CAS. In this case, in every way, he really has done it to himself.

This one little pamphlet teaches me so much. I do not know if it is there to read or take. When there is no one in the hall, I sneak a copy into my purse to review again later.

Finally, it is my turn to go into the meeting room for an update. What Alida told them is the same as what she told me and they say she needs to attend a sexual abuse survivors group run by the CAS.

It surprises them how articulate Kevin is for a boy ten years old. I catch myself in time before I say aloud, "Why are you surprised? We aren't stupid." I keep my mouth shut. Even without prior exposure to how CAS operates, I know they have power and that sarcasm and defensiveness will most likely be construed as me being argumentative and uncooperative.

Maggie and Detective Kingston keep right on talking, hardly giving me a chance to process everything they are saying.

When they mention Kevin, it dawns on me that he may also have been victimized. They say there is no evidence that Fred molested Kevin, but what stumped them was when my son said, "First Opa and now my dad." They think I should be able to explain this, but I have no idea which grandfather Kevin was referring to or why.

They say this part is complete and they will be in touch. I get up to leave with more questions than answers.

Through a heavy fog, I hear someone say, "Have a good weekend."

I wonder if it will be possible to have a good day ever again.

Once we are home, Kevin wants to know why we went to that office to see those people. He apparently did not grasp the implications of the questions or that the plain-clothed man was a detective.

I tell him, "Your dad touched Alida in places he should not have, and they wanted to talk to you to ask if anything like that happened to you."

Kevin tells me it had not. All the same, my son's distress is obvious when he asks, "Am I going to be like that, too? If I am, I want to be dead."

I explain how his father made a choice and Kevin can choose differently. The question gets me wondering how this will affect my son as he matures. What a burden for a boy who, in a few years, will begin to come to grips with his own sexuality and identity. It seems he escaped the physical act of incest, but his father's behaviour is nonetheless emotionally destructive. When incest occurs within a family, no one comes away unscathed.

I notice that neither child is distressed that their father is gone. Instead, they point out good things about our situation and we write them down.

- Talking about it will stop Daddy from hurting others (they have no idea that he already did).
- Our home will be peaceful.
- There will be no more yelling or lying and no more broken promises.
- We will get more of Mom's attention.
- Mom will no longer need to be afraid of Daddy.

It seems I did not hide my fear of Fred from them after all. Darn. I did not want them to know. I did not want anyone to know. Apparently, in this home, I only fooled myself. My children also come up with the idea that someday we may be able to help other people going through the same thing.

My kids do not want to sleep in their bedrooms, so we camp in the living room with pillows, blankets, popcorn, and ice cream floats. We stay close to console each other. When I go to the bathroom, Kevin stands outside the door anxiously chattering. It seems to me that he is seeking comfort. Alida buries herself in a book and is quiet.

After the kids fall asleep, I mentally review what today brought. My kids are amazing. They give me strength. It is not all bad if they can see the positives. Still, the situation is rapidly becoming dire. Alida is withdrawing. Kevin's talk of death is worrisome. I am already overwhelmed and I have not even begun to help my traumatized children, let alone myself.

Saturday, 11 July 1987

Fred asks for his personal belongings, including his dresser. It takes a few hours to drive around town to find boxes and then to pack his clothes, vinyl LPs, binoculars, cameras, books, coin collection, and everything that is remotely personal. When I pack his books, I realize that two of them—the V.C. Andrew's novels *Flowers in the Attic* and *Petals on the Wind*—are sexualized stories of brother-sister incest. It is disturbing that these are popular books and that they were sitting on our bookshelf.

I drag everything out to the porch so Fred does not need to come inside to get his stuff. I do that for myself as much as for my children.

Sunday, 12 July 1987

Taking my kids back to the Kettles is the last thing I want to do. It feels as if I am abandoning them. If I did not need to work or have to repay the bank the mountain of money owing, I would not leave them. It is unsafe for the kids to be home alone. Kevin needs close monitoring, and although Alida is old enough to watch her brother, right now Fred is too unpredictable and she is too withdrawn for that to be a good idea. I do not know of any babysitter I might hire who could handle Fred or his father if they come to the house while I am at work. I cannot take the kids to work because Fred turns up there and because they would be bored out of their minds. Even though I feel like a heel for bringing them back to the people who betrayed us with their silence, I do not know what else to do.

Monday, 13 July 1987

It works out well that the children are not home when Maggie makes an appointment for a home visit. I want to tell her about my sisters, which my children should not hear about. I am also a basket case worrying that Maggie will take the kids into foster care. Having them away from Abingville buys me time. The CAS does not know where the Kettles live, and if I get a notion Maggie is considering apprehension, we will go into hiding. I will not give my kids up without a fight. While I do not know where we would go, I would max out my business line of credit and take the risk. It would be worth it. If the CAS takes my children, what happens to me will not matter.

I repeat to Maggie everything I told the Task Force counsellor. Maggie already has all the details from the counsellor, and she does not appear particularly interested. When she wants to know what caused me to suspect Fred of molesting Alida, I explain how my awareness unfolded. She says the dream of them in bed makes her uneasy. I understand that. It also made me uneasy. I wonder if she thinks I am a kook. Does she think I should have known earlier or that I did know earlier?

On the external level, I carry on a calm and reasonable conversation. Internally, all my parenting mistakes and failures preoccupy me. I have a hard time waking up in the mornings and the kids often make their own breakfast before I get up to see them off on the bus. I have yelled at them. My dinners are not always home-cooked feasts and I have spanked the kids.

Maggie knows about my sisters' allegations and she says the police will follow up with them. When I express horror that Fred hurt so many girls, she tells me that some child sexual abusers have molested up to seventy victims, with a statistical average of 11.8 children per offender. With four victims, Alida and my three sisters, Fred is well below average.

She mostly wants to discuss my plans for the future.

I say, "We are separated for now. I told Fred that getting back together depends on whether he gets help, but I am pretty sure we will be divorcing."

Maggie lowers the boom. "If you ever let Fred move back home, the CAS will take your children and place them into foster care."

"In that case, I promise you he'll never come back."

"Yes, for sure Alida will attend the CAS group and I will call to arrange for individual counselling for her."

"Of course I will see my lawyer about getting custody."

"Yes, I will ensure all visits are supervised."

She obviously does not know that I had ignorantly allowed Fred an unsupervised visit with Kevin. I do not push my luck by telling her. It does not dawn on me to ask who is supposed to do the supervising. I am ready to agree to anything she demands of me so that I can keep my children, and I do not think things through at all.

Before she leaves, in order to complete a home check, Maggie has to see my children's bedrooms. She comments on my lovely house. "Abusers live in nice houses, too," I think.

Then she looks in the fridge and cupboards to see if there is enough food. Because the kids are away, and because I find eating challenging, the fridge holds only a few condiments, a block of cheese, cream for my coffee, and a bag of apples. She raises her eyebrows, and I shrug and say, "It's time to get groceries." Thank goodness the cupboards hold enough canned and packaged food to satisfy her that I am not starving my children.

I have myself so worked up that it comes as a surprise when she says I am doing a great job of protecting my children. The CAS will place Fred's name on the Child Abuse Registry. This is for CAS workers only.[5] If he moves elsewhere in Ontario and is alleged to abuse another child under the age of sixteen while in a caregiver position, the CAS will have his history. This is a tracking registry with no preventive benefits. The CAS will close our intake file and the police will follow up with Fred.

Maggie leaves and I contact the children's counselling centre. They will call me back to set up an initial interview, although the waiting lists are very long and counselling will not begin for a while, maybe upward of two years. I arrange an appointment with the divorce lawyer to start the proceedings for custody and divorce.

Fred is pissed off when I arrive at work late. I am late because I am dealing with his crap, and he uses it as an opportunity to be miserable toward me. I do not tell him about CAS because we are on opposite sides now. I am the victimized child's mother and he is the victimizer. He has become the enemy.

Since Fred returned to the office last week, it has been hopeless. We recognize working together is impossible. In a surprisingly civil conversation, we are able to look at our four options: we can sell EuroMed Importing, we could liquidate, Fred can stay to manage it, or I could run the company. Each option has pros and cons.

The first option, selling as a going concern, will be difficult, particularly since word of our separation getting out will reduce the value. I am unsure why Fred opposes the second option, liquidation.

---

[5] Every Canadian province has their own legislation and tracking system for sex offenders, and these systems have changed considerably since 1987.

The third option is for Fred to take over management of the company. That would be fine if he could take over the financial obligations, which he cannot do. If I walk away, I would have to trust him to repay the debt I owe the banks. I cannot do that because I do not trust him with my money any more than I trust him with my children.

By noon, we agree the only viable option is the last one, that I operate the business. Fred will work for two more weeks to teach me the tasks he typically does, and then he will leave. I will help him out financially until he gets a job.

When I return from a late lunch, he is angry because I have not coordinated my time with him. He rants about that for an hour and then changes his notice to one week. At 3 p.m., he leaves the office, saying he has an appointment. When he comes back to work, he informs me he met with the EuroMed Importing bank manager to review and arrange all of my financing and inform the bank he is leaving the company.

We fight again. All loans are in my name, and if financing needs arranging, I will do it since we decided that I am running this company. Fred appears bewildered that his good intentions have upset me and he makes it my fault.

"Carlyn, can't you see I am just trying to help you? Don't be such a bitch. No matter what I do for you, you don't appreciate anything and always complain."

I am definitely bitchy about his so-called help.

Although EuroMed Importing's annual sales are well over $1,000,000, because we sell exclusively to one store per town, our customer base is limited and each one is critical. This evening, my Orangeville customer phones me at home to let me know Fred called her at dinnertime. He told her he was leaving the company, and that I should be able to manage the work because I am *"a good kid.*" He asked her to please, for his sake, continue buying from me. I spoke with another customer, and he received a similar call. I imagine all of the EuroMed Importing customers will hear from Fred over the next day or two.

Tuesday, 14 July 1987

Fred comes into the office emotionally distraught. He is crying, albeit without tears, stumbling around as if in a daze, and clutching his chest. I assume the police must have taken him in for questioning. I do not ask and he does not tell.

I offer to take him to the hospital, which he declines. Fred thinks he just needs rest and finally agrees that I may drive him to his new home. A few hours later, Herman informs me Fred will never be returning to work because it is too difficult for him to have to deal with me. Fred quits for good, effective immediately.

Wednesday, 15 July 1987

Happy birthday to me. Not.

Detective Kingston comes to see me at the office. He says that after he interviewed Fred, he spoke with the crown to decide on what charges they would lay. The crown attorney is the lawyer who prosecutes on behalf of the state. In criminal court proceedings, the person alleging harm does not have their own legal representation. The crown attorney is, in effect, an alleged victim's voice in court.

Fred confessed to sexual abuse of Alida beginning in 1979, for which he will get one charge. Fred further confessed that he had molested some sisters. The detective does not remember the names of the sisters, but he does know there has been no follow up and none is planned.

The next step is for Fred to go to the police station for fingerprinting and mug shots. That is when police will lay the official charge. Because he is cooperative and it is a first offence, police will release him on his own recognizance, which means they trust his word to show up in court. He will not spend any time in jail at this point; not overnight and not even an hour. Criminal court will follow.

If the detective had not been so understanding and I was not so distressed, I would not have blubbered about the failure of our marriage being my fault.

He presented a new concept. "It takes two. You cannot do it alone when someone is working against you."

Such simple words are a revelation.

(Personal note: On May 16, 1997, I attended a scheduled appointment at Abingville Children's Aid Society office to review my file. Because they had redacted the file, what I saw had more black streaks than words. Later, I inserted the recordings into my journal where they fit chronologically, so there are times the workers knew things of which I was unaware. For integrity of this account, I have maintained these discrepancies even though at times it may appear confusing to the reader.)

```
17 July 1987
CAS Opening/Closing Recording,
Intake Worker Maggie
```

Current Situation

```
The Task Force on Domestic Violence reported
the following: Carlyn Smit alleged to
their counsellor that her husband sexually
abused her twelve-year-old daughter Alida.
After Mrs Smit learned of the alleged
incidents from her daughter, she arranged
to have the children stay with relatives
out of town.
```

The following day, Mr Smit spoke to the counsellor and admitted to the alleged incidents.

Mrs Smit reported that approximately one month ago she had a dream in which she saw her husband in bed with Alida. Two weeks after that, when her sister was visiting, they were discussing their rocky marriages. She told her sister about the dream. She stated that her sister's face went white.

The sister acknowledged her concern with the fact that Mr Smit was showing Alida too much attention and affection while disregarding their younger child. Mrs Smit recalled seeing her husband grab Alida around the waist but didn't think anything of it. She also noted that her husband referred to Alida as *"Princess."*

Her sister also disclosed that when she was between thirteen and fifteen, Mr Smit made sexual advances toward her.

Following the conversation with her sister, Mrs Smit stated she took a couple of days to think about what they had discussed, during which time she kept a very close eye on her children and their father. She then went to see a counsellor at Salem Christian Counselling Centre in Toronto for assistance on how to deal with this situation. When she returned, she spoke with Alida, who acknowledged that her father had been touching her where he should not be—places he should only be touching her mother.

Alida also told her it happened daily when her father was home. Although that was all Alida disclosed, Mrs Smit suspected there could be more to it.

She stated she made arrangements for the children to stay with relatives out of town, then confronted her husband who admitted to doing what Alida said, and a great deal more.

After their discussions, it was mutually decided that Mr Smit would move out of the home and they would obtain a legal separation with her having custody of the children.

Assessment

Sexual abuse perpetrated by Mr Smit against his daughter Alida has been substantiated and police are following up with criminal charges.

It has become evident that once Mrs Smit confirmed her suspicions, she acted in a protective manner by placing her children outside the home, then confronted her husband and began making long-term plans to ensure that the children were no longer at risk with their father.

Alida has expressed an interest in attending the sexual abuse group offered by this agency. Mrs Smit referred themselves to the children's counselling centre for adjustment to the separation and the circumstances around it.

The police intend to further investigate the matter regarding Mr Smit's involvement with other family members as well as this other person in the community whom he admitted to molesting.

The children are not in need of protection and this worker recommends the file be closed.

CAS Director to the Child Abuse Registry: Toronto, Ontario
Date Reported to CAS: July 10, 1987
Place of Incident: Child's home
Dates Incident Occurred: 1979 to July 1987

Mr Smit admits to sexually molesting his daughter on an ongoing basis since she was four years of age, and this includes touching, fondling and penetration. His daughter claims the abuse occurred on a daily basis.

Up to this point, this man has been highly cooperative. The children are not considered in need of protection at this time and the protection file has been closed.

Sunday, 19 July 1987
I hug and kiss the children goodbye after spending the weekend with them and notice myself feeling awkward and self-conscious. Can a hug be construed as abuse? Might a kiss feel inappropriate to them? My hugs and kisses have always been spontaneous. I do know children need loving, non-sexual touch. If I let myself withdraw to reduce my own anxiety, it would punish them, and they might think good touches are bad. I decide the only thing to do is be extra sensitive.

As I drive home, I think about how the Kettles were not sensitive to our boundaries. Following the Dutch tradition, at adult birthday parties all the guests would always sit in a big circle around the perimeter of the living room. As children, we were required to go around the room to greet everyone twice: when the party started and again before heading to bed.

I had been okay with the cheek kisses from my aunts and most of my uncles. However, I dreaded having to kiss the two "funny uncles" who would grab us girls and force us onto their laps. They would tickle until we struggled, while they held us tight against their laps. In front of everyone, they even gave us yucky kisses on the lips and jokingly pushed their tongues into our mouths. When we tried to stop them, we would get into trouble from whichever parent noticed our resistance. Through my adult eyes, it is appalling that these boundary violations were permitted.

I arrive home at midnight and am still outside when Fred drives by.
    I scurry into the house,
    like a scared little mouse.

Thursday, 23 July 1987
Since there is much to be done and the kids are still with family, I work extremely long days to learn what I need to know and to get

caught up. At least meals are easy. The only things I can stand to swallow are apples, McDonald's chocolate milkshakes, and coffee. And I smoke too much.

Fred is still calling customers, and they in turn phone me for assurances that I can deliver the merchandise they pre-ordered at the June trade show. I am flying on a wing and a prayer when I say I will come through.

Because the familiar routine had been Fred appearing at their stores every few weeks to take orders, they now ask when I plan to make the rounds. By offering a discount for phone orders, my customers are willing to change how we do things. I am learning and innovating as I go and it all takes so frightfully long. Not only am I learning Fred's job, I am doing the work of two.

I take an hour to meet the Task Force counsellor, who is no longer seeing Fred. It sure helps to talk to someone. I tell her about work stressing me out. She helps me prioritize which problems to deal with first. I must hire office help to have time and flexibility for the children when they come home, but I am afraid that if I place an ad in the Abingville newspaper, Fred will see it and plant someone in the office. The counsellor knows an unemployed secretary who may want the job and will check if she is interested.

Another worry I have is that my two main Dutch suppliers might not want to do business with me if they find out I am now operating the company alone. The solution is to phone them, tell them Fred had left the company, and confirm they will continue as is. They will.

I became anxious about suppliers on Monday when Fred came to the office. He insisted the equipment supplier's price lists belonged to him and that he needed them to start his new life. I refused to give him anything, so we had a shouting match. Now those price lists are missing.

I am so angry with Fred that whenever he wants something from me, I forget my safety is on the line. When my calmer mind prevails, I realize how vulnerable I am working alone and arrange for the office locks to be changed. Then, for self-protection, I leave the door locked during work hours. The courier and mail carrier both give me strange glances when they have to knock. It is weird to operate a business with locked doors. It cannot be helped. Safety takes precedence.

Sunday, 26 July 1987

The Kettles tell me they had a very nice visit with Fred last week. I am not sure I believe their assurances that Kevin was in the barn with Bert and Bart while Fred visited. I do not trust the Kettles, which tells me I need to get the kids safely home as soon as possible. I also cannot be sure my kids would be safe at home, and this leaves me in quite a predicament with no good solution.

The Kettles are convinced Fred is a born-again Christian and genuinely sorry. They claim he is doing well, found a new church to attend, and he is planning a new import/wholesale business.

"So ven are you going to give dis silliness up and let Fred come home?" Mom does not believe the CAS meant it when they said my choice was Fred or my kids.

It keeps surprising me that my mother honestly believes divorce is worse than sexual abuse. For three years, they allowed their daughters' abuser to put his ass on their couch, served him coffee, and engaged in civil conversations with him. Now that the Kettles know he also sexually abused their granddaughter, nothing has changed. They still invite him into their home. Incredible.

I suspect Fred's purpose in seeing them had been to trash-talk me and ask if he said anything about my past. "Yes, Fred said you had a lot of affairs."

I ask if Fred said anything about the things he did with other women. They say he only talked about what I did and I should not say bad things about my husband. They are aligned with Fred, and nothing I say will make any difference.

Mom snuffles about how humiliating it is that her daughter is divorcing. I am well aware that my marriage break-up damages our entire family's reputation. It is a topsy-turvy world when abuse goes on shamelessly behind closed doors with reputations intact, but the person stopping it is blamed for damaging the family. I am not just fighting against an abuser and those who side with him, but I am pushing back against the skewed priorities of the social order of my church and family.

After church, one of my cousins drops by the Kettle home. She is very serious and asks if we can sit on the deck for privacy because she has something important to tell me. In September of 1985, my cousin began a college program in Abingville. We had a plan that she would board with us for two years and I set up a room for her. Instead, she stayed only a few weeks, and then moved out quickly without explanation. It had distressed me and I thought I had done something wrong.

From gossip, my cousin had already heard that Fred was charged with sexual assault. What she wants to tell me is that she had seen Fred in Alida's bed. At the time, she had the sense he was doing more than tucking Alida in, but saw nothing concrete. It made my cousin feel uncomfortable and that is why she moved out.

I understand it would have been difficult for her to tell me then. She was a teenage girl from the same tribe as me. A family where silence is the norm. That she is willing to talk now is an act of bravery. Although vague, this account raises my concern that Fred did more to Alida than I know about. While I thoroughly appreciate my cousin's courage today, it saddens me that her silence resulted in an extended period of sexual abuse for Alida that could have been stopped sooner. Of course, I am assuming I would have acted on my cousin's feelings. In all honesty, two years ago, this ambiguous account would have been a small piece of a puzzle with no context, and I probably would not have known what to make of it.

What my cousin actually saw is similar to the bedroom dream I had and I find that discombobulating. I wonder if I, too, had actually seen him in bed with Alida, but with my desire to get out of the marriage, I cannot imagine I would have ignored that. All the same, it is weird when my nightmares and reality merge.

Yesterday evening, my sister Ellie, her husband and I take our kids out for dinner in London. While the kids are at one end of the table having some fun cousin time, Ellie quietly tells me about what Fred did to her.

Because Fred lived an hour away, when he started taking me out, the Kettles offered weekend overnight stays in the boys' bedroom. Our family never went on holidays, not even for day outings, so we sisters created stay-at-home vacations. As soon as the weather was nice, we would pitch a tent behind the house and "go camping."

On a Saturday night, Dorothy and Ellie, sisters two and three, had slept in the tent. The following morning, Dorothy had already left the tent when Fred slithered his way inside. He made inappropriate sexual comments and then reached over to make the moves on thirteen-year-old Ellie.

Before Fred could touch her, Ellie said, "Fuck off and get away. If you ever try that again, I'll kick you in the nuts."

You gotta love that girl! Fred left the tent and never again tried anything with her. Ellie defines what Fred did as an attempt, and she is positive her assertive reaction prevented physical molestation. Ellie has no idea where, in our tight religious community, she learned such language, except maybe from our brothers.

That Sunday morning, Ellie saw Fred park himself beside Dorothy who was sitting on the ground outside of the tent. Ellie heard Fred make suggestive comments but assumed that because she was keeping a watchful eye to protect her sister, Fred did not touch Dorothy.

According to Ellie's husband, a year ago, he saw Fred in a Toronto bar throwing money at strippers for lap and private dances. That explains what happened to Fred's unaccounted for "allowances." My brother-in-law claimed he had to go into that particular bar for business and just happened to see Fred there. I am not gullible enough to believe that the two men accidentally saw each other in a bar two hours away from home or that watching skimpily clad dancers is ever required by a legitimate business.

Until now, Dorothy told me what Fred had done to our younger sisters, but she has said nothing about herself. The past few years, Fred often told me Dorothy was the best-looking sister in my family. I now wonder if he was doing more than pitting Dorothy against me. In actuality, Dorothy and I look like twins but are not because of our eleven-month age difference. Looking alike has been fun when people mistake us for each other. I did not laugh the time Fred told me he went into the bathroom, thought Dorothy was me, and intimately grabbed her. He claimed it was an honest mistake. Dorothy and I never discussed it.

I wonder if, in recent years, Fred was up to no good with his frequent excuses to stay overnight at Dorothy's place rather than make the one-hour drive home to his family. It occurs to me to ask her if anything had happened and all she says is, "kind of." I am not clear what that means and she will not explain. I suspect it is quite a bit more than kind of, or else she would not be so secretive.

Back home in Abingville, I phone Fred's sister, Allison, to let her know I have left her brother and why. It shocks me when Allison says Fred molested her, starting at a time before she was ten and he was around fifteen or sixteen years old. She told her mother who responded with "Boys will be boys." Fred's father had told him to leave his sister alone, and after that Fred became sneakier and meaner. She feels badly about not telling me earlier.

This indicates that Fred's father already knew what his son was capable of doing before I told him about Alida. He knew! It makes his accusation that I put Fred up to it by sexualizing my daughter that much more disgusting.

Allison tells me Fred's former girlfriend, the girl he told me he had had sex with, had a pregnancy scare. After that, the girl dumped Fred and she told Allison that Fred had forced himself on her.

Holy moly. This new information that Fred sexually assaulted two girls before he met me, proves that no matter what Fred now says, he started molesting not because of anything I may or may not have done. Nothing we had, nothing from the start, was as it seemed. His deviance tainted everything and I was clueless.

Monday, 27 July 1987
I am obsessed with revisiting all my past memories through the lens of my current knowledge, looking for other vital information I previously missed. It seems like I am looking at my past through a kaleidoscope, where the view I thought was reality shifts and changes into something entirely different.

There are several more incidents that I found uncomfortable when they occurred. Now I worry that my discomfort was deadened intuition, and that in actuality more ominous things were going on.

Back when Kevin was a baby and Fred went off on his month-long buying trip to Europe, he stayed with a cousin and her husband at their tiny apartment in Rotterdam and slept on an air mattress in the living room. He came home, bursting to tell me a tale that titillated him as much as his swinging magazines. He told me that, while his cousin's husband was sleeping, she came into the living room to tuck him in. Fred gave me a bawdy description of how she was inappropriate with him. It stopped because, of course, he ended it.

In 1977, as an overwhelmed and depressed young mother, I thought the story was preposterous. Now I can see that Fred's pattern of telling me a little bit of an event, but twisting it enough to blame the girl, is probably what happened. I suspect that he told me a seed of truth, and that the actual story is that he forced himself on his Dutch cousin.

When a single mother took over operation of one of the stores supplied by EuroMed Importing, Fred befriended her and her adolescent daughter. He took them out for dinners, always claiming to me that the outings were work-related.

During the fall of 1986, Fred got the mother's permission to bring her twelve-year-old daughter home with him for a weekend. It was a surprise for Alida, he said. It was also a surprise to me to have an extra child under our roof that weekend. The two girls took an instant dislike to each other, and our young houseguest was distant and rude to all of us except Fred. It had been weird. On Saturday, Fred took the girl to the office to do some work for him.

In hindsight, she had been alone with him for at least six hours driving to and from home and another eight hours on the Saturday. That was many hours of opportunity for him to have done something. He claimed the girl worked hard and he paid her extremely well, too well. Now, I am inclined to suspect it was hush money. What if the girl was not rude, but traumatized?

If my concern that he could have molested the girl has validity, she is certainly still at risk with Fred on the loose. I swallow my humiliation and phone the mother. She is quick to say nothing happened to her daughter. Fred would not do something so awful because he was their friend and such a nice man. She clearly knows only his Dr Jekyll side. The mother is certain that if Fred had tried anything, her daughter would have told her. I ask her to speak with the girl. She refuses, positive that I am overreacting.

I am afraid that my customer is another mother Fred did a good job of grooming. With her and my mother, Fred had used flattery. That begs the question how he groomed me. I suppose that in the very early days of our relationship he had used flattery with me, too. As time went on, threats and degradation overtook flattery as his preferred method because they proved more effective in shutting me up.

Similar to the customer's daughter, Fred also brought my young niece Nakita to our house for surprise visits. Fred had a dark aura about him, a squinty eye smirk, when he had kinky ideas on his mind. He had the same swaggering attitude each time he brought home either the customer's daughter or Nakita, and now I have a better idea of why that was. I am venturing into feelings rather than facts, but do not dare ignore my awakening intuition.

I phone Dorothy, and urge her to ask Nakita if Uncle Fred had ever done anything uncomfortable to her. Once again, I am told that I am overreacting. She is sure that Nakita would have told her if anything had happened. I remind her that, until recently, I also believed my daughter would tell me, and I had been wrong. My pleas that she re-consider and speak to my niece fall on deaf ears.

Wednesday, 29 July 1987
Tucked between bills and junk mail is a letter to Alida. After the July 6th letter on my desk, I will not take a chance. I think it is fair to open my daughter's mail to protect her from her abuser, regardless of his relationship to her.

Although the letter is brief and relatively benign, I find fault with, "*Maybe someday we can go back to where we were.*" That he wants his daughter to go back to the relationship they had is ludicrous. I believe withholding my daughter's mail is the right thing to do.

Saturday, 1 August 1987
It smacks me between the eyes. Detective Kingston said Fred confessed to first abusing Alida in 1979. Alida was four years old. Only four.

In Alida's baby book, I see that at four years old, she had not yet begun to lose her baby teeth and she weighed only thirty-three pounds (15 kg). She had not yet started kindergarten. So young. So tiny.

Four years old was about the time when she seemed to become more headstrong. She threw impressive temper tantrums and I would send her to her room for timeouts. In her bedroom, Alida carried on even worse. Bedtime was the same. Neighbours across the street heard her screaming once and they asked what was going on. I had no idea. Mom said the problem was that I was too lenient. In reality, the stricter I was, the more Alida's outbursts escalated.

The only way I could calm her would be for us to sit together on her bedroom floor. With Alida curled in my lap, I would rock her and sing, and she would slowly settle. Talking did not help. I switched up her bedroom, but it was no better. Now I understand that she probably did not yet have the language to describe what was happening. All along, I thought my parenting was at fault or maybe that she was just a difficult child. It is now apparent what caused her tantrums, her increased agitation in her bedroom, and her difficulty to settle down at night. Fred knew why she was upset, but her distress did not stop him.

I try to recall if there was a change in Fred's behaviour around 1979. All I can think of is one incident that happened around that time that always had me feeling something was off. I had gone to a Calvinette counsellor convention in Grand Rapids, Michigan, and my mother looked after the kids. When I arrived home, Alida was there with Fred. It was not the fact that four-year-old Alida was with her father that bothered me, but the reason he gave. Fred said that he had felt unwell and he wanted her home so she could dial 911 in case something happened to him. I questioned why he would not have walked the block to the hospital emergency department rather than drive two hours, and he said he had not been that sick, but needed someone there with him just in case.

I had found Fred's story peculiar, and thought it was reckless of him to put his daughter in the position of being his caregiver. Strange, but in itself not an indication he was molesting her. Now I recognize this incident is another piece of the puzzle that, by itself, was insufficient for me to see the whole. All the same, it will take me forever to forgive myself for not knowing.

Then, it dawns on me. Of course, Fred did not change behaviours in 1979. Alida was not the first girl he molested. Fred had been abusing girls for at least 23 years, starting at least eight years before he showed up at the Young People's meeting where we met. He did not change habits; he just changed whom he victimized.

Four years old! He is not even safe with wee kids. Until now, I thought that he preferred teen girls and vulnerable young women, but a four-year-old? My four-year-old little girl.

I wish I were a wolf so I could howl in the wind.

Tuesday, 4 August 1987

Detective Kingston let me know that Fred appeared at the police station to have his mugshot and fingerprints taken. It makes me ill to think I married a sex offender. I wanted to be proud of my husband. I always tried to maintain his good image. My reward for the wasted effort is mortification that my husband is charged with the crime that criminals abhor.

The official charge is that, "Frederick Pieter Smit, dob December 13, 1946, did between January 4, 1983 & June 30, 1987 inclusive, at the City of Abingville, Ontario, sexually assault Alida Smit. Contrary to Section 246.1(1) of the Criminal Code."

The detective explained that there were changes in the criminal code laws on January 4, 1983; therefore, they were not pursuing charges for the sexual assaults that Fred perpetrated against Alida between 1979 and January 3, 1983.

Poof. Four years of my child's molestation evaporate with no legal consequences for her offender.

Wednesday, 5 August 1987
The latest business development is suspicious. I have two primary Dutch suppliers, one for medical equipment and the other for medical supplies. The main contact for the equipment supplier is a man Fred calls a friend. That company's price list is the one missing from its folder in the filing cabinet. Today, the equipment supplier informs me that going forward they are changing how they will be doing business with EuroMed Importing. They insist on payment before shipping instead of the original agreement of paying cash on delivery. The other change is that they need greater lead time to process orders.

Friday, 7 August 1987
The Task Force counsellor has good news and bad news. The good news is that the secretary she knows is interested in the job. The bad news is that the Task Force was a pilot project and the funding has expired. Since I will no longer be able to see this counsellor, she suggests I attend a support group at the women's shelter. I find that odd since I was only beaten up once. She tells me physical abuse is only one of many forms of domestic violence.

Monday, 10 August 1987
With the changes in conditions my equipment supplier imposed, I need to come up with $50,000 sooner than I counted on. Even by slashing expenses as much as possible, my cash flow remains tight. The bank manager insists I need to eliminate one of the vehicle loans. The only vehicle I can do without while still operating the business is Fred's Chrysler Fifth Avenue. I persuade the banker that if Fred assumes responsibility for the loan, I may give him the car. By registered letter, I advise Fred that we must make alternate arrangements, and I give him until next Friday to decide if he wants to either return the car, or to keep it and assume the $4,000 loan. Keeping the car would be accepting a $10,000 gift, a financial no-brainer.

The secretary comes in for an interview. Going on instinct, I hire her on the spot without checking references. I look forward to her being in the office because she has the biggest and greatest laugh I have ever heard, and I can do with some genuine laughter.

Today I saw my mother-in-law at the grocery store when I almost tripped over the wheels of her walker. I say hello and all she says is, "I cannot help de vay it is."

Then she hobbles away as fast as her arthritic legs will take her. I have not spoken to her since mid-June and suspect contact with me is *verboten*. I wonder what she believes is going on. Her unwillingness to speak to me confirms the battle lines are firmly drawn and she is not on our side.

Tuesday, 11 August 1987
I arrive at the courthouse early for Fred's first criminal court appearance for the sexual assault charge. It is my first time ever in a courtroom and I am probably as nervous as I imagine him to be. As

I sit there alone, Fred approaches the bench dressed in his newest, made-to-measure, three-piece suit. He bought a new silk tie and a pocket square the same shade as his baby blue eyes. His appearance brings to mind a clean-cut mortician, not a slimy creep who does nasty things to young girls. Court is put over one month, "to be spoken to."

Thursday, 13 August 1987

This long, hot, hellish summer is winding down. I still sleep for only an hour or two per night, even after I drink a few glasses of wine (and sometimes more) to dull my frenetic thoughts. Meals continue to consist of apples and milkshakes and my weight is plummeting. Out of desperation, I make a doctor appointment. He listens and prescribes two sleeping pills: not two kinds of pills, but two tablets.

He says I need counselling, not medication, and refers me to a social worker who opened a private practice. My doctor asks about my drinking habits and tells me alcohol acts as a depressant. That explains why I feel worse when I drink. When I get home, I pour all the booze down the drain. I think I just had a narrow escape. If he had been generous in prescribing pills, I would have taken them. I have enough problems without adding substance abuse to the list.

Friday, 14 August 1987

I clean and rearrange the furniture in our bedroom. I suppose it is my bedroom now. Sleeping on the couch with a butcher knife in my hand is abnormal. From the office, I drag home an old filing cabinet that locks. It will prevent the kids from reading my growing collection of journal entries, letters from Fred, and the pamphlet I took from the CAS office.

The children are home, back where they belong. Until school begins, it will be touchy with Alida watching her brother. With someone I trust in the office, I can go home every few hours to check in on them and rush home if the kids need me. I am thankful for my blessings.

Despite nothing feeling normal to me, my goal for the next few weeks is to get us back into regular schedules of eating meals together, bedtimes, and chores. Life goes on, and I hope these routines will help us move forward.

Friday, 21 August 1987
Today is Fred's deadline to decide about the car and I have heard nothing. I find the vehicle parked in front of Herman's garage, so I walk to their door to ask for the key. Fred answers. He was waiting for me and says he is returning the car. He refuses to give me the key until I sign a document he has prepared that is full of legal gobbledygook meant to bamboozle me. I refuse to sign and leave with Fred hollering a trail of obscenities behind me.

It is late afternoon when the locksmith finishes making a key from the little metal coded tag I found in the file with the car's bill of sale. Lena watches my children, and my next stop is the front desk of the police station. I tell them I expect problems retrieving my company car and ask if they will send an officer along for my safety. The police try to convince me this is a domestic dispute. I show them the bill of sale proving the car is a business asset, and therefore, I argue, it is a business dispute. When I shrug my shoulders and say someone will call them from the hospital, they grudgingly relent and assign an officer. By this time, it is getting dark.

The officer stays well out of sight as I walk up to the car, unlock the door, and climb in the driver's side. I notice Fred sitting in a lawn chair right beside the passenger door. Before I can put the key in the ignition, Fred is on top of me. He pins me down and pounds on my head, face, and arms. It is clear his plan is to beat me silly, but of course, he has no idea there is anyone nearby to hear my screams, and boy, do I scream. The officer hauls us out of the car and tells me to leave. I drive the car away, park it inside the warehouse, have Lena pick me up, and we all go home.

Later, the officer comes to the house to see if I want Fred charged with assault. Apparently, it is up to me. I desperately want him charged, but dare not say so. It could push him over the edge. I know from my life insurance agent that Fred cashed in his policy, meaning he has funds to buy a gun or carry out his threat to hire a killer.

The children have seen more police in the past two months than they have in their entire lives. I do not tell them why the officer came. I will be hiding behind heavy makeup and long sleeves until the bruises heal.

Tuesday, 25 August 1987

I do not know how far Fred actually went with Alida, but knowing he had been in her bed makes me wonder why the CAS worker never said that Alida should go to the doctor. I recall that Fred recently had an infection or STD or something. What if Alida was infected? While confidentiality prohibits our family doctor from telling me what Fred had, he said it should suffice for her to have a urine sample and blood work done. If avoidable, neither the doctor nor I want to put her through an intrusive swab.

I keep my attitude casual when I bring Alida to the lab. I do not want to worry her, so my cover story is that the lab tests are standard for girls her age. Thank goodness, she does not ask me for details. The doctor promises to call if the results show any reason for concern.

The business credit card bill arrives with a substantial charge for a call to Phone Fulfillment Inc. in New York, the 1-900-Sex Talk call Fred admitted to making. Fred played, and I paid.

In the world of Fred, paying for his sexual fetishes with money is an inexpensive cost. What no one knows, another secret, is that I paid with another extreme sacrifice.

I became pregnant again in 1979, and near the end of the first trimester, I had a spontaneous abortion, an unfortunate miscarriage. Because we never told anyone another baby was on the way, I never had to tell anyone I lost the baby. The doctor identified the cause as an invasive chlamydia infection. Since then, I have been barren due to scarring.

Fred had known about his infection and sought medical treatment for himself, but he never suggested I get checked. My doctor said I was one of the 75 percent of women who are asymptomatic. Fred could never understand why losing the baby should bother me. He threatened that, if I told anyone about the baby or the STD, he would have no choice but to spread rumours that I brought chlamydia home from one of my many affairs. It did not matter that my last encounter had been seven years before. Fred set it up so that his reputation stayed intact and I was stranded in my grief, alone.

Thursday, 27 August 1987
I meet with the divorce lawyer to prepare for family court. My goals are to get custody, limit Fred's access to supervised visits, and start on property settlement.

It appears Fred is thinking along the same lines because he mails me a lengthy, detailed proposal. It takes a while for me to wade through the wordiness and grasp what he wants. If I have it correctly, he sees our options as black and white. He gives me two choices.

Option number one is for reconciliation. It takes Fred four pages to say this option requires we admit our wrongs to each other, I must tell him why I am so angry, go for Christian counselling, and sell the business. He is clear he wants this option, and then we will live together happily ever after according to God's will.

Option number two is *"legal separation"* which Fred says, *"is a Biblical description of divorce and does not allow re-marriage. If you select this, I will fight for custody as soon as possible and get an injunction barring you from disposing assets."* In this option, I need to give his parents $45,000 and a new car as per oral agreement. I never made such an agreement with them, orally or otherwise.

Saturday, 29 August 1987

Fred asks to see the children, so we plan a visit that I will supervise. I only ask that he does not discuss our relationship. The kids are quite anxious, so I help them make a list of things they need to feel safe. Their requests are

- We have the right to say a topic is off limits and Dad will drop it.
- We do not want interruptions when speaking.
- All touching must be approved by us.
- The car is our safe place where Dad will leave us alone.

Because Fred readily agrees to all our requests, I think it is safe to proceed. We plan to meet at Rotary Park after lunch. At the last minute, Alida does not want to come along, stay home, or go to a friend's house. She threatens to run away if I make her go. She will not consider anyone staying at the house with her. We do not find a solution when it is time to go, so I tell her to come along and wait in the car.

Near the park, Alida curls up into a little ball in the back seat. When we get there, Kevin hops out while I try to comfort Alida. She retreats into a trance-like state. Meanwhile, I see Fred has a Bible in one hand and with the other he takes Kevin to the picnic table furthest away from the car. I feel torn in two, with two children who require my attention.

Alida does not respond to me except to push me away when I try to comfort her. Eventually, I signal that we have to leave. Thankfully, Kevin takes it in stride, but then Fred yells and curses, blaming me for cutting the visit short.

At bedtime, when I tuck my son in, he asks, "Mom, why did you have so many boyfriends? Dad said that's why you two fought so much all the time."

Monday, 31 August 1987

Kevin receives a letter from his dad that makes me wonder what Fred did for which he needs his son's forgiveness.

> *Dear Kevin,*
> *Yes. I did some bad things. I was wrong and I know it.*
> *All I can say is that I am so, so sorry. I need you to forgive me.*
> *Love,*
> *Daddy*

Alida is quieter and more withdrawn, Kevin is depressed, and I am a mess. I call my lawyer to ask for advice because I cannot supervise Fred's visits. I have no alternatives to suggest because I do not have faith that the people supporting Fred (his parents, my parents, or Herman) will take the risk seriously, and I am afraid that anyone I trust will be subject to Fred's harassment until they either give in to him or give up on me.

While on the phone, I ask the lawyer if he can do something to stop Fred from telephoning, sending letters, following me around town, and driving by the house all the time. By the heavy sighs, I understand my lawyer is quickly growing impatient with me.

Thursday, 3 September 1987

> *Dear Alida,*
> *I know that I was the one who destroyed the trust you had in*

me. I hurt you and am very, very sorry for what I did. I understand you can't trust me right now. I hope someday you will be able to do so again.

I miss you every day and want us to be okay again, just like we were. I will always remember that when I was away, it was always you who came running to greet me when I came home. We had such good times together.

I've sent along a devotional to help you forgive me and to be closer to God.

I pray for you every day, and I really do love you.
Dad

It is good he says he loves her, but what does his love mean? He loved her and abused her. She was distraught and he continued to abuse her. Now, it is possible that she will have to testify against him. I worry that hearing about all his love will make Alida waver. Fred is capable of using threats. He used code words to shut me up, and my concern is that his letter has coded references to keep her silent. I hold this letter along with the others, not sure if, or when, to give them to my kids.

Labour Day Weekend, 1987

The Kettles, my little sister Juliana, my kids and I piled into my work van on Friday to go to Parry Sound for the long weekend. We went because I had business concerning the log structure and the two properties, the lot where we planned to build a new warehouse and the house property. I had also wanted us to have a bit of a vacation, which we did. We had fun and caught a break from drive-bys, Mr Nobody phone calls, and daily pressures.

Friday night, I finished reading a book that the Task Force counsellor recommended. I am beginning to understand why she thought the women's shelter group might be helpful. The book describes emotional and verbal abuse. For the first time, I realize there are definitions for how Fred mistreated me.

Being with my own father this weekend and re-experiencing his temper brings back unpleasant memories from when I was growing up. Without my rose-coloured glasses, I can see that my childhood was an unsafe time where I had no one whom I could trust to protect me.

I remember my father shouting all too well. I always considered myself lucky when all he did was yell. That, I could effectively shut out. When I was less lucky, he applied his interpretation of the Bible's childrearing philosophy, "spare the rod and spoil the child." Then I would receive a spanking, a swat on the head, a twisted ear, or kicks. I coped with the physical stuff by making jokes, like how he kicked me halfway up the stairs. He did, more than once, and I had plenty of bruises from him.

I was probably too young to remember when Dad started pulling down my pants to spank me. I do recall the last time. I had been frantic about keeping the sight of my naked puberty hidden from my brothers and little sisters.

One of the more dramatic fights I had with Dad was when he refused something and I questioned why. He went ballistic, yelling and chasing me, while my little sisters cried, "Don't kill her." I ran outside and climbed into the lilac bush, staying hidden until my father left to go to a Men's Society meeting.

Sometimes, I was clueless as to what I did to deserve Dad's punishments. When I said so, Dad would get angrier. He would say I was a *stommeling* and give me extra punishment for being so stupid. My crying also made him more violent. "Dat vas vor vat you did and now you get it again vor crying."

The challenge was to keep the tears back until I could find a safe place to cry. With time, I became better at watching him administer my beatings from outside of myself and gain distance from my feelings, thereby not holding a grudge toward Dad. Understanding how I coped with my father helps me recognize that mentally stepping away was also how I managed Fred's moods and shenanigans.

Mom also physically hurt me. From her, I had constant bruises on the fleshy part of my upper arms. When I did things I knew were wrong, I deserved her twisting pinches. Most of her punishments were for things I did not understand, infractions unclear to me such as looking at her in a disrespectful way or referring to her as "she" or "her" instead of saying "my mother."

Mom hurt me in another way, too. I believe what she did was because she was oblivious and that she probably meant well, yet all the same I experienced it as a violation, an assault on my body and my sexuality. I was already in high school, and puberty had begun, although Mom had not yet thought to buy me a bra. I had a cold and Mom forcefully insisted on rubbing Vicks onto my chest. She pushed me down on the bed and slapped my hands when I tried to stop her. My mother rubbing my chest while pretending I was not developing made me want to disappear. Shortly afterward, a mysterious six-week illness began; the illness that I now know was a major depression and not something curable with antibiotics.

My mother also overlooked my development when she failed to explain menstruation or provide appropriate products. I was too shy to ask for what I needed, and that left me stuffing toilet paper in my pants on a monthly basis for two years until my bolder sister Ellie neared puberty and informed our mother she needed to provide her daughters with feminine hygiene supplies.

The scales have fallen from my eyes, and for the first time I can see clearly that I shifted from the familiarity of commonplace violence in my childhood home into dating and marriage where the abuse, albeit in slightly different forms, continued unabated. I did not recognize it as abuse because, for more than thirty years, I accepted physical, emotional, and sexual violations as unexceptional facts of my life.

Next week, I will register for the women's shelter group and hope to learn something about staying out of all types of abusive relationships. I want to be a positive role model and teach my children that relationships should not be about fear and manipulation. I cannot change the abuse that happened, but I am determined to change how my little family will go forward.

Thursday, 10 September 1987

My divorce lawyer said it was unnecessary for me to attend the first appearance of family court for our separation and divorce. He calls me when he gets back to his office after court to advise me that he successfully got me temporary possession of the house, an order for interim custody, interim supervised access for Fred, and a restraining order for Fred not to communicate with us. Fred successfully got an order restraining me from depleting property. This means I cannot sell anything like vehicles, equipment, store shares, or land the company owns to free up working capital to repay my enormous debt, unless Fred consents. It is very good news that I no longer need to supervise visits, since that did not go so well for anyone. The bad news is that the judge ordered CAS to supervise access, so I will again be under their scrutiny.

Friday, 11 September 1987

I was still at work when a man came to the house after school with gifts from Fred for the kids. Kevin opened the door because he recognized the man from church and thought it was safe. It is not a special occasion and not a coincidence the delivery of gifts occurred within one day of the restraining order issuance. Fred taunts me and uses a church person to do so.

Each child received a neatly gift-wrapped Bible. Each Bible has a verse written in Fred's beautiful handwriting.

In Alida's Bible he wrote, *"Suffer the little children and forbid them not to come to me, for of such is the Kingdom of Heaven. And He laid his hands on them, and departed thence. Matthew 19:14-15."*

What incredible gall to quote that verse to the girl upon whom he has laid his filthy hands. It is diabolical that he obscures his darkness with an inappropriately used Bible verse.

Because my lawyer helped me get the restraining order prohibiting communication, I call him. He says I should phone the police. The police say they can do nothing until I have a copy of the court order and tell me to call my lawyer. My lawyer cannot help me until he gets a copy of the order from the court. After going in circles for an hour, all it adds up to is, restraining order or not, there is nothing I can do today.

Tuesday, 15 September 1987
Criminal court is put over to October 20th, again "to be spoken to." I am surprised to see that Fred has hired the reputedly best criminal lawyer in Abingville. The only reason he would do that would be to get off as easily as possible. If he were accepting responsibility, he would already have admitted guilt and accepted the consequences. While I wait to go into the courtroom, I sit on a bench across from Fred and he smirks. He finds all of this amusing.

Wednesday, 16 September 1987
I do my own customs brokerage work, again with no issues, and receive a shipment from my Dutch equipment supplier. I had to wire the funds prior to them shipping the order, which was a financial squeeze. When we unload the container, I become suspicious that there is a plot to sabotage me. Is it possible Fred's business friend in Holland purposely messed with my order? I am short-shipped about $5,000, and a lot of the merchandise was already damaged prior to shipping.

The day finishes with the equipment supplier refusing to refund the $5,000 that was short-shipped or to compensate for the damaged stock. Then they withdraw their commitment to sell in Canada exclusively to EuroMed Importing. Fred must have been in touch with them because they tell me they have no objections to deliver to both Fred and me.

At our church, the Young People's Society has co-advisors, usually a married couple, but always a male and female. Gus and I have taken on this role for the past four years. It made Fred jealous whenever Gus and I met to plan the meetings, always at my place so I did not need to get a sitter and also to make sure Fred could see that I was doing nothing wrong. Whenever Fred was home, he would glower, turn the TV up too loud, and stomp off to bed when he did not get a reaction. Then, of course, he would accuse me of having an affair. Gus was never a lover, but he became a friend.

Over the past few weeks, Gus has been visiting for more than just planning meetings. He is younger than I am by several years and unmarried. We have moved beyond a hug and he stays later than he did before, but we are not dating. Gus would never commit to a relationship with a woman who will be a divorcée. I know nothing will come of it, but he does provide me a bit of relief during this stressful time. That blew up today.

Somehow, Fred found out I was spending more time with Gus than I had in the past. Fred complained to the *dominee* who summoned Gus to the parsonage office where he was scolded for the grave sin of seeing a married woman (me). The *dominee's* big issue is that Gus is interfering with the possibility of reconciliation. Gus feels he must listen out of respect, and because he is afraid for his reputation. He decides to stop seeing me unless we expressly meet relating to young people meetings. Whatever.

According to Gus, the *dominee* said that Fred was regularly perching in the pine tree outside my dining room window to spy on me with his binoculars. That is how Fred knew Gus visited me.

In frustration, I phone Fred to ask that he stop talking about me. I also ask him to quit driving by and to end the Mr Nobody phone calls. Fred says he will not stop any of it because, legally, he is doing nothing wrong. Phoning him was a dumb thing to do. Now Fred knows he is getting to me.

Friday, 25 September 1987

It is no surprise when my elder calls to request a meeting. Worrying that it might become contentious, I arrange the visit during school hours.

The first thing I do is give my elder notice that I resign as a co-advisor of the Young People's group as soon as they can arrange a replacement. I figure it is better to quit voluntarily before they dismiss me.

Overall, the elder's attitude turns out to be a pleasant surprise. He says I do not need to go into details about my past, nor does he bother me about seeing Gus. He understands why I remain separated from Fred. He is supportive instead of judgmental. I was wrong. My church community does have our backs.

Sunday, 27 September 1987

At church this morning, Alida beats me to the bulletin. She shoves it into her pocket instead of passing it to me after she reads it. Kevin gets me another and then I understand why she is upset. The consistory meeting report says they accepted Fred's resignation from the CRC. Kevin reads it and, in a whisper, asks if that means Daddy is going to hell. I tell him no. Then Alida starts to cry and people in front of us turn around to see what is going on. To quiet both kids, I give them enough *dropjes* (black licorice) to stuff their mouths full.

In the CRC, resigning from the church is shameful. I almost walk us out, but that will draw more unwanted attention. Alida drops so low in the pew she almost lays on the floor. It is not surprising that Fred resigned and no one owed me an explanation. Still, my elder would have known two days ago, and he could have let me know so that I could have prepared my children for this shock. Instead, they are forced to absorb the blow publicly. I cannot imagine this oversight was accidental, which means my church community does not have our backs after all.

Leaving the sanctuary after the morning service, we get a few quick hellos before eyes rapidly shift. We all know resignations generate much gossip and speculation. I scuttle away with my children following me like two sad little ducklings.

Friday, 2 October 1987

I guess I have to find a replacement equipment supplier after all. The latest telex from the current supplier indicates, "that effective immediately, due to streamlining in our company, we are discontinuing all export activities to Canada, to both Fred and yourself." I can only assume Fred has caused enough of a ruckus that they decided I am more trouble than I am worth.

Monday, 5 October 1987

My Orangeville customer had a visit. "A strange visit," she said.

Fred told her his plan to open a store just four blocks from our home, selling the same items as Abingville Home Health Solutions, the store his father sold in May. He also said I still owe him the money he stole. It is striking that he can spin tales so convincingly that she does not realize how ridiculous this is. At equalization, Fred said, he will get half of EuroMed Importing's value as of the date of separation. He told her that he also plans to start a new import/wholesale company selling the same items EuroMed

Importing carries. She understandably needs assurance that I will be able to consistently provide stock for her store.

I am baffled. I understand Fred wants to get even with me, but why is he undermining our assets of which he will receive half? Right now, I am still giving him weekly cheques and the company profits are the only income we have.

This afternoon, another customer calls and says that he is leery about buying from me. He is afraid of depending on my company because of the uncertainty of what Fred might do. This customer refuses to tell me whether Fred has been to see him, but it is not difficult for me to figure it out for myself.

Sunday, 11 October 1987

I cannot relax in this house worrying about peeping Fred perched in the pine, peering in the windows. Home is not our haven. It is the place of fears, nightmares, and bad memories. We cannot do this any longer. To feel safe, we need a fresh start.

Monday, 12 October 1987

Fred sent a $100 cheque for child support and a letter. Another letter, despite the restraining order.

> *Although I have forgiven and buried your past, I still need to talk about all your dirt and your affairs to Herman, Herman's wife, your elder, my therapist, and my 'shrink.' They need to know everything about you so that they will be able to help me. To rebuild my future, there are a lot of other people I will need to talk to, too. Despite your mistreatment of me, I still care deeply about you and send my love.*

To the rest of the world, love and revenge are separate ideas. To Fred, they co-exist. Psycho. And the screw tightens on me.

Fred phones this evening to discuss reconciliation and

equalization. It is a useless conversation. I know that with the letter and phone call he is breaching the restraining order twice. Yet, without the paperwork, I can do nothing. It is difficult to comprehend that it takes more than a month to get a photocopy of a court order.

During the call, I ask Fred if he will co-sign the mortgage renewal due this week. Despite the fact that Fred's name is not on the deed or the mortgage, the bank is now insisting on his signature because of his claim on the matrimonial home. Fred hems and haws until I tell him the bank is threatening eviction if he does not sign—then he outright refuses.

Friday, 16 October 1987
Maggie reopens our CAS file and arranges an access visit for Fred at their office. When it is time to go, both children refuse, so I cancel. Maggie said it is okay that I do not force them. She also says the CAS is not supposed to supervise access in divorce cases. That makes me feel like an inadequate mother who cannot manage access. I break down and tell her about the one time I supervised a visit at Rotary Park and how poorly it went.

Fred calls later, none too happy about the cancelled visit.

He manages to get in a dig that I allow to get to me. *"I know you can't get out to sell to the customers like I used to because you are tied up with the kids and all, so do you want me to say hello to the folks in Acton, Orangeville, and Barrie for you?"*

Monday, 19 October 1987
A Dutch man who EuroMed Importing pays to organize shipping from Holland calls to ask what is going on between Fred and the equipment supplier, the same company who said a few weeks ago that they would not sell to Fred or me. There are rumours in Holland that my supplier and Fred are now in business together. All

I can tell him is that I have also heard rumblings of Fred importing but know nothing concrete. It is startling to find out first-hand that rumours have no international boundaries.

The bank finally agreed to accept only my signature on the mortgage renewal. By extending the amortization period and decreasing the monthly payments, I will have the option to rent out this house if Fred refuses to sell it. This is a step forward in moving to a new home. With that settled, I make a number of phone calls to find a house to rent. By the fourth call, I grasp that property owners do not want to rent to single mothers. Each one is eager to show me their house until they realize I have children and no husband. Discrimination and stigma of being a single parent may not be legal, but I now have first-hand experience.

Tuesday, 20 October 1987

I am unsure if Fred saw me in criminal court or if he was just ignoring me. He still needs to enter a plea. The charge of sexual abuse has been reduced to "matter" and "the matter" is put over to April 7th, 1988, for "Election and Disposition." I do not know what that means. With the delay, "the matter" will hang over Alida and there is everything the matter with that.

Friday, 23 October 1987

At the office, my secretary places a registered letter on my desk. Underneath the date, Mr Amateur Lawyer typed "*WITHOUT PREJUDICE.*" The dictionary says that means, "Without dismissal of or a legal right, claim, etc." The gist of the letter is that Fred has been to the Supreme Court of Ontario in Bankruptcy and got an Absolute Order of Discharge. He is disappointed I have not yet paid him $20,000 for the money he stole, and I have one week to do so before he takes further action.

Without prejudice, Fred is trying to intimidate me into forking over a large chunk of cash outside of our separation agreement, and that would be a good investment for a new business. *"Further action"* in his lingo means legal action. If he thought he had a fighting chance to win, he would have already initiated a lawsuit. I hold firm to the position that I will do nothing until I get notice from Price Waterhouse Bankruptcy Trustees or from the Supreme Court of Ontario in Bankruptcy.

Saturday, 24 October 1987

This morning, I see my father-in-law drive by again. I am fed up. The drive-bys at school bus time need to stop. With a paper copy of the restraining order finally in my hands, I am sure I can do something about us being harassed. The part I think can help me is:

> ```
> This Court Orders that the Defendant is
> restrained from molesting, annoying or
> harassing the Plaintiff and the children
> of the marriage or from communicating
> with the Plaintiff and the children of
> the marriage.
> ```

At the desk of the police station, a constable looks at the order, shakes his head, and says it only applies to Fred. If I had wanted it to apply to other people, the order should have specified Fred is "directly or indirectly" restrained from harassing or communicating with us. Even if it had said indirect contact, there is no distance restriction in the order. The constable said that the way the order reads, Fred, or anyone for that matter, is free to drive past the house, the kids, and me as often as they like. There is also no legal issue with Fred, formerly in his Chrysler and now in his father's car, following my car around town with his front bumper right up against my back bumper. Being that close is apparently not annoying or harassment.

The police constable says he is sorry he can do nothing. "However, if it would make you happy, I will caution Fred and have him talk to his parents."

It would have made me happier if I had a court order that included the terms needed to keep us safe. I had assumed that my lawyer would know the wording I needed. That assumption has become my mistake, but how was I to have known?

If the constable spoke with Fred and if Fred talked to his parents, it did more harm than good. They are back at it this afternoon. At one point, the parents drive so slowly I think they might stop. I give up doing laundry and join the kids outside. We have a blast jumping and rolling around in the maple leaves. Everyone is tired and happy this evening.

Sunday, 25 October 1987

I started seeing the social worker my doctor recommended for individual counselling. It helps to have one person outside of my day-to-day life with whom I can speak. She tells me that not all mothers believe and support their sexually abused children and some stay with the abuser. For me, it was not an option to ignore what Fred did, which might in part have been because I was already desperate to get out of this marriage before the honeymoon was over.

At the women's shelter intake appointment, I tell the counsellor, "I'm pretty stressed and can't reduce it because I have to take care of my kids."

I must have sounded whiney because she pointed out that caring for my children is a choice. If it is too much or if I do not want to parent, I can put my children into foster care. Ouch.

I had not realized how sorry I was feeling for myself. That is exactly what I wanted to avoid, yet there I was. Now when my kids drive me nuts, reminding myself I am a mother by choice empowers me to feel strong and in charge.

I think the shelter group is going to be helpful. It has a psychoeducational format and the first thing we learn is the cycle of violence or abuse. There is the incident of abuse—reconciliation (kiss and make up with flowers, gifts, and sweet talk)—an increase in tension—fight again and back to abuse. The night I drugged Fred was the first time I became conscious of a predictable progression to his abusive behaviour, so the cycle of abuse makes perfect sense.

Having some insight into how we functioned as a couple makes me wonder about what I now recognize as confusion when I speak with Fred and the anxiety when we have no contact for a few days. It may be how I go through the tension phase of the abuse cycle, but it feels like something more sinister. Whenever I talk to Fred, his voice begins as hypnotic and soothing. After a few minutes, I become flustered and feel myself sucked into a black cloud of bewilderment. While this has probably always been the case, the distance I now have from him allows me to see it clearly. I have taken big steps to pull away from his coercion. My next goal is to wean myself from needing to speak with Fred and to live with the withdrawal anxiety.

Monday, 26 October 1987

My children have already been "latchkey kids" for an hour after school for more than a year and it has worked. They are good kids, and if something comes up, I can drive home from the office in less than five minutes. They always call me when they arrive home, and today they are in a tizzy. I rush home to find my generally unflappable Alida sobbing. Their Opa had been loitering around the school bus stop, making mean faces at them. The kids got on the bus, and he followed until they got off at home. Then he sped away. The bus monitor confirmed that Fred's father had been there and that he appeared angry and stern. The kids do not want to take the bus anymore. I promise rides for a week and then we will try again.

Wednesday, 28 October 1987

Things are looking up! I find us a new home and we are moving. Through the grapevine, I hear of a place in a decent neighbourhood that will soon be available for rent. Before it hits the market, I talk to the owners who are relatives of relatives, and they will rent to me. I am hoping Fred will agree to sell our matrimonial home, but if not, I will rent it out.

My brothers Bert and Bart offer to help me with some urgent repairs to make this Victoria Street house rentable or saleable. They understand my need to get us out of here and do not think it is silly. I have other friends who also support me. Tessa does. Lena listens and is always willing to help when I need her. John has dropped by a few times, and he does not seem to be judging me. At work, I have my wonderful secretary and the warehouse staff, and we are getting through our Christmas rush without working overtime. I feel hopeful when I feel supported.

Monday, 2 November 1987

Fred has made the rounds again. Two customers say he told them of plans to sue me and he audaciously asked them for loans to help with his legal costs.

At 11 p.m., the phone rings and it is His Highness again. His reason for phoning is to get several coins he says I stole from him. He is so bloody unreasonable and I cannot convince him that in July, when he picked up his belongings that I had set out on the porch, he received his entire coin collection.

I ask him to rethink instilling apprehension in the customers, since their unease will not help the value of our assets or feed our children. Fred claims it is a free country and he may visit my customers if he wants to; he does not need to answer to me about what he does, and if the assets depreciate, it is my problem. He will get half the value at the time of separation, and if I run my business into the ground, it is no affair of his.

It is clear Fred does not want to settle peacefully. He wants the fight. To add insult to injury, he tells me that one of my customers lent him a $25,000 stake to begin his new life. I am guessing that whoever lent him the money did not anticipate Fred would use it to buy a sporty red Mustang. I see this new car when he stalks me around town and hear it when he revs his engine driving past our house multiple times a day.

He tells me he has a job cutting grass and will soon start paying $40 per week for child support. Grass does not grow in Ontario in November unless you are smoking it.

He finally gets to what I suspect is his underlying reason for phoning. There are apparently a few lawsuits in the works. Fred plans to sue me to recover the money he stole. His parents are going to sue me for breach of contract. Fred is going after custody. I know at this point these are only threats, but they all worry me.

I call the police to report a breach. The officer says that a phone call is not proof. It is a matter of he says/she says that will not hold up in court and therefore a waste of police time.

Tuesday, 3 November 1987

After speaking with Fred just before bedtime, I fret all night. I always pick up the phone to screen incoming calls because my kids think their lives are over without hourly contact with their friends. An answering machine may be the solution.[6] What would I do if I could not afford the luxury of buying things to make life manageable? Simple things mean so much. Simple things like answering machines and window blinds to stop peeping Fred from looking inside.

---

[6] In 1987, all telephones were landlines and caller ID was not available to residential customers. The only way to "screen" calls was to have the caller leave a message on an answering machine.

I am starting to worry about money. Although I have been able to pull it off up to now, with the supplier issues, all the distractions, the court order freezing assets, and the extra expenses, I do not know if EuroMed Importing is breaking even. It will be next spring, when the accountant completes the financial statements, before I find out how the company is doing. If Fred competes with me the situation will become serious, of that I have no doubt. He is out to destroy me, and he is an extremely persistent and capable man when he sets his mind to doing something.

Thursday, 5 November 1987

Fred produces another financial statement for court. This is ridiculous. Three days ago, he told me he was cutting grass, and today he identifies his employer as *"Fred's Medical Equipment & Supplies."* Fred claims a weekly income of $150 and proposes to pay $15 to charities. I wonder if he thinks that a judge will consider him a nice person because he makes donations. Charity, apparently, does not begin at home.

In this financial statement, Fred values our joint assets at separation $200,000 higher than he did in August. He thinks his valuations mean something, but they are all just numbers he pulls out of thin air. This valuation is quite a hike, and when divided in half it means that for his half, he now expects to receive more than 100 percent of my holdings.

Friday, 6 November 1987

Not to be a drama queen, but I believe the odds are in favour of me meeting a premature death, and I plan accordingly. Without fanfare or alerting the kids to my fears, I have put all my affairs in order. A new will is in the filing cabinet. Lena is the only person I fully trust and she knows where I hide the filing cabinet key. She promises that "if something happens to me," she will destroy my journals without reading them and make sure my executor gets my will. I think Lena just believes I am being conscientious and doubt she realizes I fear for my life.

Monday, 9 November 1987
Last night, when I kissed Kevin goodnight, he lifted his right arm and asked me to look at his armpit where it had begun to hurt. We see our family doctor first thing this morning. He contacts a surgeon who immediately admits Kevin to the hospital. The surgeon will be operating tomorrow morning. Kevin is being brave, although he is as scared as I am. He asks me if the lumps might be cancer.

Thinking Kevin's father deserves to know, I look up Herman's number in the phone book. At first, Herman refuses to take a message, but when I say it is something urgent to do with the children, he gives me a phone number to contact Fred. I call and a woman answers. When Fred is on the line, I tell him Kevin is having emergency surgery in the morning. In totally predicable Fred fashion, he is angry that I tracked him down and intruded on his new relationship. Shame me once for thinking he cares; shame me twice for apologizing.

Tuesday, 10 November 1987
Time distorts and every other care recedes as I pace the waiting area while my son is in surgery. In real time, it is only two hours from when they put Kevin on the gurney until the surgeon comes to talk to me. He successfully removed three tumours from Kevin's lymph nodes. In his opinion, they are not cancerous. However, we have to wait for confirmation from the lab report.

The full impact of being a single mother hits me hard. Being single is not about sitting alone with the children at the dinner table, walking into church alone, or being solely responsible to pay the bills. Being single is about facing life's fears alone. Alone. Today there are no friends or family with me, it is just me against the unknown. I fight the urge to feel too sorry for myself.

Friday, 13 November 1987

Kevin is home and it is not cancer. What a scare. What a relief.

My lovely, laughing secretary is a godsend. She made lists of urgent things for me to do when I was able to come in and she kept the office under control. That, during our Christmas season rush is awesome, particularly for a new employee. My intuition about her certainly proved correct. I brought her flowers. Daddy sent Kevin a prickly cactus.

Monday, 16 November 1987

Weekly talks with the social worker help me to understand a few things. She tells me I sometimes act child-like. I find that disgusting. I now recognize I act immature when I speak softly and peek through my eyelashes. I call it my Princess Diana look. When I speak, I raise the pitch of my voice at the end of sentences, so statements sound like questions. It makes me sound uncertain, insecure, as if I do not deserve to have a voice. I do these things more so when I am scared and that is almost all the time.

The social worker's area of practice is personal growth and she tells me it is as much about learning new things as it is about letting go of things that no longer work. Sometimes it means letting go of people. That makes sense to me. I have to let go of my marriage, Fred's family, and other people who are detrimental to my well-being. Letting go really hurts.

The women's shelter group gives me good information and insight about my relationship with Fred, and errors I never want to make again. Neither the group nor counselling gives me the understanding I most desperately need about how to parent my wounded children. Kevin sees a private counsellor. Alida started the CAS group and has a leader whom I have yet to meet. I have not heard from my CAS worker since the time when the children refused the access visit. I am still waiting to hear from the children's counselling centre.

It is exhausting for me to integrate our piecemeal, fragmented professional support. We each get help within our own silo. I am in the dark about what goes on in therapy for the kids and my therapy focusing on personal growth and domestic violence has very little to do with the kids. Yet, my task is to fit all the pieces together into a functional family system.

```
16 November 1987
CAS Transfer Recording,
Intake Worker Maggie
```

Current Situation

```
An order dated September 10th, 1987,
indicates that Mrs Smit shall have interim
custody of the children, and that Mr Smit
shall have interim access to be arranged
and supervised by the Children's Aid
Society.

Mrs Smit reported that neither child
is currently interested in seeing their
father. She arranged one meeting in a public
park; however, Alida chose to stay in the
car. They have also reported seeing their
father driving around the neighbourhood.
When they have spotted him, they have run
and hid somewhere. Alida quit her paper
route for fear of having contact with her
father. Alida is currently involved in the
sexual abuse group.

According to Mr Smit, he and the children
have a close bond and they adored him. He
cannot understand their refusal to visit
```

him and feels that if they could go back to what they had, the children's concerns would quickly fall away. He feels he was the glue that held the family together, and with his absence and things he heard by way of rumour that Mrs Smit is telling the children, their emotional instability is becoming cause for concern.

Since Mrs Smit has taken appropriate measures to ensure her children's safety and well-being, they are not considered to be in need of protection at this time. However, this case has been passed on to a protection worker in accordance with the court order. Also, the children's resistance to seeing their father is an issue of concern.

Thursday, 26 November 1987

My divorce lawyer says that for legal reasons, I cannot move next month. I try to explain to him why, for emotional reasons, we cannot stay in this house. He shakes his head and says I make it very difficult for him to do his job. I have no doubt about this lawyer's capacity, but he does not seem to grasp the extent of our distress. Moving may not be good for my case in family court, but moving is good for the rest of my life. If we do not move, I am going to be another case—a nut case.

I look in the yellow pages of the phone book for a female lawyer. I am sure a woman will better understand my dilemmas. I phone a few with no luck, so opt to leave things alone for the time being. Although I would feel more comfortable with a female, sexist Fred will be more resistant to a settlement if my lawyer is a woman. I am still hoping we will be able to negotiate a settlement out of court.

Monday, 30 November 1987

Overall, today was a magnificently awful day. It started this morning when our new CAS family service caseworker, Bea, did a home visit. Fred got to her first and he reported that I pulled down Kevin's pants and fondled his privates. It supposedly happened in the kitchen and both he and Alida saw me do it. If Fred believes I sexually abused my son, he is delusional. If he wants to get back at me, he succeeded, in spades.

Bea and the police again need to interview my children. She thought they would do it at the school and I beg her not to. The Dutch community does not need to add my CAS involvement as grist to the rumour mill. She makes a phone call and then agrees to follow me to the school. I take the kids out of class and they go in her car to the CAS office. This is a precaution so I do not have an opportunity to coach the kids as to what to say. Now that Fred made a sexual abuse allegation, the CAS procedure definitely demonstrates a lack of trust in me.

We repeat the July process. Detective Kingston is waiting for us. I sit on the cold, orange furniture in the waiting room. Alida goes in first. Kevin is next and his interview is the longer one this time. When they call me in, they tell me the allegation is not substantiated. Bea is closing this investigation, although the file will continue to remain open for access supervision. Both Bea and Detective Kingston say they believe that Fred's complaint was maliciously driven. All the same, I am aware that the fact the allegation was made will hang over me forever. It is impossible to prove something that did not happen.

I drive the kids back to school and then go home. I give myself fifteen minutes to swear and cry. How dare he allege that I molested my son? This is a heinous underhanded move on Fred's part. Exhausting every swear word I know in English, Dutch, and Primal Scream, barely touches the rage. When the time I allotted is over, I wash my face and heavily reapply my makeup to cover my swollen eyes. Returning to the office, I pretend everything is fine.

Tuesday, 1 December 1987
Bea's supervisor, a man who is also the supervisor of Alida's group, phones me to set up access. I explain that the kids are not ready to see their father. He agrees I should not force them. I ask how my daughter is doing in the group. He says that since counselling is confidential, he cannot tell me anything other than that Alida seems to be "making good progress." I have no idea what that means.

Friday, 4 December 1987
At 4 p.m., after the kids arrive home from school, Bea makes another home visit. She offers to arrange all access going forward, which means there is no longer any need for me to speak with Fred. She asks the kids about seeing their father and both say they do not want a visit yet. Bea tells my kids their father blames me for their lack of interest in visiting. I have not told them that because of concern it might sway their loyalties away from their own feelings. I do my best to not put my children in the middle and this CAS worker just plunked them there.

Monday, 7 December 1987
Every year, on the first Monday of December, EuroMed Importing hosts a customer appreciation dinner in Milton. Everyone looks forward to spending time catching up with colleagues in the same business. Stopping the tradition would cause customers to lose confidence in me. Besides, I have not seen most of them since early summer. Fred has been visiting them, so I can be certain he knows the dinner is happening and that I will be out of town. Even with a sitter, it is irresponsible to leave the kids home, so I arrange for them to stay with friends for the night where they will be safe.

The couple who bought my father-in-law's store back in May offer me a ride. We leave early so they can do some buying from a specialty company in Toronto. It is none of this Toronto vendor's business, but once he realizes who I am, he tries to pump me for details as to why Fred is out of EuroMed Importing. There is obviously no love lost between the man and Fred as he gloats over Fred's misfortune. It freaks me out that people I do not know are gossiping about my family. I escape to the car to wait, and the last thing I remember is crying.

When I again become conscious of my surroundings, I am sitting in the Milton restaurant with all my customers. I feel disoriented throughout the dinner I am hosting. It is a struggle to appear professional and remain emotionally present.

It seems Fred made the rounds yet again, according to what my customers tell me. Yesterday evening, he was at the home of the Leamington customer asking to borrow money. This morning, Fred visited my Chatham customer to ask for money and complain about me.

After the dinner, my Orangeville customer insists I stay back to talk to her about something important. She tells me Fred spent almost five hours at her house on Saturday evening, and she made notes of everything he said. The primary reason she wanted to talk to me was to give a heads up that my father-in-law is suing me for an awful lot of money. The papers were to be served this afternoon. I left Abingville earlier than Fred would have anticipated, and assume this is probably why it had not happened.

Fred is apparently quite concerned about my stability. She shows me her notes where she quoted, *"Carlyn needs to get counselling."* It is a relief Fred does not know that I am doing both group and individual counselling. It is obvious my customer cares about me, yet I am not confident I can trust her sufficiently to share that information.

Fred complained that he did not know Kevin had surgery.

(Liar. Why did he send a cactus?) Fred told her I am having an affair with Gus, not that she cares, and Fred claimed that is why he left me. (Liar.) Finally, Fred said his counselling was a success. The therapist discharged him because he is cured. (Liar.) I recently bought a book about sex offending and the author said that to be even marginally successful, sex offender therapy takes years (not weeks).

Tuesday, 8 December 1987

By a stroke of good fortune, I come home at noon. There are three envelopes in the mailbox, a letter for each of us and a $100 cheque for each child. I add another daily chore: go home at noon to screen the mail. I read the letters and then they all go into my filing cabinet.

> *Dear Carlyn,*
> *I wrote letters to the kids today and am mailing them all together. CAS said I could do this. You may read them if you want.*
> *You were not to blame for what I did to Alida. It was not a rejection of you. When we dated, you mentioned something about your small bust size to me, but you were wrong. I loved your breasts because they were a part of you, just like your eyes, your face, legs, everything. If you had had warts on your nose, I would have loved warts. Because I loved you.*
> *I wasn't trying to have sex with Alida. That doesn't justify what I did. Nothing does. I was totally wrong, and feel very ashamed of that.*
> *Don't blame me for what I didn't do. Irene came on to me when you were in the hospital. I gave Helen a back rub, nothing else. And Grace and I went for dinner and drinks. She tried to make out with me and I stopped her. That wasn't child abuse because she was sixteen and an adult. It also was not sexual assault because she was more than willing. Too bad if her conscience bothers her now.*

I won't accept the blame.

With Alida, it was technically sexual assault because I touched her breasts. I can't undo what I did. I can help her, and Kevin, by admitting what I did. I am doing that. I thought I'd be going to jail but it turns out I won't be.

Going through the courts is a long process, but I can't do anything about that. If I had a choice, it would be over already.

I'll go in April and plead guilty. Then sentencing. None of you will have to come to court.

Love,
Fred

I go to the police station to report Fred breaching the court order three times with three letters. The police officer rolls his eyes and, in a monotone voice, suggests I speak with my lawyer or take it back to family court. He blows me off. A family court judge issued the restraining order and the police department's role is enforcement. I brought proof of three blatant violations, so it is not a case of he says/she says. The issue for me is that the cops have discretion about laying a breach charge. Cops can take it or leave it, and when they leave it, women can die.

John visits again and his agenda appears to have shifted from support to reconciliation. I let him read Fred's letter that arrived today and he wonders if reunification or an out-of-court settlement is still possible. He then says he visited with Fred and his parents earlier today, and they are all up in arms about me. Of course they are.

I am no longer certain that John is a neutral party. It appears that he is now aligning with Fred and his parents, making it four-against-one. I feel mislead.

John asks me why I am so hyperactive. As we sit in my living room, I do counted cross-stitch because counting is soothing. I often catch myself counting things such as the number of meatballs I put into a pot of Dutch soup, the pieces of vegetable for a stir-fry, and the steps from my car to my office door. Today, I notice myself counting my chewing before I swallow a bite of my apple. I know this is not good, yet the harder I try to stop, the worse it gets. Counting stitches seems less insane than counting everything else.

The social worker I see for private counselling knows I am stressed. I have not told her about the compulsive counting, nor will I. She audiotapes our sessions and that adds to my fear and concern about what I say. If she ever has to report to anybody about me, it is better if there is no proof that my stress is building.

Wednesday, 9 December 1987
I am running out of steam between trips to school, my own appointments, driving Kevin to Cadets at church, Air Cadets and counselling, Alida to Calvinettes at church, gymnastics, and both kids to and from their friends. I have all the parenting responsibilities including things such as helping with homework, cleaning the house, groceries, cooking, laundry, and paying bills. In addition, I am doing my best to help my hurting children, attend counselling, and meet with Bea. I am also learning to run and operate a million-dollar business, managing the stress of the drive-bys, Mr Nobody phone calls, criminal court, and somehow finding time to hammer out a settlement agreement with Fred. Every day is a juggling act. If I had a job elsewhere, I would be in a terrible position and probably be forced to quit or be fired. Because I am self-employed, the lost time becomes my financial loss.

Everyone keeps telling me that things will get better and that is a hope I cling to. It is worth taking a pause to look at what has already improved.

Someday, I will be divorced. The kids and I are better able to express our feelings. We no longer need to pussyfoot around Fred's moods. The kids are doing well in school. It has been a few weeks since the principal called about Kevin fighting with other kids or back-talking to staff. The children invite their friends over more often and we are moving out of this haunted house in a few weeks. Those are many good things.

Bea stops by and I find out she did not give Fred permission to send us letters. Then I make a big mistake by telling her about the mail that I am keeping from the kids, including the letters and $100 cheques. I thought withholding the letters was the right thing to do to protect my kids. I explain my concern that Fred may be using coded words or that Alida may feel the money is to buy her silence. It also breaches the restraining order. All the same, Bea says it is illegal for me to withhold the children's mail and I must give it to them. I feel bullied. It seems to me she does not appreciate my concerns and that she feels she knows better than me what is the right thing to do.

I have a love-hate relationship with the CAS. On one hand, Bea tells the kids far too much, and I think she is wrong about needing to give the kids the mail; on the other, I am thankful for the support they do offer. Bea says she will arrange volunteer drivers to take Alida to and from group meetings. She assures me the drivers have undergone police checks and are safe. It may be taking advantage of their resources since I have a car, but she has no idea how much I appreciate this assistance.

Alida reads the letter from her father and is confused about who reported the abuse to the police, so I go over the details of how it occurred. Then she gets angry with me over something silly. I know why she is angry—who in her shoes would not be? I understand why she takes it out on me. I am here and she knows I will love her no matter what, making it safe for her to rail against me. All the same, it is not easy for me to handle.

There is further tension between Alida and me, mostly around who is in charge. Sometimes it seems like Alida misses being the favoured child. I understand she is trying to control her world because of what Fred did to her, but I will not abdicate my role as mother. Group therapy at the CAS or the stress of upcoming criminal court or something else seems to be making her more short-tempered and less reasonable. It is becoming increasingly difficult to know how to meet her complex emotional needs. I hope that being loving, understanding, and consistent will help. All the same, it is difficult to be unflappable while I spiral around on my own emotional magic carpet.

Friday, 11 December 1987
The bank notifies Kevin that his father put a stop payment on the $100 cheque. He already spent some of the money. I doubt Bea, who told me I had to give the kids their mail, or the CAS for that matter, will compensate the bank, so that falls on me.

My lawyer says Fred opposes listing the house for sale. Fred is unaware that we are moving regardless of his stance. He will find out soon enough that what he says does not matter. Using Lena's phone number as the contact, I place an ad in the paper to rent the house. I get a call right away and two young professional women with enchanting Scottish accents come to see the house. I promise them a year, and they understand that I hope to sell the house at some point after that. They are happy to sign a rental agreement.

Thursday, 17 December 1987
A lawsuit from my in-laws has gone from threat to reality. At the office this morning, I no sooner hang up my coat when a process server is at the door with court papers. The case centres on my father-in-law's position that he was verbally promised an income for life. The person who will testify the verbal promise was made is Fred. Thank you, gentlemen.

Fred incites his parents to sue me and the same day I am served the lawsuit, I receive a letter that makes my head spin.

> *Dear Carlyn,*
>
> *The adults of our church are having a dinner on Saturday, December 19th at Herman's house. I would very much like to take you. I need to you let me know ASAP.*
>
> *With love,*
>
> *Fred*

I do not call him. Instead, I go to the police station. With a copy of the restraining order and Fred's letter, I am sure I have a clearly documented violation of the court order. The police disagree. Fred's ability to bury a wolf in sheep's clothing convinces them that the letter is sweet. The benign appearance does not change the fact the judge made the restraining order for valid reasons. It appears that only I can see that this will escalate if Fred is not held accountable for breaching the order.

Friday, 18 December 1987

The CAS supervisor contacts me again. On December 1st, he supported me in not forcing my kids to have visits. Now he has changed his tune. He says that as a responsible mother, I must take control and insist they attend. He believes it is important for my children to maintain a relationship with their father, regardless of what happened. Finally, he admits that Fred has been incessantly calling about access and threatening legal action against them if the CAS does not comply with the family court order.

Today, these are my struggles, inconsistencies, and dilemmas

- If I let Fred come back home, the CAS will take my kids away, but CAS insists that my kids need to maintain a face-to-face relationship with him.

- My kids still say that they are not ready to see their father.
- Fred's words say he is sorry, but his actions say otherwise.
- No protective parent would insist his or her child spend time with a sex offender. It is disgusting that the agency meant to protect children is advocating for a man who molested children to have rights to see one of the children he molested.
- I am not convinced access is good for my children and no one can adequately explain to me why it might be.
- Forcing my kids to have visits is too much to ask of them or of me.
- I am uncertain if I should allow Alida to continue group attendance. This (male) group supervisor may not be an appropriate person to be in charge of my daughter's healing.

Sunday, 20 December 1987

I have a ridiculously huge extended family with over fifty first cousins. Now that I have pulled my thumb out of our family's dike of silence, more stories are spilling out. There are certainly more "funny uncle" stories.

One incident typical of the duo that happened to me was at a cousin's wedding reception a few years ago. When I went to use the restroom, they had staked out the hallway and blocked my path. "Hey cutie, how about a kiss?"

One of my uncles firmly grabbed me by the arm while his free hand groped my backside. I can still recall the feel of his hand on top of my silky dress.

Trying to wrench myself away, I snapped. "Do you mind?"

"We don't mind. Do you?" The uncle who was feeling me up, and the other one who was encouraging him, thought this was hilarious.

This incident stands out because, at age thirty, it was the first time I dared to try to stop them. When he let me go, their taunting laughter echoed down the hall as, without using the restroom, I dashed back to the safety of the crowd.

If I had told Fred, he would have said I was flirting and deserved it.

I did tell one of my aunts that my uncle groped me. I should have expected the response I got. "Carlyn, you know how these two uncles are. You should just stay away from them and not put yourself into such as risky situation."

As if going to the restroom in a church basement is a risky situation.

While I have many relatives, Fred has less family in Canada. I am pleased when his cousin Jeannie and her husband drop by to say Merry Christmas to us. About our separation, she is not the least bit surprised by the reason. Years ago, I heard Fred's version of what he called their childish explorations. Today, I hear Jeannie's side.

As a child, Jeannie had been very vulnerable because of her family dynamics. Fred, eleven years older than her, said she was his favourite little cousin. As a pre-teen, she had been thrilled to be someone's favourite until his sexual advances began. She did not know how to stop him and had nobody who would listen.

Fred had resumed pursuit of Jeannie when she moved back to Abingville after some time in Toronto. Over the course of several years, first when I believed Fred was campaigning for City Council and later when he said he was working, he would actually be harassing Jeannie. She was in her early twenties when Fred began showing up with cases of beer and pornographic movies, doing the *"we are kissing cousins"* routine. He would force himself on her, and as a young woman she had been as unable to stop him as she had been when she was a girl. It surprises Jeannie that I had no idea Fred had been coming over because he told her I knew. She had avoided me as a result, and it is a relief for her to tell me now and be believed.

Today, Jeannie and I feel closer than we ever have before. It strikes me that genuine connection with all the girls in my family has been compromised. I always thought it was that I was unlovable and now see that it is likely they all stood back from me because I am their abuser's wife. I wonder if Alida also struggles with me for the same reason. The social impact of Fred's molestation isolated me within his family and mine.

I have been keeping a mental tally of girls Fred molested and those I suspect he may have abused. I move Jeannie's name from the suspected column to the confirmed side. Originally, I titled my tally "The Victim Count." I now change it to "The Count." Saying someone is a victim gives the person an identity based on vulnerability vis-à-vis an abuser, and in my opinion, that gives an abuser too much power.

The Count:
- six confirmed (my sisters Grace, Helen and Irene, my daughter Alida, Fred's sister Allison, and Fred's cousin Jeannie),
- one attempted (my sister Ellie), and
- five suspected (the teenage store employee, Fred's former girlfriend, our customer's daughter, my niece Nakita, and Fred's Dutch cousin)

Monday, 21 December 1987
It is another challenging day that begins after midnight. Gus had been abiding by the *dominee's* directive not to see me, but last evening he decided to stop by for coffee. The kids were asleep upstairs and we were sitting at the dining room table when, just after 1 a.m., I heard Fred drive by. Ten minutes later, I received a

Mr Nobody heavy-breathing phone call. Gus was intimidated and left in a hurry.

This morning, John visits me at the office to ask for an explanation as to why Fred phoned him at 1:20 a.m. to report Gus being at my house. John seems disappointed that Gus was visiting, and so late, too.

There is a stop payment notice from the bank for Alida's $100 cheque. She already spent it, so I need to repay the bank. Again.

In the mail, there is also a letter for me.

> *Dear Carlyn,*
>
> *I hope we can put our unresolved differences aside and live in the spirit of Christmas. At this time of year, we think of loving and sharing as the true meaning of Christmas comes to mind. For me, Christmas has a special meaning as I think of what God's gift of salvation means in my life. At the same time, it is bittersweet because much has been lost in the past year.*
>
> *Carlyn, I want you to know that I treasure the years we spent together. I'm very thankful for all the happy times we had. I remember Rock Glen on our first date, feeding Alida bacon and eggs at the restaurant near Balsam Lake, or you goofing with the kids on the drives home from Muskoka and Parry Sound. You have given me a lot, including two beautiful children. Words alone can't express the feeling in my heart. I don't regret the time we've spent together. If I could choose all over again, I'd still choose you.*
>
> *Thinking of you, and loving you every day,*
> *Fred*

This makes me cry and cry. It is all so sad. During our years together, we did have good times. I feel myself wavering, which is his intent with this letter. Soon after his latest shenanigans (putting his parents up to filing a big lawsuit against me, getting the *dominee* involved, badmouthing me to my customers, and planning to destroy my business), he seems to be smack-dab back in the middle of the reconciliation phase of the cycle of violence. I believe he means for me to jump back into the familiar routine and overlook why I left him. My emotions wobble until I remember, and then my resolve returns.

Alida and her friend are playing a block from home at Centennial Park when Alida sees her Opa hanging around. The girls run home as fast as possible, and both are upset. At this rate, I wonder how long other parents will let their children continue to play with mine.

So as to not interfere with my Christmas, I have my kids open the gifts that their father, for once respecting the restraining order, forwarded through the CAS. I think he made sure there were many presents, which makes him look like a generous father to Bea.

I tell the kids they may only keep their gifts if they write their father a thank you note. It surprises me when they ask how to address him. They would rather not call him dad. I give them permission to call him whatever works for them. Kevin and Alida huddle together before they write. When they finish, they ask me to read their letters. I see that they both address him as Mr Smit. He will love that.

Alida hands me her letter and asks me to okay it before it goes into the mail. Similar to me, writing seems to be her way of working out feelings.

> Thanks for the stuff for Christmas. I am not sure I believe everything what you say in your letter. You say you will plead guilty in court. I will be in court, and will believe it when I hear you say the one word: guilty. You also said that your

> intense [sic] was not to sexually abuse me, but I think it was. If you knew what you were doing was wrong, why the Hell didn't you just stop? Why do you write so much bullshit? Just get to the point and I think you are just trying to regain my trust with crap. You really damaged my relationship with my family. That hurts, you know.

A long time ago, in a faraway life, I would have thought it important to reprimand my daughter for her language. Now, I am happy she has a way to express herself.

Monday, 28 December 1987
We got through Christmas, and I am thankful that hurdle is over. Once I had a signed rental agreement for "the matrimonial home," I told the kids we were moving. We were able to get a tour of our new house. They picked out bedrooms and were quite excited.

Today is moving day. The help we receive is heartwarming. Lena, Tessa, Bert and Bart, and their wives all show up early this morning and they tell me to quit fussing about not being fully packed. Everything is moved by early afternoon. In the old house, I just need to say what I am taking with us and they put it in the moving truck; whatever is "junk" goes to the garage for a dump run, and anything "for Fred" goes into the work van. I make sure to give Fred all he needs to set up a small apartment.

Looking inside the work van at the end of the day gives me a good idea of their feelings toward Fred. Everything is turfed in, including quite a lot of what I had said was junk. Bless my family and friends.

They also do their best to make our new home feel safe. My brothers adjust the blinds I already had to fit the windows in this new house, and when there are more windows than blinds, they go shopping. They buy deadbolt locks and put them on the doors. I arranged for us to have new mattresses and a new, unlisted phone number.

This is our first evening in our new home and we are all ready for a fresh start. I have accomplished a lot since June, and moving houses is near the top of the list of positive things. Sitting in my new living room, I feel secure. Even the kids' moods are lighter and they smile more today than they have in a long time. I hope we can all leave some of the nasty memories behind.

Tuesday, 29 December 1987
John offers to drop off the load of things to Fred. When he returns the work van, he remarks on the deplorable packing condition. I do not explain the mess because I have no intention to implicate my family and friends. That Fred has to sort out a bit of mess does not stress me out. He only has a vanload; I have a shitload.

This afternoon, both my father-in-law's car and Fred's Mustang drive back and forth on our street. They slow down when they pass by our new home. The only valid reason for them to drive in this direction would be if they were heading out of town toward London, which they have no reason to do a dozen times in one afternoon. It is fair to assume their purpose for driving this route is solely to resume their stalking and harassment. Our respite is short-lived.

I call John to ask if he gave Fred our new address. He denies it. So then, who was it that told Fred we moved?

**30 December 1987
CAS Ongoing Recording,
Caseworker Bea**

Current Situation

On November 30, 1987, Mr Smit reported to this worker that he and his daughter witnessed his wife Mrs Smit sexually abuse Kevin. He alleged this occurred in the kitchen of their home. An investigation ensued and the complaint was not substantiated. This worker will monitor the situation in regular visits between Mrs Smit and the children, and also in 1:1 private visits with the children.

Mrs Smit is a strong-willed individual who is coping well with the pressures of being a single parent. There appears to be a close attachment between Mrs Smit and her children.

This couple remains legally separated at this time. Mrs Smit has already filed for a divorce, as she has no interest in reconciliation. Mr Smit, however, would like to reconcile for the sake of the family's future.

Although Mr Smit has expressed an interest in visiting the children, they voice strong opposition with this plan. At this point, Alida and Kevin are still bitter toward their father and are not prepared to give in to his wishes.

When visiting with this family, it appears Mrs Smit is supportive of the decision that the children make concerning visitation. She encourages the children to freely discuss their feelings, and this is apparent through the children's openness with this worker.

At the present time, Alida is attending the sexual abuse group at the CAS office. She is enjoying this opportunity to share common feelings with her peers. Mrs Smit has also arranged counselling for Kevin with a therapist in private practice.

Mrs Smit has good insight into the issues of sexual abuse. She has gained a better understanding of the perpetrator and victim. She is handling this situation appropriately, and she is able to keep it in perspective and not allow it to overwhelm their family life. Mrs Smit's strong nature has allowed the family to adjust quite well to their new single-parent status.

Mr Smit shows an interest in seeing his children. At this point he has not succeeded in visiting the children and has corresponded with them through the mail only. Mrs Smit intercepted these letters as she thought they were a violation of the restraining order and that he overstepped his boundaries. During a home visit on December 9, this worker educated Mrs Smit that holding back mail from others is a criminal matter. She reluctantly agreed to give the children their correspondence that evening.

At this time, the children are not in need of protection as Mrs Smit is acting in a protective and responsible manner. This worker continues to visit the home. Mrs Smit has taken appropriate measures to ensure the welfare and safety of her children.

Reassessment

An investigation of a complaint made by Mr Smit that Mrs Smit sexually assaulted their son was not substantiated.

Mrs Smit has taken appropriate measures to ensure the safety of her children. The children remain resistant to seeing their father. However, in the event that the visitations do take place, this worker will ensure the appropriate supervision of the contact.

Friday, 8 January 1988

John and our black-suited, stern-eyed, head-shaking *dominee* show up in my kitchen and turn up the heat. They gang up on me to settle out of court with Fred's parents.

The *dominee* has lots to say. "Can you not just pay them out? It is awful when two members of one Christian family sue each other. If you don't resolve this, you are placing a black mark on the entire church."

These men do not understand or care about my grim realities that make handing money over impossible. I did not make the promises to my in-laws that they claim. I did not file the lawsuit. I have a sizeable debt that is worrisome. Fred is interfering with my operation of the business. Fred and his parents each want considerably more money from me than I have, and I cannot settle with the parents without also settling with the son.

"No, we didn't talk to Fred's parents about the criminal charge. We are here about the money you refuse to pay. You should learn to keep these things separate, Carlyn."

"Yes Carlyn, children are important and this isn't about condoning sexual assault."

What conclusion am I to draw about the CRC's priorities when there is all this hoopla about money and no indication of concern for the welfare of my children?

Monday, 11 January 1988

Detective Kingston comes to the house to update Alida and me on the status of criminal court. He takes his time to answer our questions. The words "Election and Disposition" means Fred intends to enter a guilty plea on April 7th. The court will not be accepting new evidence and there will be no opportunity for witnesses to speak. Sentencing will be a few weeks later, after a probation officer does a pre-sentence report. That report is to update the judge of the current situation and inform his sentencing decision. There is nothing for us to do until the probation officer is in touch for our input when the report is prepared.

The detective says we are not required to attend court but are certainly welcome to do so. Alida says she wants to go to hear her father say one word: "Guilty." Of course we will go. It makes perfect sense to me that hearing it will give Alida some closure.

Alida asks why it is taking so long. The detective explains that waiting is a smart move on the part of Fred and his lawyer. The time allows Fred to start counselling and get a positive progress report. Positive reports will make his sentence lighter. Detective Kingston confirms court could have gone much faster if Fred had entered a plea at any one of his previous court appearances.

So much for Fred's claim, "*Going through the courts is a long process, but I can't do anything about that. If I had a choice, it would be over already.*"

Tuesday, 12 January 1988

Bea worries the children are bitter toward their father. You think?

She says I should encourage them to express positive feelings and asks if I will allow them to forgive their father so they can see him again? What a stupid question. Of course, I will. Why do I send them for counselling if I want them to remain hurt and angry?

I wonder, but do not ask, why Bea does not accept my children's anger. When they express their feelings, she thinks I am putting them in the middle and coercing them to take my side. She must think I am dumb. Everyone knows it rips children in half when divorcing parents insist kids take sides. My kids can think for themselves. We are on the same side, if sides are to be taken. I want Fred to get help and be on our side, the side where our children matter.

If, after eight years of sexual abuse, a child escapes her molester, no one in his or her right mind would expect the child to resume the abusive relationship. The Kettles and the CRC would, but they are not in their right mind. I think Bea is not rational either, since she expects my daughter to forgive and resume the relationship with her father a mere six months after she finally got away. With all her chatter about forgiveness and bitterness, I am under the impression that Bea is religious. Just what I need, another zealot, and this one with power over me.

Kevin has trouble sleeping. During the night, he often wakes up upset and crawls into bed with me. Sometimes I allow him to stay, but that is a huge risk. I am not sure what the CAS would do if they found out, particularly since there is already a sexual abuse allegation against me on file. Most nights I carry Kevin back to his own room. Then I feel bad because I am not giving him the comfort he craves.

Friday, 15 January 1988

Apparently, Fred met with John again to discuss settlement. This evening, John is at my house to present what he calls a proposal from Fred.

The general idea is that Fred will pay $500 per month for child support if I settle. If I want a separation, then I have no right tell Fred what to do with his life. I need to trust him not to destroy me. He made promises and is now obligated to import for a few of my biggest customers. If I refuse this proposal (what it actually entails is unclear), Fred will write to my bank, customers, and suppliers (to say what is unclear). If I take this matter to family court, he will give me all-out-competition, meet with the Kettles, and inform my father's church consistory of my dad and brothers' involvement with his theft.

This is not about settlement. Despite John's well-meant intentions, all he has done is endorse blackmail and relay threats. Fred, manipulating John's good heart, is pulling the strings and John has become a puppet.

I have decided to take a new stance with the black suits. "John, please give Fred the message that he can pass the proposal on to my lawyer. From now on, all negotiating will be done through him."

John shakes his head in frustration.

Sunday, 17 January 1988

The Kettles come for a visit to see our new house. I tell them about the latest "proposal" that John forwarded on Fred's behalf. Dad thinks I should just fight Fred all the way and try to get everything. Dad does not understand the law, and even if I could fight for everything, that is not what I want. I want to be able to look at myself in the future and feel that no matter what Fred and his family do, I handled this divorce with fairness and integrity.

Friday, 22 January 1988
Herman irritates me. He requests a meeting with the Kettles before February 1st, and despite my objections, they agree. The Kettles also irritate me. There is nothing to resolve between them and Fred or between them and Fred's friend.

Friday, 29 January 1988
Last Sunday morning, we sat in the same pew as another woman who left her husband two months ago. Imagine the scandal of two separated couples in one church!

Her situation came about because the man had mental health issues and it was not safe for her to stay. She did the right thing to get out of an unsafe situation and, miraculously, she has church support. In the long prayer, the *dominee* again prayed for her family, but not mine. Every single Sunday, they pray for that man, his wife, and their children. Not that prayer by itself means anything, but what I understand is that in some cases, marital problems are worthy of prayer.

My family apparently does not qualify. Not once, during the six months of Sundays, have they prayed for my family. This is not a marital problem; it is a sexual abuse problem. I am quite sure they are not publicly acknowledging us because that would be admitting a man, when he was a member of their congregation, molested his daughter.

Later than I hoped and sooner than anticipated, I have a telephone intake with the children's counselling centre. Regretfully, they will not provide what we need. They only offer counselling for Alida and she declines. They have no other services to offer my family, so the file is closed. They terminate services before the first appointment. Finding help there is a dead end. Alida's CAS group is finished and Kevin is "progressing" with his counsellor.

Kevin seems to be doing the best of all of us and that is not too great. The school is again calling me regularly with concerns about Kevin's behaviour. They know what happened in our little family, yet there is no consideration given for what he is going through. Kevin should not get away with misbehaviour, but a bit of understanding would go a long way.

Tuesday, 2 February 1988
The significance of February 1st. is public. *The Abingville Shopper*, a weekly newspaper delivered to every home in town, has a half-page advertisement for the grand opening of Fred's Medical Equipment & Supplies. Fred invites everyone to see him and enjoy great deals on commodes, catheters, and enemas.

The products he is retailing are the same ones carried by the store Fred's father sold less than a year ago. As part of that sale, my father-in-law signed a non-competition agreement. Neither Fred or I had store ownership, and probably because we were moving to Parry Sound, the new owner had not asked us to co-sign that agreement. Opening Fred's Medical Equipment & Supplies is legal, but in my opinion, it is an underhanded move.

The past few weeks, my headache has been so severe that it extended down to my toes. My chiropractor said he has never had a client with such tight muscles. He asks me what is going on. Explaining is too complicated, so I treat it as a rhetorical question and laugh.

Wednesday, 3 February 1988
The Kettles have their meeting with Herman. They tell me it had nothing to do with the opening of Fred's Medical Equipment & Supplies. Because they evade my questions as to what Herman wanted, I am left not knowing why the meeting was necessary.

My sisters are all home for a visit. The police never contacted them, so Helen takes the initiative to file a complaint. She wants Fred charged for what he did to her. I am very proud of Helen for her courage. Tomorrow morning, she is meeting with Detective Kingston at my place.

Thursday, 4 February 1988
Helen gives her statement and Detective Kingston says that, while there definitely is sufficient evidence for a charge, the police will not proceed. His reason is that Fred already has one charge and there is no benefit to laying a second one. I can see that Helen is crushed, so I argue on her behalf to no avail. I think the Detective had already decided the outcome before he came to the house this morning.

In addition, he adds, if there were a trial, it would be at the crown's expense to fly Helen to Abingville. He suggests that Helen, at her own expense, can file a civil suit that would give her compensation. Helen's interest is in justice, not money. Justice, to her, would be to carve another notch into Fred's criminal record.

Fred gets away with it. The law will not hold him accountable. It is unfair. I hurt to see Helen go through the agony of this dismissal. I can do nothing to make it better for my sister.

Friday, 5 February 1988
It is gruelling to make sense of my conflicting emotions. That police do not endorse Helen's experience with a criminal charge makes me feel sad, and my helplessness to change the outcome

leaves me ashamed. Helen telling what Fred did was demoralizing for her. It made me heartsick, but because it was my husband who did it, I felt that I had a responsibility to be resilient for her. I hope I acted stronger than I felt.

Fred drove a wedge between my sisters and me. Initially, their collective silence divided us. My knowing did not make it better, and as much as it shames me to say, knowing made it worse for me. I recognize that Fred was the perpetrator and none of the girls are to blame for what he did to them. I understand and feel deeply for their pain. At the same time, I struggle with incredibly strong feelings of resentment that my sisters were "the other women" in my husband's life and that they hid what happened from me.

It would be terribly hurtful to say any of that to them, and I am much too humiliated to tell anyone about these feelings. Even in counselling, it is not something I would ever say out of fear that the social worker would think badly of me. If she reported me, the CAS might construe my feelings as cruel, lacking empathy, and victim blaming. Without confidence that I will not be harshly judged for my feelings, I keep my thoughts to myself.

Sunday, 7 February 1988
The kids and I spend the weekend on the Kettle farm. Yesterday evening, my grandmother, my Oma Ketel, has her eightieth birthday party. I almost skip the party because of the shame of being the first grandchild in the family who will be divorced. I brave it and none of my Ketel relatives hassle me. Oma and her daughter, my aunt, take it a step further and tell me I am doing the right thing.

Oma is the most blunt. She says, "Don't even tink about going back to Fred." I wonder if she speaks from general wisdom that comes with age or from her own direct experiences. Most likely the latter: Opa was no treat to live with.

In my experience, when he was alive, Opa was a volatile and unkind man. Opa and Oma each lived on their own side of the kitchen table with their own window sill piled with their own things. Oma's ledge held knitting needles and yarn; Opa had a book about birds, a jack-knife, an ashtray, and farm magazines. The only words that passed across the few feet of vinyl tablecloth were demands and cutting insults from him to her.

I had been too young to comprehend the meaning when I heard the Kettles whisper about Opa's female friend. Once, when I stayed with my grandparents, Opa took me to her house. He stayed inside for a long, long time while I waited in the car for him to return. At the door, the woman laughed and waved us off. Opa said he had finished his business with her and I was a good girl for staying in the car.

I was a quiet kid who learned things by watching and listening. I understood that my Oma was unhappy. She, too, always put up a façade, behind which she hid her melancholy. She never spoke of her childhood, and she never once gave me a grandmotherly hug. Oma lived in her own world, stoic and aloof.

My theory is that Oma's painful silence ate away at her body. Opa and Oma were together forty-some years, and during that time, Oma had forty-some surgeries for a host of ailments. After Opa died, other than age-related complaints, Oma has been healthy. Maybe Oma's hospitalizations were the only socially acceptable way she could manage time away from her volatile husband.

Wednesday, 10 February 1988

Herman arrives without an appointment, interrupting my workday. I seat him in my office and make him a coffee, not to be sociable, but to give myself a moment to get a grip on my emotions. I listen to him just long enough to realize his visit is all about money. Then my mind shuts down. Really shuts down.

The next thing I recall is standing at the door with him shaking my hand saying, "Well, you'll call me tomorrow then and let me know that you agree with this settlement proposal."

I say I will, with no idea what I am supposed to consider. I am sick of men in general, or at least the ones knocking down my door trying to get me to settle with Fred. They do not understand or care about the implications of what Fred wants from me. I sometimes think that there is a male conspiracy rallying around Fred to protect him with a goal to force my submission.

Later in the day, all the girls in my family go out for dinner. While we wait for appetizers, I say something or other about my situation. One sister emphatically says, "Just drop it, will you?"

Throughout the meal, I am detached, observing. They seem oblivious that I shift my food around on the plate without eating more than a few bites. I can accept if they are uninterested in what is happening to me because of their own wounds. The alternative is that they do not care. Who would fault them, given what my husband did to them? Either way, because of Fred's abuses, the divide between my sisters and me is widening.

Thursday, 11 February 1988
I call Herman to refuse the proposal. I hide the fact I have no idea what I was to consider and what I am declining.

Fred is hammering at me from all fronts. Today, he and his lawyer meet with us at my divorce lawyer's office to present a new proposal. Fred's offer is that I sign all assets over to him, keep my personal guarantees on all loans and lines of credit, leave the loans and lines of credit limits as they are, and I get no security and no profits. For that, I will get one lump sum payment, broken into instalments, but only if he can get financing, and the total payout he proposes is 10 percent of EuroMed Importing's book value.

I think, "Now I know how women get taken to the cleaners."

In order to be done with Fred, I agree in principle with a few minor changes. My counter-proposal is a condition for security with company assets and $100 support per month per child. My lawyer presents the counter-proposal and Fred rejects it outright.

I accomplish very little work today between phoning Herman, the settlement meeting with Fred and the lawyers this morning, a counselling appointment with the social worker over lunch, and a meeting with the CAS worker after school. There is barely time left to run a business.

My staff expressed concerns that they were due for a pay raise. In contrast to the conservative values of my families of origin and marriage, my liberal leanings make me strongly object to underpaying employees. It is true that it is time for a pay increase and I have been too preoccupied to think of it. Behind the closed door of my office, I do the math. If I increase their hourly wage and shorten the hours we work, my budget remains on track. They are happy that from now on we will all take Friday afternoons off, and they will receive the same weekly pay. At work, I come up with a win—win solution. I wish I could do the same in the rest of my life.

Friday, 12 February 1988

It is snowing this morning, so I call a day off for all of us. The snow is not very bad, but I give the kids a day off school, close the office, assure my employees I will pay them for today, and cancel all our appointments. The kids and I play computer games, eat junk food, and lounge around in our pyjamas the entire day. Snowflakes are the fireflies of winter, sparkles from heaven giving me an excuse for a bonus day with my children, away from the madness of life.

Sunday, 14 February 1988

Saturday morning started with family photos. The Kettles have a thing about family pictures, and this is the first one without my husband at my side. I grit my teeth and hold back the tears when the photographer says, "Smile."

Having our pictures taken sets me thinking about my wedding picture still standing on the Kettle fireplace mantle. Three times now I explained to my mother that it is hurtful to see Fred's face when I come to her house. Three times I asked her to put it away, and three times she said no. Yesterday afternoon, I took it down. This morning the photo is back on the mantle. Mom says the fact we were married stays the same, so the photo stays. With the picture in view of everyone who comes into the Kettle home, my mother does not need to admit to reality.

I know how I feel about it and cannot help but wonder what my sisters think. It makes sense that, after years of parental inaction in response to their abuse, they just shrug when I ask them.

This weekend I notice that Alida receives extra consideration and attention from my family and that they push Kevin aside. This feels too similar to Fred's unfairness for it to be comfortable. I also feel sorry for Alida because of the incest and the upcoming criminal court, but favouring her is a tragedy, too. I try hard to give both of my children equal treatment, so maybe I am being too sensitive. That is what they all say when I ask them to regard both children equally.

They think that because of the severity of abuse, Alida deserves special attention. They know less than I do about what happened to Alida. My theory is that my family is overcompensating with Alida because they knew enough to pray and yet did nothing to stop her abuse. They are assuaging their guilt by being overly solicitous, and it comes at Kevin's expense.

When we pack up to go home, my father tells Kevin, "Take care of your mudder and sister. You are de man in de family now."

I make sure Kevin hears me tell my father that, as their mother, taking care of the children is my job. Kevin is still a boy and he does not need to assume the burden of being responsible for his family. My kids have already experienced too much adultness, and I want to preserve what I can of their childhood.

The issues shattering me also seem too much for most of my friends. There are a number of ways to tell they are growing fed up with me. The first clue is the familiar glaze that comes over their eyes when I start to speak about what is happening. Then their eyes shift, and they look away, at the walls, at the table, over my head, anywhere except my eyes. Their hands begin to fidget. They move coffee cups and ashtrays an inch to the right, and then two inches to the left. They have sores to scratch and teeth to pick. The faces are different, but the words sound the same.

"I really don't want to get involved."

"You should not let this stuff bother you so much."

The "you should" unsolicited advice has become excessive and contradictory. I should be firmer with the kids *and* give them more latitude. I should quit work to be home *and* work hard to support my kids. I should give Fred what he wants *and* fight for it all. I should reconcile with Fred *and* get divorced as soon as possible. I should focus on myself *and* my children *and* God.

My problem is that I still want to please everyone and it has become impossible. From now on, when I get "you should" advice, I will thank the person for their concern, and then continue to do what I believe is best.

Monday, 15 February 1988

It has been a long, stressful day. My bank manager starts my morning by letting me know the bank is recalling all my business loans. Their reason is receipt of updated company information from Fred, of course.

I call my divorce lawyer and we arrange for a meeting this afternoon. In a room full of bankers, we get copies of a letter written by Mr Amateur Lawyer, who is acting in true form. The general idea of Fred's letter is to advise the bank that I am being sued by a third party for breach of contract, and that he is pursuing legal action for his interests. Because he has a matrimonial interest in the company, and because he gave his guarantee to the bank, he opposes any loan extensions.

I am grateful my lawyer is at the meeting to do the talking. When he explains to the bankers about my in-law's lawsuit, I realize that if I had spoken, I would have dwelt on the sexual abuse. For me, everything boils down to what happened to my daughter, my children's safety, and my ability to protect and care for them.

The meeting ends with the bankers agreeing to leave the current loans and lines of credit as they are, pending further review. Fred is systematically cutting my legs out from under me, and at this rate, eventually there will be 50 percent of nothing to give him.

Fred copied his criminal lawyer, and one might think his legal advice would be to stop the insanity. It is curious that he is not copying his divorce lawyer.

Moreover, he claims all the EuroMed Importing loans have his guarantee. Another lie. If Fred meant he gave a handshake guarantee, even he knows that to a bank, a handshake is as worthless as lips on a chicken.

I am trying my best to keep this business going since it provides us with a good income. I am wondering if my efforts are worthwhile. I am so very, very tired.

Over the phone, Dorothy reads me a letter that arrived in her mailbox this morning.

Dorothy,

I am writing to thank you for your help in making the present situation what it is.

Before you get the idea I'm trying to get out of anything, I'm not. I am guilty and will soon answer to that. I realize that I was a nasty person. That is enough to make the present situation a mess. But it's little pearls like yours that makes this all entirely hopeless.

Yeah, I kissed you and I touched your breast. Yeah, I made advances toward you. But why don't you tell people about your part in it. Nothing more happened until you told me you loved me. I couldn't believe my ears. You started this.

After that I made advances to you because, yeah, I was totally frustrated in my marriage. I was looking for love since I certainly wasn't getting enough at home.

If you are going to contribute to the picture that your family is painting of me, why not be honest and tell the whole truth?

Fred

c.c. Fred's criminal lawyer.

It sounds like Dorothy told someone something and they told Fred. Who was it? What further mystifies me is why Fred would be writing her a letter now, and why she is sharing it with me when she knows I was only "kind of" aware until now.

Last June, when we discussed my bedroom dream and why my family was praying for Alida, Dorothy spilled the beans about our sisters, while saying nothing about the secrets she had with Fred. Later, in July, when I asked if anything had happened, she said "kind of." Now, with the receipt of this letter, she tells me that more did happen. Despite giving me the impression there was coercion involved, she remains secretive. Fred makes it sound like she was the instigator, but I know he lies like a snake's belly. Without knowing for sure, all I can do is add her name to the suspected column of my count.

The Count:
- six confirmed (my sisters Grace, Helen and Irene, my daughter Alida, Fred's sister Allison, and Fred's cousin Jeannie),
- one attempted (my sister Ellie), and
- six suspected (the teenage store employee, Fred's former girlfriend, our customer's daughter, my niece Nakita, Fred's Dutch cousin, and my sister Dorothy)

Monday, 22 February 1988
The man in Holland that EuroMed Importing hires to arrange shipping lets me know that the company where I purchase medical supplies received a letter. He reads me the letter, and it is along the same lines as the one Fred sent to the bank. I immediately book an international flight to Holland for next week to address it. My kids will stay with Lena, so I know they will be safe.

Wednesday, 24 February 1988
    Dear Mrs Smit,
    With reference to our meeting on February 15, 1988 regarding the correspondence received from Mr Smit, we are concerned with the implications civil actions against your company might cause. We wish to fully re-assess our participation with the financing of your operation. We will monitor your account very closely, so going forward we require you to discuss with us any purchases prior to being ordered.
    Yours truly,
    EuroMed Importing bank manager
    c.c. my divorce lawyer

The bank is tightening the screw on EuroMed Importing's financing and, objectively, it makes sense, given how ominous their informant made the situation sound. There is an order already packed into a forty-foot shipping container. The container is standing at the loading dock of the Dutch company where I purchase all my medical supplies. Later today, it will be delivered to Rotterdam harbour where it will be loaded onto a ship that will take it across the Atlantic Ocean. Once it lands in Canada, it will be loaded onto a transport truck and delivered to my warehouse where it will be unloaded and given final clearance by Customs Canada. I rushed to see my account manager to ensure this could all still happen. He approves use of the line of credit, this one time, for this one purchase.

Friday, 26 February 1988
When Irene returned to Moose Jaw, there was a letter waiting for her that she forwarded to me. It arrives in today's mail.

> *Irene,*
>
> *I wish somebody had clued me in earlier to what you and your sisters have been saying. A lot of misery could have been avoided. Now we're in this mess. As far as the situation with Alida is concerned, I will face the music. Yeah, I'm guilty of wrongdoing, but intent was never present. It certainly was not what you and your family are trying to make out of it. Once that is handled, we'll have to tackle the rest.*
>
> *It doesn't end with my "trial." Too many insinuations have been made, and in order to clear those up, all these things are going to have to be brought up and handled. And I know, Irene, that I'm not blameless in these things either. Only God and me know what a totally nasty person I've been. But I also don't feel that it is fair that I'm a piece of dirt that your family can just dump on in order*

to get rid of your own guilt and try to make yourselves look "holy."

I have it from good authority that you have been saying that I molested you when your dear sister had the car accident. It was you who offered to come and spend a few days with me to help with the kids. I did not pressure you.

When I came home for lunch that Friday, I found you lying on the couch. The shorts you had on were so short I could see your pink panties, and I could tell you were wearing nothing under your T-shirt because I could see your outline. I told you I wanted a nap and you did not get off the couch. I jokingly tried to push you off and we had a play fight. Your left breast pushed against my hand and then your leg brushed against my crotch. So yeah, I did go further, but don't forget, baby, that you started it. Now you are trying to blame me, probably because your guilty conscience cannot accept you were a willing participant.

Someday, the whole truth will come out, including why I did what I did. And your dear sister contributed a lot more than she'll ever know. But your family will no doubt never believe it, cause you're just too busy trying to push your own guilt on someone else.

May God forgive you for what you've contributed to the mess we are in. I know someday I'll have to, as well, but right now I'm not ready for that.

Fred

c.c. criminal lawyer

This is disgusting. He recalls every little detail. I wonder if it arouses him to relive what he all did?

I call Irene to make sure she is okay. She is reeling and then reveals that when this all happened, Fred not only told her I knew what he did to her, but that I approved and encouraged him. I hope she believes that I did not know, approve, encourage, or condone anything.

The *dominee* has become Fred's most recent puppet. Other than one visit last month where he and John tried to coerce me into settling with Fred's parents, I have had no contact with him. On the phone he lets me know that he is now well versed about the affairs (mine of course) and the trials (the lawsuit and the divorce), but he claims to know nothing about the upcoming criminal court (sexual assault sentencing).

The *dominee* has me come to his office for a more serious discussion and immediately starts tightening the noose. "Fred is a Christian and truly sorry for what he has done; therefore, Carlyn, it is your duty to reconcile."

Evidence of Fred's Christianity, he claims, is that Fred takes his Bible everywhere he goes.

I push back. "A bit of showmanship doesn't make a Christian. Just watch, Fred's religious act will end when court ends."

"No Carlyn. You don't know that. Judge not lest ye be judged."

The *dominee* says he received a letter and vaguely wiggles his fingers toward the stack of papers on the corner of his desk. He refuses me a copy or a chance to read the letter. He feels it would not be fair, given confidentiality and all. He is protecting Fred and does not give me the opportunity to defend myself. I am a woman charged and convicted without knowing what crime I committed. I feel like a Kafka trial defendant or a Salem witch.

Given Fred's prolific letter-writing campaign, I wonder who else has received such letters. I call the sisters I have not heard from. Helen and Grace both got letters and they say they destroyed them. Ellie has not heard from Fred, and as far as I know he has no reason to send one to Julianna.

Fred is sucker punching me through people in every area of my life. I feel like a Bobo doll, an old-fashioned cone-shaped toy weighted at the base. Every time a Bobo doll is knocked, it wobbles and eventually rights itself. I wonder how many blows this Bobo doll can take before she falls over, never to right herself again. Soon I will fall and shatter. Just a little bit more, one more swipe, and all the king's horses and all the king's men will not be able to put Carlyn back together again.

Tuesday, 8 March 1988
I return home from the business trip to Europe, bringing back mixed feelings. On the positive side, I still have a provider of medical supplies. The CEO of that company bowled me over when he gave me a copy of a personal, handwritten letter from Fred. He got this letter along with the typed one Fred sent to the company itself. Imagine my mortification, sitting in an office in Holland, trying to keep a professional demeanour while reading.

> *Dear Mr de Vries,*
>
> *I apologize for not contacting you in the last seven months. At first, I couldn't because I was literally set out onto the street without a cent. After that, I could not personally risk it. Another supplier of EuroMed Importing stopped delivering late last year, and through my wife's lawyer, I was blamed for that. Therefore, until that is dealt with, I must be very careful about what I say or don't say.*
>
> *It is regretful, and totally a surprise to me, that this situation occurred. I have done everything to come to an arrangement in the past seven months, but unless I sign over everything to Carlyn, and I sign an agreement to never go into the import business again, there is nothing to be done. These two things I can't do because Carlyn's business will have to be dismantled to divide it.*
>
> *As soon as possible, I will contact you again, also with plans for the future.*
>
> *In the meantime, thank you again for the fine working together that I had with you and your company.*
>
> *With kind regards,*
> *Fred*
> *Fred's Medical Equipment & Supplies*

I am dumbfounded at the extent to which Fred will go. Even the world closes in.

During the business trip, I learn that I am fully capable of operating this company. I have a few other insights about myself as well. I realize how fearful I am of everything. In Holland, I use room service and even go without meals because I am too frightened to eat out alone. Leaving the hotel room to explore Utrecht on the weekend takes all the courage I can marshal. It is worth the effort.

During this trip, nightmares are particularly awful. One night I wake up in the hotel screaming and soaked to the skin. At Schiphol Airport in Amsterdam, I buy a bumper sticker that shouts my unfortunate truth. It is already on my car. I am fully aware that it is a blatant cry for help.

I AM GOING CRAZY
DO YOU WANT TO COME ALONG?

Tuesday, 15 March 1988

Dear Carlyn,

Since you agree that ending our relationship is the best solution, given the situation, and since dividing the assets is very much a part of this solution, I would ask you to genuinely consider a meeting between the two of us in order to achieve equalization of assets as quickly and cost effectively as possible. Your unwillingness to communicate effectively and negotiate fairly has led to a lot of problems. Perhaps a resumption of respectful interaction between us can still make this split a civil one.

Please let me know your feelings on this.

Fred

Another tangible proof of breach. Another time the police do nothing.

Thursday, 24 March 1988
We started this week with Fred driving by at 8:20 a.m., precisely the time the bus picks up the kids for school. Because the weather was nice and the kids planned to bike to school, they were still in the house and did not see or hear him. On Tuesday morning, Alida was taking the bus. I went to the bus stop with her to make sure all was fine when we saw Fred. Alida ran back into the house, rattled. After she calmed down, I drove her to school.

Today, Alida is biking home from school when her Opa drives slowly alongside her. Then he pulls his car across her path and stops. Alida bikes to the other side of the street and peddles home as fast as she can with him following the rest of the way. She comes home very upset, calls me at work, and asks me to help.

I take Alida to the police station to report that she was harassed. We get the same old story. Nothing can be done. I cannot comprehend why it should matter what the relationship is between the harasser and the harassed. It is scandalous that a twelve-year-old child, and a sexually abused child at that, must tolerate being stalked and harassed by the father of her abuser. Police refuse to do their part to protect my child.

Sunday, 27 March 1988
Mr Nobody has our new unlisted phone number. The phone calls and the drive-bys really get to all of us. The kids think we should pretend we are spying back by planting a dummy in the car. The largest teddy bear Alida has is now sitting behind the steering wheel of my car, cuddled in a red coat, with glasses perched on its nose. From a distance, it appears to be a person. We make some fun out of our misery and laugh so hard we cry. Our antic will not hurt anyone.

Monday, 28 March 1988
Mr Nobody phone calls go on from morning to night.

Thursday, 31 March 1988

Most of my employees are young and single. They go to the bars on weekends and tell me Fred is always there trying to pick up young women. He no longer carries his Bible. I get the impression he is quite unconcerned about his upcoming criminal court appearance.

Friday, 1 April 1988

I barely finish telling John, once again, that I will only discuss financial settlement with my lawyer, when the *dominee* appears at the door. He says he is doing his best to help me do my Christian duty and settle out of court. People like John and the *dominee* think they are helping. In reality, Fred is masterfully manipulating them. What they are doing is repeatedly delivering threats.

The *dominee* feels sorry that poor, destitute Fred has cash flow problems with his new store. He thinks it is un-Christian of me to swindle Fred and his parents. He relays Fred's message that if I continue to fight in court, Fred will make sure I end up with nothing. If I take the offer (the *dominee* is unsure what offer this is), I should trust Fred to give me child support.

The *dominee* is quite willing to fight Fred's cause against me, taking Fred's word for all the figures and assuming I have disposable funds to give way. I try to explain I do not have the money he was told. He shakes his head and says I should be willing to part with my assets to support the family I committed to when I married Fred.

When the *dominee* is sufficiently frustrated with me for not accepting what he calls Fred's settlement proposal, he moves on to my next sin. "Oh, by the way, are you still seeing Gus? You are? Oh, no. Carlyn, you are making reconciliation between you and Fred impossible."

Preacher. Preacher. You do not get it. I will never reconcile with Fred. I am using Gus as a buffer, and I do not feel bad because Gus is also using me. He will not appear with me in public and he sees other women.

The *dominee* is still sitting at my kitchen table when Lena stops by. She urges me to check out the parking lot at Fred's store right away. I send the *dominee* on his way and do my own drive-by. There is a large, portable, roadside sign at the corner of one of Abingville's busiest intersections.

HAPPY EASTER
CARLYN
ALIDA & KEVIN
LOVE FRED

About the sign, the police say, "It looks like the guy spared no expense to tell you and his kids he loves you. We are not going to charge him with a breach for that."

It is not only that Fred thinks he is above the law, but with the unwillingness of the police to enforce the restraining order, he *is* above the law.

Sunday, 3 April 1988
Allison comes for a visit. She is fearful that her family will find out she saw me, and I swear not to tell anyone that we continue to have contact. That is an easy promise since no one else in her family is speaking to me.

The fact Allison is scared tells me the aftermath of her brother's abuse and the lack of support from her family significantly affects her. What Allison's parents and my parents have in common is that they know and believe their daughters, but they will not do anything to actively support them.

Monday, 4 April 1988
I find myself in a meeting with Fred in the *dominee's* parsonage office. For the life of me, I do not have the foggiest clue how I got here or why. Since the discussion is about money, I assume we are meeting to discuss financial settlement. Fred seems rather cavalier for a man facing criminal court in a few days.

At some point during the meeting, Fred talks about our kids. He is mad they will not visit with him. Fred says he will give the kids six more months. If they do not see him by then, he will write them out of his life. In my opinion, that would be the nicest thing he could ever do for his children.

When I seriously start thinking about smacking both men, I gather my purse and keys. I hear Fred say my name and both men snicker as I walk out the door.

Wednesday, 6 April 1988
Lena offers to go to criminal court with us tomorrow. It is a kind offer that I decline. Court is something I need to do alone with my daughter. Lena listens and is respectful.

Alida is furious when she finds out the *dominee* is planning to be there. I am sure shame has a lot to do with it. I advocate for her by calling the *dominee* to request that he not attend. He points out it will be a public hearing; therefore, anyone who wants may attend. He says it is his pastoral responsibility to support us, and Fred too, by being there. He is deceiving himself because Alida does not want him there, and Fred resigned from his church more than six months ago.

Alida's voice is disregarded, and she again has to take what a man forces on her. This so-called support is re-traumatizing my daughter, and I am powerless to stop it.

Thursday, 7 April 1988

The dreaded day has finally arrived. It takes Alida a while this morning to get herself ready. She is clearly very nervous. So am I. During the short drive to the courthouse, I fill the silence with babble about court protocol, at least what little I know about it.

Alida says one thing, the same thing she has said all along: "All I want to hear is one word. Guilty."

My timing is good and we arrive before Fred. His flashy Mustang is not yet in the parking lot. Being early is good because Alida is in no shape to see her father ahead of time. I assume they do not post Fred's name on the docket because they are sensitive to Alida being a minor. This is the first time the court gives this consideration and, for Alida's sake, I appreciate it.

We find seats in the crowded courtroom and rise when the judge enters. The first case is a shoplifting charge. Then there are a few drinking and driving cases and a theft. Time drags on and we hold our breath after each case. Are we next? After a while, the judge calls a recess. We both check the courtroom, and although there is no sign of Fred or his lawyer, Alida and I both spot the *dominee* sitting in the back row and Detective Kingston standing in the doorway.

The Detective sees us and looks surprised. A few minutes later, he slides along the bench to sit beside us and asks, "What are you two ladies doing here?"

I remind him, "Today Fred enters his plea. Isn't that why you're here?"

He grimaces. "No. I'm here for another matter. Didn't you know they changed the date? It was yesterday. He pled."

I ask whom I am supposed to talk to about the pre-sentence report.

"You don't. Fred was already sentenced."

"What happened? What did he get?"

He says, "Check with the court office. I think he might have gotten probation, but they can tell you for sure."

"No." Alida sobs. "No."

I wave the *dominee* out of the courtroom and tell him court is over.

In the car, Alida stamps her feet and smashes her fist into the dash, the door, and the window. She lashes out at me. "You knew I wanted to hear him say that one word. You must have screwed up the date."

At home, I show her my date book, my notes of the last court appearance, my journal entry written after the last time Detective Kingston was at the house, and the copy of the criminal court docket record he had given me.

"See Alida, I did not make a mistake. Everything says court was supposed to be today, April the seventh."

"Oh, you and your dumb papers. I don't want to see them. I'm sick of your stupid self-help books, too."

Since I am consistently present and safe, I understand that Alida makes me the target to absorb her anger.

Alida goes to her bedroom, and I lock my papers back in the filing cabinet.

I phone the court office and the clerk says that the lawyer for the defendant (Fred) would have changed the date. Since the court was aware Fred intended to plead guilty, they were not required to notify the victimized child or the child's mother.

The clerk refers me to the crown attorney's office. The person who answers my call tells me that yesterday, the crown accepted Fred's plea bargain from the charge of sexual assault to a downgraded charge of a common or simple assault. The court sentenced him to one year of probation with four terms or conditions:

- Report to his probation officer.
- Live in Ontario.
- Not change his address without notification.
- Take counselling as directed.

That is the entirety of his penalty. I did not expect that Fred would have to grovel for life. I did expect there would be a meaningful consequence. He has gotten away with years of molesting without spending one hour in jail.

Simple assault is a grab, push, or slap. How is a simple assault proportionate to my daughter's loss of innocence and her father's violations for eight years, starting when she was four years old? The criminal justice system doubly betrayed my daughter; first when they gave him a meaningless sentence, and then by denying her the one crumb, the one word, she has consistently needed. There is nothing fair or just about this.

Alida's door creaks and she tiptoes into the kitchen. As I prepare lunch, Alida gives me a feeble smile and I give one back. I can see that something very fragile inside of her broke this morning. All I know to fix this is to love her. I want to keep Alida under my wing this afternoon, like a duck trying to keep her chick safe. It feels like a rejection of me that she prefers to go to school to see her best friend.

I go to my office long enough to ask my secretary to lock up at closing time. Letting Lena know the verdict is okay, but letting my molested sisters know is brutal. They feel the insignificant sentence also minimizes what Fred did to them. The court, and by extension all of society, communicated to Fred and all molesters that sexual assault is no big deal. This meaningless sanction weighs heavy not just on Alida and all those Fred molested; it is a heavy weight felt by all who have suffered the violation of sexual abuse, and all their mothers.

When Alida comes home from school, she fights with her brother and then hides out in her room. She refuses to talk to me or to join us for supper. Mother and daughter's hearts are shipwrecked and floating away from each other on rafts amid a sea of pain.

Heartbroken is a lame word for my feelings.

Helpless. Hopeless.

Full of sorrow.

I am afraid to cry outwardly because it might erode the thin membrane between sanity and lunacy. On the inside, I am drowning in a rain of tears.

Friday, 8 April 1988

Bea phoned to tell me, "Now that criminal court is over, the children need to re-establish their relationship with their father. Everybody knows that children need two parents. It will be good for them all. Just because Fred sexually molested Alida does not mean he lost his rights as a father. He is sorry, on probation, and no longer a risk. You make sure you have them here at the CAS office on Monday, promptly at 9 a.m."

Sunday, 10 April 1988

All weekend I agonize over what Bea will do if the kids refuse to go to the visit tomorrow. When I ask why she is sure there is no risk, Bea said it is because he is on probation. Does she really believe two days of meaningless probation has changed him sufficiently, so she can now gamble with my children's safety?

I keep saying it, but I will never understand why any sex-offending father without genuine remorse and having undergone no effective treatment should have any rights to see the same child he molested, or any children for that matter.

I think CAS is misusing their authority and power by forcing me to place my children in a situation for which they are not ready.

It is terribly wrong that the same agency that first told me never to allow Fred to return home or they would take my children away, now makes it impossible to for me to keep my children safely away from the same man.

Bea is on my case again about being too bitter. She thinks bitterness is getting in the way of my objectivity. Less than two months ago, the man they are pressuring my children to see wrote horrible letters to some of the girls he victimized. He has zero remorse and Bea thinks I should be chill.

In a religious context, bitterness is an attitude of extended and intense anger and hostility, and the remedy is forgiveness. I will get to forgiveness when I am darn well ready, and I am quite sure it will take a long time, if ever. For what Fred did to Alida, I have the right to be bitter for decades. When I take the whole picture of what he did to me and those I love into account, forgiveness may not happen until I am a hundred years old. These things cannot be rushed.

A one-year term of meaningless probation does not assure me Fred is miraculously safe with my children. As the mother entrusted to protect her children from further sexual violence, it is entirely fair of me to say that my trust is something that Fred needs to earn.

Fred could start by taking responsibility for everything he did to every girl, starting with Allison and Jeannie. He could quit minimizing his actions and quit displacing blame onto those he molested or onto me. He could stop stalking and harassing. Pleading guilty to common assault was a ploy to receive a lighter and less meaningful sentence. The bastard arranged it so that Alida was not present in court, even though he knew she planned to be there and needed to hear him say "guilty." Why could he not have given her that morsel of validation? It was all she asked from him.

The CAS makes no sense to me. My anger and bitterness give me strength to keep fighting for my kids' safety, while Fred continues to generate misery and destruction. I am an angry, bitter, protective mother who is navigating this journey the only way I know.

Monday, 11 April 1988
Self-hate and self-disgust are my predominant feelings this morning. I vowed I would never force my children to visit their father and because I am afraid to oppose the CAS, here I am fighting with the kids about it. Alida does not want to go. She is furious and yells at me for forcing her. Kevin follows suit. It becomes quite a ruckus. Finally, I bribe them with lunch out at their choice of restaurant and the rest of the day off school if they will please, please, just get in the stinking car.

It is so wrong that I buy off my molested and hurting children to do what they do not want, just to keep the fucking CAS off my back. I assure my kids that I will stay in the building the entire time. They ask me to join the visit and I promise to try.

Bea listens to the children tell her they want me to stay and, to my surprise, allows it. In this visit, their first since the Rotary Park fiasco eight months ago, Fred uses his children's audience to talk about their Aunt Grace. This is no lie. The children knew nothing about it until today. Fred told them about taking Aunt Grace out for dinner, to his motel, and that Aunt Grace came on to him with passionate kisses. He shamelessly went on to tell his children their aunt tried to take his pants off and that he stopped her.

Alida shows her distress through body language and by crawling under a table when her father says he is taking Grace to court to *"set the record straight."* Fred looks over at Bea who is engrossed in paperwork, curls his lip into a smirk, and keeps talking. He knows he is in total control of this visit.

Next, he snaps his fingers to get Bea's attention. He asks for her assistance because, he says, I am denying his parents the right to see their grandchildren. I cannot believe it! It has been almost a year and they have driven by hundreds of times without stopping. They never once requested a visit. Fred takes this opportunity to ask Bea, since Carlyn is too unreasonable to deal with, if she will kindly arrange for grandparent access. Bea thinks they should be seeing each other and offers to set something up for them in the community. Fred catches my eye and gives me a diabolical sneer.

I decide it is better not to be in the room than to let my children see me powerless, so I leave and sit on the ugly orange furniture in the waiting room until the visit ends. Both children choose to stay, even Alida, who had not yet spoken a word. I wonder if, by staying, she means to protect her brother.

Bea returns them to the waiting room and says Alida did not say a word after I left, either. According to Bea, Kevin told his dad how angry he is and asked Fred to pass along an invitation to his parents for Grandparents' Day at school. If Kevin wants them there, I will support it. Alida may stay home from school that day if it is too much for her. I hope, whether they talked or not, that the kids will not be so angry or so scared now that they have seen their father.

When we get to the restaurant for lunch, Alida asks me if he will also take her to court for what she told the CAS. I cross my fingers and give her assurances that will never happen.

Tuesday, 19 April 1988

The *dominee* phones in a tizzy about some proposal that is valid only until midnight tonight. If I decline this offer, Fred will "*massacre regarding the children.*"

Mid-afternoon I am back in his parsonage office. The *dominee* says he had some paperwork for me, but I go to hear more about Fred's threat. Unfortunately, the *dominee* refuses to elaborate because he does not want to get Fred in trouble. I leave shortly after with a page of the *dominee's* chicken scratches about finances that I am supposed to consider.

The proposal makes no sense, but what does frighten me is that Fred's language is getting much more aggressive. The *dominee* should stick to preaching. He is not much of a mediator.

This time, I do not go to the police station because I am quite sure the police will say the threat is hearsay and do nothing.

Sunday, 24 April 1988

The cold mechanics of the court process devastate Alida and me. It is a brutally crude analogy, but when a horse is sufficiently dominated, its spirit is broken. In the same way Alida's spirit has been crushed, and mine too.

It is unfathomable that Fred got off so easily with a downgraded simple or common assault conviction, especially when there is so much evidence that he is guilty of sexually assaulting my daughter. The evidence trail starts with him confessing to the police that he molested Alida for eight years. I could have testified as to what Fred confessed to me. It would have been excruciating for Alida, but I know she would have testified. My cousin could have spoken about seeing Fred in Alida's bed. He apparently confessed to Herman, quite a few friends, and some of my customers. Then there was Fred's never-ending barrage of letters. In ten separate handwritten letters in my filing cabinet, Fred confesses to sexually abusing Alida. Because the crown attorney did not contact me prior to accepting Fred's plea, neither the crown nor the court was aware of this mountain of confirming evidence. If there had been a pre-sentence report ordered, I would have brought this information forward for consideration. Fred was slick to plead out and accept sentencing quickly and quietly.

Fred's letters indicated he planned to confess, but he never said it was to the charge of simple assault. I had naively assumed he would be pleading guilty to sexual assault, and no one told me otherwise. No one asked Alida or me how we felt about the lesser charge or the sentence. Now that it is too late, I realize that all along he planned to plea bargain to a downgraded charge. He knew he would get off easy, which explains why he has been so arrogant.

On one side of the criminal system scale of justice, they tossed away Fred's sexual assaults of Alida and replaced it with one measly simple assault charge. They then balanced the scale with one year of meaningless probation. His consequence does not fit the actual crime. There is no retribution and rehabilitation only if he is directed to take counselling. I know him too well and am quite sure that, going forward, he will not stop abusing girls. Similar to his teenage response when Allison informed her parents what he had done to her, Fred will be meaner and sneakier than ever to avoid detection.

The court's scale of justice weighs different things than mine. I see one year of probation on one side. The other side of my scale is lopsidedly heavy with eight years of incest inflicted on Alida, along with sexual assaults perpetrated against Helen, Grace, Irene, Allison and Jeannie. This side is also loaded with the pain, loss, shame, and humiliation we have all suffered.

Somehow, I have to come to grips with the unfairness of the court's decision and find a way to carry my devastated daughter, and me, forward.

Monday, 25 April 1988
The children's grandmother, by way of letter, declines the invitation to Grandparents' Day at the school. Her reason is that "Because of the situation, we do not want any friction with your Ketel family." If she thinks seeing Kevin's other grandparents will cause friction, it is best she does not attend. However, my son wanted them there, and he is the one they rejected.

Thursday, 28 April 1988
It was worth cancelling my counselling appointment to take the kids to the circus. Fun helps a whole lot more than bemoaning my life, which is not great right now and will not be for a while. At the rate things are moving, the kids will be adults by the time everything is settled. They will not wait to grow up and I do not want them to remember our life as only negative. I do my best to choke down the chaos and provide opportunities where fun is possible.

Friday, 29 April 1988

> To my son Kevin.
> This year the only present I can give
> you for your birthday is myself.
> This coupon is redeemable for an entire
> SUNDAY AFTERNOON
> of undivided love and attention,
> doing whatever you'd like to do.
> With love,
> from your daddy

Daddy comes off as the good guy and Mommy is the meanie who says no. Kevin is too young to understand that it is not only me, but also CAS and a judge who says he cannot have a visit alone with his daddy. Therefore, he sees me as the one denying a fun afternoon of *"love and attention."*

Going to the police station is becoming a full-time job. Again, they say this is not a violation of the restraining order. I know they are sick of seeing me, but I intend to face their repeated rejection and keep going every time I have proof that Fred violates the restraining order. If nothing else, the police will have a long history of complaints on file when things escalate. Actually, they probably will not have a record because they do not even ask my name before they say they can do nothing.

This will get worse. Fred will not stop unless someone makes him. I can only keep my wits about me and hope that when he flips out, the kids will not get hurt and I will survive. I fear that the only way I might get police attention and action is to be murdered. Maybe that is what it will take for them to know my name.

I worry when I hear rumours about Fred starting a new import/wholesale company. He will do all he can to take away my customers, if for no other reason than spite. I know he will keep fighting until something gives, and that something will probably be my mental health. I want a peaceful existence, not a life of fear and fighting. As long as my income and safety depend, in part, on his actions and whims, high levels of stress will continue. As for settlement options, negotiations with our lawyers about Fred taking over the business or giving me a non-competition agreement have been exhausted. There is no short-term way to deal with this and no long-term solution in sight. What I need to do is remove myself from the storm, although I cannot see how to navigate my way out.

Monday, 2 May 1988
The social worker and I have our last appointment. Her rates are going up and this counselling is not really helping me with what I need. During this appointment, I speak about totally breaking off my relationship with Gus. All along, Gus decided if we would see each other or not. He will only see me late at night with his car hidden. He is ashamed to be seen with me in public. Initially this was okay, but as I get stronger, it feels demeaning. This has become an issue between us that we will never resolve. I am not angry with him. I just recognize that I have changed and he cannot or will not. It is time for me to move along.

Thursday, 5 May 1988
This afternoon I have an unexpected visitor at the office. Alex lives on the same country road as the Kettles. He is also single. Alex drove his motorcycle over to say hello to this woman he heard so much about. I have heard about him, too. I can tell he is shy and that this is a big step for him. He seems nice, does not go to the CRC, and we enjoy the same music. It is refreshing that we can eat lunch in public and are able to speak of normal everyday things. I am happy to, at least for an hour, put aside abuse, my ex-husband, courts, and lawsuits.

Friday, 6 May 1988
I leave the house early for another appointment with the counsellor in Toronto. I need help with some of the religious guilt all the talk about my duty to reconcile intensifies. On Highway 401 heading eastbound, a big old car follows me. For more than fifty kilometres the man's car is right on my bumper, just like Fred has done repeatedly this past year. In the rear-view mirror, I can see him making lewd gestures.

My mind leaps to the assumption that Fred hired this slime bucket in his rust bucket to kill me. At the Cambridge exit, I wait until the very last second to jerk my car onto the off-ramp. I find an open business, run inside, and someone phones the police. He had followed too close for me to get his license plate number, so there is nothing the police can do. I blubber like an idiot. What would cause me to be upset at any other time, now tips me over an edge. I am running out of edges.

Monday, 9 May 1988
It is a day of breaking ties. As much as I dreaded doing of this, I advise my current divorce lawyer I am switching to a legal counsel that seems a better fit.

I meet with Gus to tell him that our relationship, or whatever it is we had, is over. He does not take it very well. I think he is probably shocked that I took the control away from him and made it my decision.

Thursday, 12 May 1988

I see the Toronto counsellor for another session. He is the only person who makes any sense with religion and God. He reminds me of the law I have heard from the pulpit every Sunday. "Love your neighbour as yourself," not more than yourself. It is not that I must love Fred and reconcile with him, I must love myself and do what I believe is right for my little family. God is not such an ogre after all, nor is it all as complex as it seemed.

I was on the right track last summer, but with the many pressures, I slipped backwards. This counsellor encourages me to live my own truth as authentically as possible. I do know what is true and right for me. Now comes the more difficult part of finding the courage to live what I believe.

On my way back from Toronto, I spend a few hours in London with my new divorce lawyer. By the time I leave, he seems to have a good understanding of my case. It is well worth the effort to retain a lawyer who listens. This man does. I believe he will do his best to help me get divorced with custody and a final order of supervised access for Fred. I also feel positive that his unflappable demeanour will allow us to proceed with as little drama as possible. Having a lawyer that I trust to be on my side makes me feel hopeful. With these two positive appointments today, hope flows over into everything.

Sunday 15 May 1988

I am visiting my family on the Oregon country road when Alex stops by to return some tools, or so he says. He invites me to visit him later. When I tell my mom my evening plans, she thinks it improper for a single woman to visit a single man alone. It takes some doing to dissuade her from accompanying me as a chaperone. My kids might need supervised access, but their mother does not need supervised dates. Alex and I talk, smoke, and drink coffee. I feel like a delinquent teen sneaking into the Kettles' house at dawn. That I do not get up for morning church displeases them.

Saturday, 28 May 1988

For one-half of my life my safety depended on the Kettles, and the other half I relied on Fred. Neither did a good job. When things went wrong, I felt powerless and out of control. In that dependent place, I had no voice and could not take care of myself, which meant I really had no way of fully protecting my children, either. I do not mean that I am excusing Fred's behaviour or taking the blame for what he did. I am saying that I lacked self-confidence to fight for what I knew was right, and in that sense, I opened the door for Fred to take advantage of me. I hope it is not too late to teach my children that they have every right to fight for their own safety, and the only way I know how is to provide a home that is safe.

Sunday, 29 May 1988

Another new unlisted phone number that I paid for has stopped those annoying phone calls again. When Mr Nobody is unable to annoy us one way, Fred and his father drive by more often. It goes on all weekend. I become irritated enough to suggest that we should move to British Columbia or Australia to get away from the stalkers.

Alida is angry at the idea of moving. She thinks I am trying to take her away from her friends. Alida, also angry with Fred, takes my suggestion to write her feelings in a letter that she shows me when she is done. She wrote that she likes her life and the friends she has. She is not a street kid in Toronto and is safe. These are blessings. For the time being, we are not moving anywhere.

Monday, 30 May 1988

After weeks of being a scaredy-cat, I finally scratch together the courage to phone Fred's probation officer. It surprises me that he will talk to me, given confidentiality and all. Since the police are unwilling to enforce the restraining order, I hoped he might be able to help. Unfortunately, because Fred's probation order has no restrictions around communicating, there is nothing this probation officer can do.

When I explain the situation to him, he goes on a rant about how too many working in the criminal justice system are lazy. Because it is easier, the police do not charge for breaches when they should. Crown attorneys plea bargain cases, and judges accept those plea bargains to relieve court docket congestion. That sex offenders get restraining orders without substance does everyone an injustice, including the person who gets off too easy. The probation officer thinks it inexcusable when victims have no voice and when offenders get off on terms without teeth. The court should stop being so impatient to sentence before they have a pre-sentence report to fully inform them of the circumstances. When he finds out no one told me I had the right to contact the crown attorney in advance, he gets even more upset with a system that benefits the accused and not the victim.

He says he could have helped, if others who came before had done their part. The failure of one or more cogs in the criminal justice structure causes the entire system to wobble, allowing a perpetrator to walk away unscathed while those victimized remain exposed and vulnerable. Fred's probation officer says he feels for me and gives me permission to call him again if I think he might be of assistance.

Wednesday, 1 June 1988

EuroMed Importing's financial statements are complete, and this past year I still made a profit. I also successfully limit work to four and a half days per week and never need to take work home. It is unfortunate that I still come face-to-face with marital problems at the office. A few weeks ago, when I phoned my Listowel customer for an order, he put pressure on me to reconcile with Fred. It was a tightrope between standing up for my right to personal privacy and losing the sale. Since then, every time I need to speak to one of my customers, I become nauseated with anxiety.

After almost twenty years, I know Fred well enough to appreciate that he will eventually find some alleged misdeed of mine that, in his mind, will justify selling to all my wholesale customers. He will never forgive me for rejecting him and will always hound me; therefore, it is up to me to get out of his way.

Although I dislike country and western music, the words of the song *The Gambler* replays in my thoughts.[7] It is the song about knowing when to hold, fold, walk away, and run.

I am going to fold EuroMed Importing and walk away. The financial cost of getting out of Fred's way is that, at least initially, I will have very little money in my personal bank account, zero income, and no financial plan. The only thing I have is my faith that this is the right decision. I will find another job, but with only a grade twelve education, the pay will be much less than the generous income we have enjoyed. However, I can do this. I am the daughter of immigrant parents who showed me how to work hard and stretch a dollar. Youth and ingenuity are on my side. I feel blessed with the opportunity to sidestep Fred and live the remainder of my life without his manipulation and harassment.

---

[7] Don Schlitz, 1976. *The Gambler*. Performed by Kenny Rogers, 1978.

I notify my new lawyer of my intent to leave EuroMed Importing. He reminds me it will harm me in terms of financial settlement. I know that, but am doing it anyway because I cannot go on. All I ask is that my lawyer does his best to help me minimize the damage, and he says he will. He plans to call Fred's new divorce lawyer in Waterloo to advise them. If this does not shake things up, nothing will.

I give my employees a one-month notice and organize a final sales push to clear as much inventory as possible, as quickly as possible. According to my lawyer, it is within the bounds of the family court order that I tell my customers I will not be replacing stock, and I may offer the standard quantity discounts. My end goal is to sell enough merchandise to pay off all outstanding arrears. Going forward, I will have no income, but if this works out, I will also have zero debt other than the mortgage on the Victoria Street house that I have rented out.

Thursday, 2 June 1988
The front of the pretty card says, "We've both been hurt…." The inside reads, "…It is time we both forgive each other."

In addition, there is a letter…

> *Carlyn,*
> *I'd really like to take you and the kids out, either to a show on Saturday nite, or to my church's picnic on Sunday. Please let me know ASAP so I can invite someone else if you decline.*
> *Fred.*

The police think that the efforts of a poor fellow hoping to take his family on an outing does not constitute a breach. Blatantly cloaking a violation of an order in an attractive card and nice words does not change what it is, but the police remain firm.

I am furious again, and bitter. For him, the consequences of his sexual abusing are over. I am sure he believes that by playing nice in one little note, I will go back to him. I will not. Fred has absolutely no idea, nor does he care, about the depths of my anger and pain.

Friday, 3 June 1988

One of my employees receives an unexpected visit at their home, which would be an indirect communication breach had that been a clause in the restraining order. I never thought Fred would harass my employees. It reaffirms my decision to claim defeat. In letting Fred win, I win.

Fred's second divorce lawyer, the one from Waterloo, is already out of the picture. His friend, Lawyer Buddy, is now representing him. This friend of Fred's is no friend of mine.

The first time Lawyer Buddy made an advance toward me was when my kids were babies; Lawyer Buddy had known Fred was in Europe and he called me. He was insistent that he take me out for dinner, and he even offered to arrange a sitter for the kids. I refused and never told Fred. Later, when Fred was trying to talk me into a threesome with Lawyer Buddy, he said something that led me to believe he was aware of the dinner invitation.

After that, I had been able to avoid contact with Lawyer Buddy until a few years ago when Fred was having one of his infamous arguments, that time with our computer dealer. In the middle of the heated argument, Fred called Lawyer Buddy who drove over to EuroMed Importing. While the argument raged on in the foyer, slimy Lawyer Buddy wormed his way into my office. With the door wide open, he snaked around the desk and, without my consent, reached over my shoulders from behind, pinned me to the chair, and groped my breasts.

I did not make a scene. It was easier that way. If Fred found out, he would either use the incident to bully me into a sexual threesome or berate me for flirting, which I had not been doing. I was too worried about Fred's reaction later, and too used to men doing what they wanted, that it never occurred to me that I could call the police to report an assault.

Simply remembering the incident stresses me, and now I must see Lawyer Buddy again. The lawyers have arranged a meeting in Abingville to explore settlement possibilities. It is obligatory that I attend.

Thursday, 9 June 1988

It is déjà vu. We have two different lawyers, and a settlement meeting that fails to produce resolution. Lawyer Buddy and Fred ask some pointed questions around the company's financial situation. I do my best to answer them, on the condition that they will not hold me to the precise accuracy of estimated figures. My lawyer calls it a "without prejudice basis discussion," and they agree.

Unfortunately, we are unable to resolve anything and are moving toward a trial. Before the meeting ends, Fred wants it on the record that he has no plans to start a new import/wholesale company.

Tuesday, June 14, 1988

I hustle over to the school when the principal calls about Kevin being in trouble. On the phone, he makes a snotty remark about mothers who work. My children attend a private Christian school and my income pays the substantial tuition fees. I know darn well they think a good Christian mother's place is at home. I did not ask for subsidy or charity, so I resent his comments and go into the meeting feeling defensive.

In the principal's office, Kevin and I hear how "This boy has a bad attitude and he needs to change it."

I want specifics. "Which attitude might that be?"

"Everything about Kevin's attitude is bad and needs adjusting. Kevin is too much like his father."

I go ballistic. That is uncalled for and hits *way* below the belt. This man sits in the pews with us on Sundays and, with all Fred's confessions, he certainly knows what Fred did. Everyone in our Dutch circle knows.

I ask the principal if he thinks Kevin is a helpful child. He says, "Yes."

I ask if he wants Kevin to change into an unhelpful boy. "No."

I ask if Kevin is a motivated child. He says, "Yes."

I ask if he wanted Kevin to change and be lazy.

This is when Kevin cannot stifle his giggles and the principal tersely excuses him to wait in the hall. Although I know this is not going well, I can think of no other way to handle it. The principal suspends Kevin until he apologizes for mouthing off, and I tell the principal that Kevin will not return to school until the principal apologizes for his bad attitude toward us and his remark about Fred. Because Kevin deserves to be emotionally safe, he has my permission to stay out of school for the rest of the school year if that is how long it takes.

I think the principal now believes Kevin's attitude is too much like his argumentative mother.

Wednesday, 15 June 1988

John still pays me regular visits, but since he now supports Fred and my in-laws, either he is more distant, or I am less trustful. I struggle to know what is proper and what is not in terms of male/female friendships. It has something to do with the ministers saying I should not have a male friend at my house and my mother saying I should be chaperoned with men.

Although there has never been anything even remotely improper between me and John, I now feel uneasy being alone with him. It seems too complicated to tell John that I have become uncomfortable with his visits. I take the coward's way out and avoid seeing him. It is easier that way.

Thursday, 16 June 1988
This afternoon, I take a late lunch away from the office for an appointment with the *dominee*. The staff all leave the office early in the afternoon, my secretary for a personal appointment, and the men to deliver orders. We regularly swap vehicles during business hours and I use one of my employee's cars. I return to the office and work alone for a while, trying to tie things up. Around 4 p.m., Fred calls. This is the first in a long time he phones me at work and I panic. I tell him to talk to my lawyer and rush out of the office as soon as I hang up.

Friday, 17 June 1988
I feel like an idiot about overreacting to the phone call yesterday, so I get in touch with Fred to see what it was he wanted. He should not speak with me because of the restraining order, but he does.

The reason he gives for yesterday's contact is, *"I needed to let you know the court actions I'm taking are nothing personal against you."*

Fred suggests that, for the sake of the children, he should re-establish rapport with them. I suggest that, for the emotional sake of the children, we should cooperatively finalize the financial settlement. He thinks none of the business issues should bother the kids, and if the kids have emotional problems, it has nothing to do with him.

One week ago, during the settlement meeting, Fred put it on the record that he was _not_ going into the importing/wholesale business. Yesterday, when the men made the EuroMed Importing deliveries, every one of the customers sent back a copy of a letter for me. Apparently what Fred said at the meeting was another lie.

Fred's Distributing Ltd
"Importers, Brokers & Distributors
of Medical Equipment and Supplies"

Dear Customer,

After almost a year of absence from the "medical" scene, I am very pleased to advise that I am once again back in the import/wholesale business and ready to serve your needs.

I am certain many of you have wondered what was happening, particularly in view of the many unpleasant rumours which have been circulating during the past year. In that respect I fear that I can't shed much light on the matter, since I consider the problems between Carlyn and me a personal matter between the two of us. As far as the rumours concerning myself, there are obviously two sides to every story, and I can only state:

No, I did not voluntarily leave EuroMed Importing.

No, I have not been in jail, and

No, I am not living a life of leisure.

I have been busy trying to work out some of the problems concerned, and to rebuild a business life for myself starting with nothing. Early this year I was able to open a store in Abingville, which I am pleased to say is very successful. Now, with the assistance of a silent partner, I have set up a new import/wholesale company.

The remainder of the letter explains his elaborate and well-developed plan for his new business. My decision to get out of the EuroMed Importing and out of his way is clearly the right one.

Tuesday, 21 June 1988
What a day!

The school principal calls to ask if Kevin is ready to apologize. Kevin is not. An hour later, the principal phones again to say that my son served adequate punishment and may now return to school. Kevin does not get an apology, either. I leave it up to Kevin, and he wants to finish the school year as long as he does not have to say sorry. I am sure I handled it all wrong, but at this point, I have no idea what I could have done better. I still feel fully justified in defending my son.

We are heading back to family court again. In an affidavit, Fred says he saw my employee, but he writes it in such a way that reader is led to believe the employee contacted him. He goes on to report that, *"On the evening of June 14, 1988, after darkness had fallen,"* he observed my employees loading the delivery truck, found it suspicious, and reported it to the Abingville Police.

Then he reports, in great detail, what he saw while staking out my work premises on June 16th:

11 a.m. Two vehicles known by me to be the personal vehicles of two employees are parked at the side of the warehouse. The EuroMed Importing delivery truck is parked at the loading dock at the rear of the warehouse.

11:50 a.m. The EuroMed Importing delivery truck is being loaded by two employees.

1:10 p.m. The EuroMed Importing delivery truck and work van are both gone from the warehouse but the employees' vehicles are still parked there.

1:25 p.m. The EuroMed Importing van is at the Abingville Home Health Solutions store and it is being unloaded by an employee.

2:15 p.m. The employee drives the EuroMed Importing work van back to the warehouse. The employee's vehicle is no longer there. The employee uses keys to let himself into the warehouse and loads goods into the van.

2:40 to 3:50 p.m. The employee's vehicle is parked at the parsonage of the CRC in Abingville.

3:55 p.m. The Plaintiff drives the employee's vehicle to the warehouse. The EuroMed Importing work van is no longer there.

4:07 p.m. The Defendant called the office of EuroMed Importing and the following conversation took place.
Plaintiff: 'Hello, EuroMed Importing.'
Defendant: 'Hi, this is Fred. Is there a chance we can have a talk?'
Plaintiff: 'Oh. Call my lawyer, okay.'
Defendant: 'Okay, I'll do that. Thank you.'

I verily believe that all these actions are irregular and not the ordinary, logical actions of carrying on a business legitimately. To allow the employees, admitted thieves, free access to the warehouse is an irresponsible act.

I verily believe that the Plaintiff is spiriting away the inventory of EuroMed Importing in an effort to defeat the order of this court and that it is necessary to immediately remove the assets of EuroMed Importing from her control in order to preserve them.

He was the one who spirited assets away to defeat his creditors, something for which he was charged. Now he is projecting the same behaviour on me. I just do not have it in me to spirit away assets and doctor books. It looks like my goal of paying off all the debts will be accomplished, and that is a notable achievement. There will be no extra to spirit away, even if I were so inclined.

Calling my employees thieves is unkind. Fred was still involved when two employees came to us to confess to having stolen some merchandise. We had not even noticed. They offered compensation and the matter was settled. To bring that up now is just dirty and mean.

Of all the things I know, I wish I were unaware of his slithering around where I work. That he was hiding in the bushes and watching the warehouse all day makes me feel violated. I am angry with the police for not enforcing the court order and astonished that he puts into court papers an admission that he has breached the same court's order by contacting me. I am doubtful if I am safe anywhere since he knew, from spying, that I was alone when he phoned. Although there is work to finish, I am too frightened go back there alone.

I am in bed, still awake and reading, when Alida crawls into bed beside me. She tells me she just remembered her father being in her bed playing a game that she now realizes was not a game at all. With sex education in grade seven and what she learned at the CAS group, she put it together. She recognizes that his rubbing up against her and jerking movements were also sexual abuse. The dirty pig. It turns out my cousin's feelings about Fred in Alida's bedroom had been right.

My way of comforting my daughter has always been touch, but she does not want that now. I have to be content with her falling asleep beside me. This is both a sad moment and one I wish I could preserve forever.

Wednesday, 22 June 1988

Last Wednesday, I saw Fred drive through the parking lot near Alida's soccer field. I was thankful Alida had not seen him. Midway through Alida's soccer game this evening, she runs off the field, freaking out. She saw her father sitting in his car, watching her. She is crying and wants me to make him leave. I understand his spying makes her upset for many reasons. This is an opportunity for me to do something for her.

"Of course," I say. "I'll take care of it."

With another parent watching Kevin, Alida goes back onto the field to play and I storm over to Fred's car. The binoculars are on the seat. I ask very politely if he will please leave because Alida is upset.

He arrogantly sputters, *"You bitch. You've no right to impinge my legal right to watch my daughter play her game."*

I am talking about our daughter's feelings and he is worried about legal rights. My fear of Fred fades in the face of protecting my daughter and I swear. When that does not help, I swear louder. I am glad the field is far enough away so no one can hear me.

Finally, with a shrug of his shoulder and a little shake of his head he says, *"I don't deserve this. I'm going to the police station to report you for criminal harassment."*

I do not care. I accomplished my mission of getting rid of him for Alida's sense of safety. Alida is withdrawn tonight. The police do not contact me, so either they discounted Fred's complaint or he was just making an idle threat.

After the soccer game, Alex visits. It is dusk and the blinds in the living room are still open. I tell Alex about Fred watching Alida's game with his binoculars, and Fred peering into my window with those same binoculars. There is movement in the bushes outside the window, so I jump up and turn on the light. A glimpse of the prowler is enough for me to recognize Gus.

Alex is staying over, on the couch. That sounds like a line, but it is the truth. Having another adult in the house allows me to feel safe for one night.

Thursday, 23 June 1988

I know Gus and his friends hang out at Tim Hortons on First Avenue every Thursday evening after their baseball game, so I go there looking for him. I am fully prepared to say my piece in front of his friends. He is just lucky I find him outside and alone when I let loose. He apologizes and promises never to prowl around my house or peep into my windows again. Darn, that feels good.

```
27 June 1988
CAS Ongoing Recording,
Caseworker Bea
```

<u>Current Situation</u>

```
Mrs Smit and her children live a normal
life and they are managing very well.
Kevin and Alida are well-behaved children
who have maintained a strong bond with
their mother. The support system within
the extended family is helping all members
deal with the sexual abuse, divorce, and
feelings of betrayal and anger.

Mrs Smit remains extremely bitter toward
her husband due to the trauma he has
brought upon the entire family. Although
Mrs Smit says she allows the children
```

to form their own opinions, it is this worker's view that she is allowing her underlying feelings of betrayal and hostility to surface in such a manner that it has a negative influence on the children. Alida and Kevin are very bitter on the surface. However, upon visiting with their father for the first time since the abuse, their veil of hostility lifted. During this meeting, the children became friendlier with their father and exchanged some kind words. This worker believes that the children would feel uncomfortable in betraying their mother by expressing an interest in increasing contact.

Several further attempts for access made by Mr Smit have been foiled by the children's resistance. Mrs Smit explains that she will not force the children into visiting with their father. Aside from the access order, which names this agency as supervisor of contacts, there are several other issues of conflict between these parents.

Mrs Smit's in-laws are suing her for business and financial reasons, and the Smit parents are suing one another for eighty percent of their family business. The EuroMed Importing business is under Mrs Smit's name. However, Mr Smit is determined to obtain a substantial settlement. Since their separation, Mr Smit has opened up his own business, Fred's Medical Equipment & Supplies, and he has another new business called Fred's Distributing Ltd. The parents are now in direct competition.

Mr Smit pled guilty to sexual assault and is serving a one-year probation term. He has weekly appointments with his probation officer. The probation officer's reports indicate full cooperation from Mr Smit. Mrs Smit was upset upon learning that he did not receive a jail sentence for his crime.

This worker has contacted the paternal grandparents several times to set up access. However, the grandparents are not interested as they feel Mrs Smit sabotages their relationship with their grandchildren. They are aware that if they change their mind, this worker will make the arrangements.

Alida appears to be doing well. She has graduated from grade seven and is excited about her next year in grade eight. She attended two sessions of the abuse group and found it extremely helpful to discuss common concerns with her peers. Alida presents herself as a mature and level-headed teen who is adjusting well to the separation and the circumstances around it.

Kevin observes his sister's and mother's pain and has had minimal opportunities to express his own thoughts and feelings. Mrs Smit gives the children verbal permission to make there own decisions. However, one can only assume her actions speak louder than words.

The family session at the children's counselling centre was not a success, as the family did not feel comfortable with their approach.

Reassessment

The family continues to cope with the current situation. Although they seem to be slowly recovering from the sexual abuse, there remains further conflict due to the pending divorce proceedings. The tension within the home lingers.

Mrs Smit is a very strong individual who is capable of pulling her family through this stressful time. It would appear Mrs Smit is feeling the strain as time goes on. The financial proceedings are causing ill feelings within the entire family.

Alida and Kevin are very mature and responsible children who remain loyal to their mother's cause. It is hoped that the children will soon be able to feel comfortable in expressing their positive feelings about their father. At this point, the children's bitterness has created a very tough exterior.

Thursday, 7 July 1988

Yesterday, my lawyer and I prepare for family court by answering Fred's motion. I take the opportunity to, for the first time, ask the court to make an order for child support. As long as I had the business to sustain us, it was of minor consequence to me that the only child support Fred paid to date was $100. Now that he sabotaged my mental health and the company, I believe he should financially contribute toward his children's needs. We will also seek the judge's clarification around disposal of EuroMed Importing's residual assets that remain frozen by court order.

It is a rare night when both kids are out overnight with friends and I have an evening to myself. At dusk, about 9 p.m. at this time of the year, I get home from my mommy chauffeur services.

As I get out of the car, knowing I will be going into the house alone makes me nervous. I scold myself, "Being spooked all the time has to stop."

Feigning bravery, I take the garbage bags to the road for morning pickup. I am relieved when I get back to the house without incident.

"See, the bogeymen are in your own mind," I tell myself.

I stop to pull a weed out of a flowerbed and notice the trapdoor at the side of the house is unlatched. I reach over to lock it, but on a whim, peek into the chilly darkness of the crawlspace.

Imagine my shock when I look into human eyes. I start screaming before I slam the trapdoor shut and run through my neighbourhood like a banshee possessed. The men who work at the garage next door left hours ago. The neighbours are all inside their houses with air conditioners running. I am too frantic to worry about my bladder letting go. A warm gush soaks my red skirt and runs down my legs.

Two men working at a metal fabricating company about half a city block away hear my screams above the noise in their shop. They come running to my house, and when I tell them there is a man in my crawlspace, they go over and yank him out.

They ask, "Do you know this guy?"

I do, but I say no. It terrifies me that my rescuers might leave.

One man watches over the intruder, and I go inside with the other. In my bedroom, I strip off the soaked red skirt and pull on a pair of jeans. Just then, I realize that besides a "strange" man under my house, I am alone in the house with a stranger. I rush back to the kitchen where he is patiently waiting. He suggests we call the police. When the officers arrive, I finally admit to knowing the bogeyman.

The police ask what I want done. I say, "I want to be left alone and never see this guy again."

The police officers caution the man to stay away and everyone leaves. An hour later, I am still in a state of shock, unsure how to make it through the night. What is wrong with me that there are now two men stalking me, three if I count Fred's father? I know I need help, but who am I gonna call? *Ghostbusters*? I cannot ask the Kettles for help, or John, or anyone from the church. Lena goes to bed early and I hate to bother her. My new friend Alex is the only person I can think of. It is close to midnight when he arrives.

We wonder why someone might have been under the house and go outside, armed with flashlights, to look for answers. Alex goes into the crawlspace and throws out running shoes, a tracksuit, a pair of binoculars, a water bottle, a toolbox with an electric drill, several drill bits, Peter Jackson cigarettes, and some other tools.

When we call the police, they return and take all of Gus's belongings as evidence. They say he will be getting two charges, "Break, Enter & Mischief" and "Possession of Burglary Tools." I give a statement and the officers leave to arrest Gus. Police will hold him overnight. It gives me some comfort to know he is locked up for a little while, but it still takes me hours to calm down.

Alex and I try to figure out the reason for a power drill. Another trip into the crawl space shows no hydro outlets. What was Gus doing? We go around that question for a long time. Finally, it hits me. The crawl space is under my bedroom.

Sure enough, in my bedroom is the answer. Around the bed, about eighteen inches from the frame, there is a semi-circle of holes bored through the hardwood floor. Since tiny piles of sawdust lay on the floor around the holes, Gus obviously had been in my room. Back in the crawl space, Alex can see the entire bedroom through these viewpoints.

I spend the night curled up in a chair, still in shock. Alex keeps me company and his presence is reassuring.

Today, I dig deep for courage to carry on.

To conquer my shyness and boost my confidence, I have been taking a Dale Carnegie Course in Public Speaking. It is manageable because the cost is a business expense and Lena has been taking the kids for a few hours while I attend. Although it turned out to be more work than I anticipated, the benefit is I am doing something positive for my future. I am learning to use my voice. In terms of self-care, for me, gaining new skills beats warm baths and cups of tea.

During each weekly class, we need to give a talk on an assigned topic. The topic today is, "Overcoming the Biggest Hurdle of My Life." When it is my turn to go the podium, I still have not decided whether to talk about the secret of my miscarriage or about this past year.

Tears stream down my face, and the facilitator encourages me to continue as I share with the group how I discovered my husband molested so many girls, and some of the challenges I overcame this past year. The talk I give comes from my heart, and I deliver it without using the notes I had prepared.

The standing ovation is ample reward. At the end of the speeches, we all vote for the top two. Everyone has an emotional and touching story, so I am surprised when, for my blubbering performance, I am one of the winners.

The other winner was a woman whose husband kidnapped and put her children into hiding. She has not heard from them in six years. A horrific experience for a mother. She ended her talk with a poem she had written in the midst of her despair. The last line was, "Courage is the capacity to carry on, in spite of the fear and in spite of the pain."

Sunday, 10 July 1988

Several years ago, Fred and I visited with an older couple from our church a few times. I had not heard from them at all during this past year, not that I would have expected to. It is a pleasant surprise when the wife calls. She sounds so sincere when she says they want to come over to support me. My hopes rise.

When they arrive, I learn the real reason for their visit. Fred had been in Holland and asked them to deliver a huge bunch of six-dozen yellow roses he oh-so-lovingly carried home on the airplane, as well as a message.

"Fred wants you to know he still loves the girl you were when he met you. He wants to reconcile, and he wants your relationship to go back to the way things were before."

I try to get them to see my position. "I will not go back, and besides, if I did, the CAS would take my children away."

Explaining is waste of breath. Fred has already persuaded them he is a loving husband deprived of his family. He has gone to the outer reaches of our social circle and found himself some new allies. His outstanding persuasion skills again awe me.

They accuse me of exaggerating and are peeved by my stubbornness and unwillingness to accept their assistance to repair my marriage. Matrimony is sacred and my duty is to reconcile with my husband. I am sick to death of duty.

The couple is sure they are doing their part to help patch our broken marriage. They continue to believe Fred is a sweet man. What they think of me is not as positive. It does not help that I turn down the wife's offer to arrange the roses in a vase. By the time they leave in a huff, I am happy to show them the door.

My hope is crushed. This final straw cracks me.

My mind goes off like fireworks gone sideways.

I am sick to death of trying to explain my position. I am fed up with polite words that minimize what actually happened. I hate wishy-washy language like "abuse." Even words like "sexual assault" and "molesting" do not do justice to reality.

I say Fred abused girls, but what does that really mean? Saying Fred "forced himself on me" before we were married does not adequately explain my experience and makes it sound not-so-bad. Only the gritty facts will describe the brutality of what I endured. The details are not pretty, but they are real.

> *(Sensitive content warning)* He pushed me face down on the bed, tore off my clothes, and held me down by my shoulders. Then he crudely penetrated me from behind. He humped dry and hard for what felt like forever. I bled for days and it took weeks for the lacerations to heal.

I have never told anyone what Fred did to me that night in my little rented room. I had always considered it extremely unpleasant, unwanted sex that somehow was my fault. Only recently did I learn the name for it is date rape. Even when I knew the correct term, I stayed quiet because I did not want any of the other girls Fred molested to think I was trying to make it about me.

This is the first time I am prepared to acknowledge, albeit only to myself, that Fred raped me. There is no doubt Fred remembers. He admitted to it in his vague way. I check through my file cabinet for verification. The proof is in his letter to me on July 6th of last year:

> *But all the times you never wanted sex with me, from day one, that was all my fault. It was cause I pressured you, tried to get too much before we were married. Yeah, I did and yeah, I wasn't too nice about it when you didn't want it.*

The Count:
- seven confirmed (my sisters Grace, Helen and Irene, my daughter Alida, Fred's sister Allison, Fred's cousin Jeannie, and me/Carlyn),
- one attempted (my sister Ellie), and
- six suspected (the teenage store employee, Fred's former girlfriend, our customer's daughter, my niece, Fred's Dutch cousin, and my sister Dorothy)

Fred molested, or did something inappropriate to all seven of the girls in my wedding party: me, my sisters, and his. I find the photo of us in our rainbow of homemade dresses and weep at our youth. At age eighteen, I was the oldest. Each one of us was so young and so vulnerable.

Fred wants me to go back to being a timid and compliant farm girl.

Yellow roses are my favourite. He thinks an obscenely large bouquet of yellow roses can sway me. I cannot stand the sight of these flowers. Yellow roses like the flowers tucked between the daisies in my wedding bouquet. I will kill the flowers just as he killed our marriage.

Lack of water will not destroy them fast enough, so I rip the petals and leaves off each of the seventy-two stems. I barely notice the blood on my hands from the thorns.

I find scissors to chop the stems into tiny pieces. Dead flowers for a dead marriage.

A large shoebox will work as a coffin to bury the marriage.

A dead marriage deserves dead wedding and honeymoon photos. I love cutting up Fred's face. One eye, two eyes, a nose, mouth. There. He is gone.

What else can I put into the coffin? Ah, I have leftover fabric from the wedding and bridesmaid's dresses. I hack and fray the material until it is shreds. I do the same with the ribbons and lace that are still in my sewing box.

I find a full bag of confetti in the closet and, oh yes, the 8-mm home movie of the wedding with the *dominee's* chastising sermon. It is quite a job to pull the film out of the reel and snip it into quarter inch strips.

Everything swishes in the shoebox coffin until it is multi-coloured chaos. The sum of all colour is black. Black as death.

In our backyard, I find some dead sticks and flowers. They get tied to the shoe box with a piece of pale purple ribbon. Funeral flowers.

Fred is telling people this marriage is recoverable and reconcilable. While he may never grasp that it was he was who killed our marriage, the girl he met and the relationship we had are gone.

It feels urgent to deliver our dead marriage to him. My car becomes a hearse and I scour the streets of Abingville. When I finally see his red Mustang driving toward me, I squeal to a halt in the middle of the street and jump out of my car.

I am too angry to be afraid and too crazy to be rational.

Fred slams his brakes. His arm dangles out of his rolled down window in his cool dude position. He takes a long drag off a cigarette and blows the smoke toward my face, away the teenage girl beside him who has her hand on his thigh and the two girls giggling in the back seat.

I open the shoebox coffin and throw the ashes onto his lap. "There you go asshole. You killed our marriage and now all the pieces are yours."

For once, just once, he has nothing to say.

I stomp back to my car, sobbing uncontrollably and laughing maniacally.

I have completely lost my shit.

Wednesday, 13 July 1988

In weekly family court appearances this past month, Fred submits further arguments in another painfully long affidavit. Today the presiding judge heard the motions and awarded me $300 per month interim child support. With respect to the sale of the assets, the judge orders us to draw up a document called "Terms of Consent" and then bring it back to him for an order.

My lawyer needs more money since the retainer I gave him is long spent. With no income and frozen assets, I appreciate that Alex offers a loan.

Friday, 15 July 1988

It is my birthday, so Lena comes for cake and coffee. Another friend phones to ask when I am having my birthday party and I tell her I am skipping it.

She asks, "How can you not?"

"I just can't. It is just too much this year."

I want my birthday to slip away as quietly as possible. It takes too much effort to smile and go through social niceties. I wonder who knows what, what to say to whom, or who wants to talk about what. Life is too intense to socialize. Being alone is preferable. There will be no celebration in my home today.

Monday, 25 July 1988
Because Fred alleged that I depleted stock, I am obliged to honour his request to review all EuroMed Importing records. My lawyer arranges for Fred and Lawyer Buddy to meet me at the office. Fred wants to take the books away, which was not the arrangement. He throws up his hands and claims to find it utterly mysterious that I do not trust him. The meeting ends with Lawyer Buddy leading Fred out of the office and Fred yelling that he will be getting a court order to do a proper forensic analysis.

Wednesday, 27 July 1988
I had an all-out argument with the *dominee* last evening. He asked weird questions that made no sense at first. It took a bit before I realized that he was fishing for clarification of things he heard about me. The question that clued me in was, "How could you have fired Fred and his father in such a malicious and ruthless manner?"

It turned out the *dominee* was talking to Fred and his parents and planned not to tell me. I was upset and mouthed off about the CRC not helping me one iota and, in fact, hurting me more than anything. Then I apologized for my outburst and grovelled my way back into the fold. Tonight, I regret my apology.

I cannot think straight. Ideas race through my mind like squirrels in an attic. Somehow, I have to separate all those thoughts and feelings and deal with them one at a time.

I am exhausted by feeling down, tired of not sleeping, tired of being alone and scared, tired of nightmares, and I am tired of not eating enough. I am tired of the holes in my bedroom floor. I am tired of worrying if anybody is lurking outside this house. I am so tired of being tired.

I am confused. I do not know what to do about moving out of Abingville, work, money, church, school, friends, my rights, my children, Fred's parents' lawsuit and stalking.

I question the existence of God, or at least the God of the CRC. It is getting increasingly difficult to find my way to the Light.

I am lonely. No one seems to understand how intertwined everything is. When I see people, I feel even lonelier than when I am alone.

I am angry with everyone and at everything except my children, but parenting drives me to the edge. I am fed up with the army of black suited men who tell me how to behave, tripping over Kevin's broken bike on their way in and out of my house. If they would listen to my concerns, they would know that fixing that bike is something I need done. Maybe I would be able to hear what they have to say if they would offer meaningful help.

I am afraid of so many things. I fear how much I want to die. I am afraid of being dependent on anyone, that I will never get over this, that I will end up in a straitjacket, that Fred will flip out and kill me, and that the future will be as bad as the present. I am afraid of trying and failing, of not trying, of being wrong, and of not having the courage I need to carry on. The worst fear of all is that my children will be taken away. I can bear it all, but that would be too much.

Thursday, 28 July 1988

The Dale Carnegie Course finishes and I receive another award. Acknowledgment validates that, even in the midst of such a difficult and emotional time, I do not have to be perfect and still have something worth sharing.

The group went out for a drink after the last class. One woman followed me into the restroom to tell me that she suffered incest when she was a girl. Before my talk, she had never told anyone. This past week she had a candid conversation with her mother, and her mother believes her. I am glad my disclosure gave her a green light to tell her truth. And yet, another female victimized means there is another mother who needs to find a way to cope with her daughter's violation.

Sexual abuse supposedly happens less often to males, but I am starting to wonder. Not counting Fred, six men have told me of sexual abuse by fathers, brothers-in-law, strangers, and neighbours. Every man said he never told anyone before. Sexual abuse is a secret, sinister thread that runs through too many lives.

I cannot remove people's agony, but I can listen and validate their experiences. That is similar to what Lena does for me, and the importance should never be underestimated.

Friday, 29 July 1988
Something I have wanted to do for years is put all our pictures into albums. I cry as I sort the photos spread out across the living room. I see Fred and I when we met, the few remaining wedding pictures, the children's births, baptisms, and first school days, my little sisters when they were young, my sisters now, Alida at age four beside our Christmas tree. The glossy finishes only show the façade of a nice-looking family. Sweet memories, all of them superimposed over the horror of abuse.

I hate nights. As soon as it becomes dark, every creak and crack send me spinning. Not only do the doors have deadbolts, I wedge a broom against the outside door and lock every window at night, no matter how hot it is. I also hang contraptions of tin cans on the doors. When I omit the crazy bedtime rituals, sleep eludes me. When I do sleep, my mind still works overtime. In my latest nightmare, a waddle of male penguins in black suits attack me, each one gnawing off a chunk of my flesh.

Wednesday, 3 August 1988
On Sunday morning, the *dominee* announced the tragic death of the man with mental health problems. The whispers are that it was

suicide. This hit me hard for selfish reasons. I feel so terribly jealous of his wife because her hassles are over and her children are safe. Because we are part of the same social circle, I go to the funeral.

After the service, our former CRC minister and his wife knock on my door. We had known them well when they lived in Abingville. Since they heard the gossip of what happened to us, there is no need for me to share details. He admits he had no training at the Calvin College seminary in Grand Rapids regarding how to handle sexual abuse from a ministerial point of view. This honesty is both refreshing and pathetic.

Friday, 5 August 1988
I have a great big ugly cry. My eyes are numb from the ice cubes I use to bring down the swelling and, at the same time, some heaviness has lifted from my heart. By closing EuroMed Importing, I am no longer indebted to the Kettles and no longer need their sales to survive. As long as they were my customers, I had to swallow the anger I felt toward them for knowing about Fred and doing nothing. By releasing myself from our business ties, I am free to grieve. I sound unappreciative of all Mom and Dad do for me, which is not the case. Mom buys the kids things and they take their grandchildren for weekends and during the summer. The word thankful is like the word sorry; the words do not erase what happened.

Mr Nobody is at it again. The phone company will bill me to get another unlisted number unless I can get a recommendation from the police. The police refuse to track the calls since nothing is said. The calls are not threatening, at least by police definition. I find the silence chilling.

I get another Mr Nobody call right after I speak with the police. To get a reaction, they receive a string of curses befitting the mouth of a sailor, but they say nothing. Swearing feels good, but I regret doing it because I empowered Mr Nobody with the knowledge that they are getting under my skin.

Sunday, 7 August 1988

I lent our former CRC minister two books, one by an incest survivor and one about sex offending. He returns both to me after preaching this morning's church service, both tucked inside a brown paper bag. I assume he was ashamed to let anyone see what he was reading. Brown paper wrapping is what pornography comes in. Secrets go in brown paper bags.

Abuse and incest are dirty secrets to keep hidden. Church people hide my family by ignoring us. Even in today's long prayer, the minister whom I thought was empathetic did not mention my family. I interpret my church's hands-off approach a result of their revulsion, and I feel dirtier and lonelier than ever.

Saturday, 13 August 1988

On the heels of the resumption of the Mr Nobody calls, Fred phones me again. I asked how he got the number.

"*Several of your people made a point of getting in touch and gave it to me. They feel sorry for me, and asked me not to give you their names. I did not solicit to get the number, Carlyn. Yeah, they just keep on calling to update me about what you are up to. I promised them I would keep their identities secret. God knows, they are all scared of you. Nobody wants to bear the brunt of your anger.*"

I want to say my friends would never do that, but he has obviously received my number from someone. I am trusting people I should not.

"*I've been in contact with the CAS who are now out of the picture. They say access supervision is up to you, Carlyn, so what time can you bring the kids for a visit today?*"

His indignation at my refusal almost makes me believe him, but I have the wherewithal to wait until Bea confirms his story.

Monday, 15 August 1988
Bea returns from her two-week vacation and Fred reaches her before I can. Fred did not mention the Saturday phone call to Bea. I explain and she simply says, "He lied." It is scary how close I came to believing Fred.

Fred, according to Bea, phoned her to question my competence as a mother in letting the kids go swimming and biking. That he knows of these activities suggests he is stalking the kids. Bea said she informed Fred that I am very capable of caring for my children.

I spend most of today sitting on the couch like a zombie, staring out the window. I watch the spruce tree outside with much interest. It is an extremely hot summer, and we have not had rain for weeks and weeks. Farmers are predicting serious shortages as crops wither in the fields. The tree seems unaffected, standing strong in the drought. I am reaching deep to find hope, and my source today is the tree. If this tree survives, I have hope that I, too, will survive. This tree is my anchor to hope.

Tuesday, 16 August 1988
Because I was raped, I shave my head as an expression of despair. In the dream, Lena consoles me, rubs my bald head, and says, "We will work it out. You will be okay."

My nightmares are getting worse and mimic my mental health. There is less distinction between nightmares and reality, days and nights, and between light and dark.

The only thing keeping me somewhat grounded is my single-minded refusal to abandon my children. I love them and being their mother means more than my life. My children are my strength.

I cling to hope that I will eventually get out of this quagmire. All I can do is keep going. Put one foot in front of the other. Breathe.

I have a poem posted on my fridge that I read frequently, and a piece of music that I listen to many times a day. The two provide somewhat of a road map: keep swimming and hold on.

> Two frogs fell into a deep cream bowl;
> The one was wise, and a cheery soul.
> The other one took a gloomy view
> And bade his friend a sad adieu.
> Said the other frog with a merry grin
> "I can't get out, but I won't give in;
> I'll swim around till my strength is spent,
> Then I will die the more content."
> And as he swam, though ever it seemed,
> His struggling began to churn the cream
> Until on top of pure butter he stopped,
> And out of the bowl he quickly hopped.
> The moral, you ask? Oh, it's easily found!
> If you can't get out, keep swimming around.[8]

The music is Peter Gabriel's song, "Wallflower."[9] He wrote it with Amnesty International, political prisoners, and people being tortured in mind. The lyrics describe my situation as a prisoner of my community's indifference and remind me that while I feel alone, others suffer much worse. The refrain is "Hold on. Hold on." Most of the time, holding on is all I can do.

Monday, 22 August 1988

It is no longer reasonable to put off notification to the Christian school that my kids are not returning in September. I already registered Alida and Kevin in the public school system. The Christian school principal was cruel to compare Kevin to his father,

---

[8] Author unknown.
[9] Peter Gabriel, *Wallflower* from the album *Security*. 1982.

and he never said sorry, so I feel this move is necessary to safeguard my children. There will be fallout for this decision, particularly from the Kettles.

I am still toying with the idea of resigning from the church. I want to, but years of brainwashing have convinced me church resignation will assure me a VIP place in hell, much more so than I ever believed divorce would. To be emotionally manageable, I can only do big moves like this one at a time.

Thursday, 25 August 1988

For fourteen months, I never doubted that my daughter was molested. This afternoon, when Alida is pushing all my buttons, I find myself questioning her allegations about her father.

I think, "This little brat said she was abused just because she is a brat."

From there my thoughts go to, "None of it is true. It was a nightmare, not reality. I made it up, like Fred said."

Not trusting myself to talk to her, I send the brat to her room to protect her from my dangerous thoughts. After going to the bathroom to purge my self-revulsion, I lock myself in my bedroom.

I am thankful for the concrete things I have saved. The evidence in my locked filing cabinet helps me to recover from my disbelief. Both the CAS and police believe something happened. My journal and Fred's letters with his confessions assures me it is real. There are too many girls saying the same things and none of them would have reason to lie.

It takes me an hour to realize that I am overwhelmed and not coping, or more appropriately, simply coping. I have read that grief can include episodes of denial. With my mental health slipping, everything caught up with me today. My mind was overwhelmed with truth's harsh reality, and I flipped headfirst into denial. Experiencing denial does not mean I am a bad mother.

According to the professionals who had become involved since Alida's disclosure, my initial reaction to believe my daughter was supposedly atypical. Ideally, professionals would be patient with mothers who are in denial and give them the support, information, and the safety they need to accept the truth. That is not what happens because maternal denial places children at risk. It seems to me that mothers who deny are denied a perfectly normal reaction.

If I had known ahead of time that denial could happen this long afterward, it might not have upset me as much as it did. It made me feel terrible, and yet I am proud that I was able to withhold my doubts from my daughter. If it happens again, I will know what it is and that my file cabinet holds what I need to counteract it.

Wednesday, 21 September 1988

Fred has a new buddy, someone I have never met, who phoned me last weekend. He got our unlisted phone number from Fred and called to tell me what a nice, generous fellow my husband is. The man was slurring his words and I hung up as soon as I dared without angering this new, apparently very drunk, friend of Fred's.

Drunken Buddy phones again to check with me if there is a reason to be concerned about Fred hanging around his daughters. That catches my attention. He is a widower with three daughters who are all young teens. He tells me Fred, now a regular visitor at their house, arrives with fancy boxes of chocolates and bouquets of flowers for the girls and beer for him. Fred takes the girls to town for meals and movies and teaches them to steer his Mustang by letting them sit on his lap. Fred photographs the girls and has life-size, sexy pictures of them hanging in his apartment. Drunken Buddy is confused because his daughters adore Fred. Yes, Fred has taken them out this evening and yes, Drunken Buddy has been into the beer.

I suggest the first thing he should worry about is his drinking and the second is to keep Fred from being alone with his daughters.

Drunken Buddy whines that CAS has been at him for months, saying the same thing. Everyone seems out to get Fred.

The modus operandi Fred uses, the method by which he grooms both girls and parents, is recognizable. I suspect that by now, Fred has crossed the line with these girls.

It is the father's job to protect his daughters, but society is also responsible for keeping those three girls at risk. If there had been a pre-sentence report before criminal court sentencing, I could have asked for a probation order condition that Fred not be alone with under-aged girls. How was it the crown attorney did not insist on conditions aimed to prevent Fred from being free to groom, and possibly abuse, other girls?

Furthermore, if Fred's name were published like the names of other criminals, everyone would know he is a risk to children. Publication of the offender's name can occur without naming whom he victimized. Molesting one's own daughter should not afford protection from public exposure. For offenders, sexually abusing their own children is the safest bet. They get protection, perpetuating the whole cycle indefinitely. I have read enough to know that the best predictor of a person being a future sexual offender is a history of sexual offending, yet we place children at risk because we give sex offenders protection along with indecently meaningless consequences. Society is not yet prepared to do what it takes to protect children.

I just re-read the last paragraph and I am mistaken. Fred was not convicted of sexual assault, so publishing his name for a common assault would do nothing to protect children in the future. That an offender benefits from another level of silence is an unintended consequence of a plea bargain.

The Count:
- seven confirmed (my sisters Grace, Helen and Irene, my daughter Alida, Fred's sister Allison, Fred's cousin Jeannie, and me/Carlyn),

- one attempted (my sister Ellie), and
- nine suspected (the teenage store employee, Fred's former girlfriend, our customer's daughter, my niece Nakita, Fred's Dutch cousin, my sister Dorothy, and Drunken Buddy's three daughters)

Thursday, 22 September 1988
I receive an extensive handwritten proposal, valid only until midnight tonight. Each new proposal is increasingly complex, and with each, Fred's imagination conjures up higher amounts that I supposedly owe him.

Fred ends the document with a section he titles Custody and Access.

"While I agree that my past actions account for a very small part of the feelings the children have toward me, I strongly believe that the greatest reason for their negative attitude is because of your persistent negativity about me during the past fifteen months."

He threatens to go to court for a judge to decide custody and access, since I am too unreasonable to come to an agreement in this matter.

Another breach.

Again, no police action.

Saturday, 24 September 1988
This evening, Drunken Buddy phones to invite himself to attend church with me tomorrow morning. I speak with him long enough to find out Fred brought over two cases of twenty-four beers and has taken the girls to town. I decline his church invitation and he calls me an uppity bitch, a goody-two-shoes, and says it makes sense to him why Fred dumped me.

Seeing Drunken Buddy would be foolish, even for the sake of helping his daughters. It is up to CAS now. I am thankful that I have the strength say no and avoid another miserable situation.

As the evening grinds on, I worry that Drunken Buddy and Fred might come here together and gang up on me. It is amazing what kind of panic I can brew with one phone call.

Now I lay me down to sleep, I pray the Lord my soul to keep. If I should die before I wake...what a morbid thing to teach kids. If I should die before I wake, it might not be such a bad thing. I worry more about waking before I die.

By 5 a.m., I assume the Drunk and Fred are either sleeping or passed out, so it must be safe to go to sleep.

Sunday, 25 September 1988
(mailed Monday, 26 September 1988)

> DAD,
> I trusted you, once upon a time
> Then you molested me, made life a hard climb.
> I loved you from when I was a baby
> Now that love is just a maybe.
> You broke three most important things
> My heart cries instead of sings.
>
> You broke my trust, something hard to gain
> Now instead of trust, all I feel is pain.
> You broke my love I had so much.
> Darn it! Why was it me you had to touch?
> Most of all you broke my family
> Why did you have to be so unmanly?
>
> All I felt was anger, pain and guilt
> That I had put my family on a tilt.
> But now the whole truth I do realize
> You put our life in such jeopardize.

Now I feel no more guilt and pain
No more anger, only sane.

So I ask one thing only
Even though Bea says you may be lonely
Please stop you and your family from driving by
Then will I feel relief, and sigh.

Alida (age 13)

Tuesday, September 27, 1988
(hand delivered in our mailbox before noon)

> *Alida,*
> *I know you trusted me, and you loved me too,*
> *When I went on a trip, the one who cried was you.*
> *Then I went and touched you, when I knew I was wrong.*
> *I've wanted to face you, to tell you for so long.*
> *They've told you what I wanted ... the reason why.*
> *Alida, I can't stop you from believing that lie.*
> *Perhaps someday you'll know what really is true,*
> *And just what it was I was trying to do.*
>
> *Still, it was wrong, so like a man I stood,*
> *To take the blame, and spare you what I could.*
> *I'd betrayed your trust, that to see was so plain,*
> *And I'd broken your love, and caused you such pain.*
> *I know how it hurts, I honestly do.*
> *You see, I've been betrayed and through hell too.*
>
> *I'm glad you do realize that you had no part,*
> *In things that caused our family to come apart.*

But you blame me, and call me unmanly,
Sorry Princess, but I didn't break apart our family.
I did things wrong, and not a little bit,
But that's not what caused your mom and I to split.
Every marriage needs a certain kind of glue,
You have to be able to trust each other to be true.
I'll take the blame for whatever I do,
But others are responsible for their own actions too.

You kids are in the middle, and it'll probably get worse,
Before Mom and I are through with our divorce.
I wish there was something that I could do,
But to set matters right will really take two.

Now we've grown so very far apart,
I miss you all and it really breaks my heart.
I just hope that someday, each other we'll see,
Cause I'm still your father, and you'll always my kid be.
You can do things to hurt, and yes, even make me cry,
But I'll keep on loving you, and I will till I die.

But Princess, one thing really did make me glad.
When you wrote your letter you called me "DAD."

Love,
Dad

Monday, 3 October 1988
Before our divorce goes to trial in family court, we must go through a process called discovery. This is where the other person's lawyer questions us under oath. Both sides can also request and receive

any documentation they require to go to trial. Last Friday, late in the afternoon, I receive a five-page list of what Lawyer Buddy and Fred require. I gather what I can over the weekend and schlep one file box full into the meeting.

A few times during Lawyer Buddy's questioning, I almost lose my cool, but overall, it is manageable. In my pocket, I hold a stone inscribed with the word "integrity." When I become overwhelmed or confused, that one word helps me stay focused. When Lawyer Buddy becomes too pushy, I think of what he did to me in my office and stare him down. He is always the first to look away. That helps.

Something upholds me today and it is more than my own strength or the support of my lawyer, of that I am certain.

Thursday, 6 October 1988

The *dominee* arrives for a ministerial visit at 9:45 p.m. It is awfully late, but the advantage for me is that the kids are in bed, so we can speak privately. The *dominee* pulls out his big guns and all his ammunition. He heard from Fred that I am seeing someone, and he wants to know if the man is Dutch or from the CRC. Since the answer is neither, he reprimands me for seeing a "Canadian." Then he goes at me for dating at all because my divorce is not final. Reconciliation is God's will. The *dominee* cannot get it through his thick little round skull that reconciling would be going back into hell. I will take my chances with God.

It is likely true I am not ready to date, and that seeing Alex might not be the wisest move. However, unwise is not sinful.

His objective is to label me sluttish. A harlot. He cunningly cloaks the insults in Biblical prattle. Funny how the sluts and harlots materialize with the *dominee*.

With his beady eyes boring into mine, he interrogates me. "Well, I know you see Alex, but are you having a sexual relationship?"

"This," I think, "is a trick question." There are three possible responses. If I deny it, it would be a lie and suggest I am ashamed of what I am doing. Not an option. If I do not answer, he will interpret my silence as a yes, and if I say yes, I will wear it. Silence and yes would have the same effect, and yes is the honest answer.

"Not that I think it's any of your business, but yes I am."

In my mind I hear, "You fool."

The pregnant silence is disturbed with the crackle of Bible pages.

"Ah, here it is," he says.

He reads John 8: 1-11. At verse number four, his voice gains pastoral supremacy, and the meaning of his biblical choice becomes evident. "This woman was taken in adultery, in the very act."

He softens his tone until the final verse when, with the force of authority vested in him, he pronounces, "Go, and sin no more."

Then, "Shall we pray?"

In dutiful submission, like a lamb led to the slaughter, I fold my hands and close my eyes.

"God, I humbly stand before you with this woman who admits to committing adultery. Carlyn is truly sorry and asks for your gift of forgiveness. We know that your infinite grace is sufficient to forgive her, just as you forgave the harlot brought before you. And Lord, please walk beside her, this woman who has sinned, and grant her sufficient strength to go, to go, and sin no more."

After the *dominee* leaves, I am destroyed.

The wooden handle fits so nicely in my right hand. A few days ago, I had my knives sharpened. The glint of the blade lures me.

Somehow, I hold on. It is the best I can do and I take it as a win.

Saturday 8 October 1988
It is not that I want to die, but holding on is the most difficult

thing I have ever done in my life. The Light is dimming and harder to see.

Every route toward something better seems blocked. No one appreciates the effort it takes to fight and claw through each minute to reach the end of every day. I want to curl up and hide. I want to sink into a place where the bombardment of my senses stops. Maybe that place is the womb of death. This morning, I woke up crying for Mommy to help me.

Tuesday, 11 October 1988
I am finally able to think about the *dominee's* visit with some rationality. If we could do it over again, I would tell him to shut his pie hole. I will never sit through anything like it again, not as long as I live. We did not attend church on Sunday and I will never return. The soul murdering has become too much.

Friday, 21 October 1988
After a ton of negotiations via the two lawyers, we work on an agreement that Fred, for a hefty fee, will dismantle and sell off EuroMed Importing and the log house. To be honest, now that all the loans are paid and I have no more financial obligation to EuroMed Importing, I am too worn down to care what happens to the rest of the assets. Before we make this agreement, also via the lawyers, I make Fred an offer to settle.

In the offer, I withhold my car and ask only for the money that I got for the accident insurance settlement. I am prepared to give Fred absolutely everything else with no strings attached. That includes the matrimonial home, the Parry Sound waterfront property and partial log house, and from EuroMed Importing the remainder of the stock, equipment, truck, and van, and all the cash in trust from the sale of the Parry Sound warehouse property.

The value of my offer to him is worth somewhere around

$250,000, and all of it is debt-free except for the mortgage on the matrimonial home. That gives him a very generous stake for his new life. He declines my offer because, in his opinion, half the value at separation is more. Either Fred fails to understand that saying something is true does not make it so, or his objective is to continue to revel in the fight and make my life miserable. Fred, it appears, does not understand the proverb, "a bird in the hand is worth two in the bush."

The cash I have left in my personal bank account is just enough to keep us afloat for another month. I break down and contact welfare. I explain my dilemmas to a worker: there are assets in my name, but they are frozen. When Fred and I divorce I may or may not receive some money, and I want to work but I am an emotional wreck. The worker consults her supervisor, and they need a letter from my lawyer confirming the assets are frozen pending resolution or further court order. My application goes through and I qualify for social assistance. Too bad I have to go on welfare. I wish I were stronger.

Because an order for $300 monthly child support was made in family court, I have two choices. One way that welfare can deal with it is to deduct the $300 per month from my cheque and any support Fred pays is mine. The other option is that I sign up with the Support and Custody Enforcement Agency, and sign over to welfare anything they collect. That way I will receive the full benefits from welfare. Since Fred will never voluntarily pay me child support, and I need the $300, I sign the papers. Fred will be livid.

Last week the two divorce lawyers and Fred started his Discovery Hearing. In the mail today is another financial statement, with Fred showing a monthly budget of more than twice the income I will receive from welfare for the three of us. His weekly budget for eating out would feed us for a month. He failed to account for his court ordered child support.

There is a new black suit in the mix, a new elder, who wants to arrange the annual *huis bezoek*. When elders come for house visitation, they do so in pairs. Two against one. It is inevitable that they will want to discuss my sin of pulling my kids out of the Christian school, my duty to reconcile with Fred, and if they noticed, my lack of church attendance. I might be able to handle God giving my soul a review, but not these men.

    Not knowing how to fight, for my sanity's sake, I hide. I tell the black suit I will not be participating in *huis bezoek* this year. That alone is defiant enough to justify discussions at consistory meetings about the errors of my ways. It is uncomfortable when others negatively judge me, but there is no other way. The black sheep is straying further from the fold. Never mind that if I stay in the fold, they will eat me alive.

Kevin gets himself into a fight and complains his ribs are sore. The other day, he and his friend were in Kevin's bedroom burning things in a wastepaper basket. I cannot decide which is worse, him keeping his feelings inside or acting them out. Either way, I worry about him. His progress has been short-lived. I have to do better. The CAS worker says I am talking to the children too much and it seems to me I am not talking enough. All the available counselling has been exhausted and there is no place else to turn for help.

Alida has some friends from her CAS group over. These girls are older and much more streetwise than Alida is. Although they seem nice enough, I worry about their influence on her. I pull out some crafts and they work together on making Christmas ornaments. Keeping the girls close is better than them running the streets.

Tuesday, 25 October 1988

For Fred to proceed with selling the company assets, he needs the keys to EuroMed Importing. I cannot bear to face Fred, so Alex drops them off for me at Fred's Medical Equipment & Supplies. Alex, bless his "Canadian" heart, is not the least bit intimidated.

Fred and his uncle are at the store when Alex gets there. Alex sits down for a minute and Fred takes the opportunity to warn him that I am not to be trusted. The uncle pipes up with his opinion, which is, "Carlyn is making a big fucking deal about nothing. All Fred did was feel his daughter up a little bit."

The uncle's attitude makes me feel terribly sad for my children's father. This uncle and Fred's father were his role models, and still are, it seems. Fred's attitude toward females is the same as theirs. They are three peas in a pod.

By 6:30 p.m., when the answering machine takes a message, I regret negotiating anything at all.

> *Hi Carlyn, it's Fred. I hate to bother you. I've been at the office and paperwork seems to be missing. [Pause] Okay. Yeah. I'm going down to the police station now to report it missing, since I do have complete power of attorney. You can contact my lawyer's office in the morning to return it or the proper authorities will be notified because the papers belong in the office. Thank you.*

Wednesday, 26 October 26 1988

> *7:30 a.m. Your lawyer will be trying to get in touch right after 9 a.m. We've got only an hour to get things straightened out, to get the paperwork back in place Carlyn, or the Corporations people and Revenue Canada will be called in, and there's nothing I can do to help you then. I don't want it to go this way. It's up to you.*

10 a.m. I'm hoping you will call me. I'm waiting thirty minutes. Okay? Then we are calling the field office in London, Corporations Branch, at Revenue Canada. We are asking for a full-scale audit into EuroMed Importing. You're the only one who can avoid this. If you don't want to talk about it, fine. You can talk to those people. I'm at the office. Yeah. Call me ASAP.

Police do not consider the three taped phone calls breaches of the restraining order.

The rest of the day we get calls from Mr Nobody, Lena and a few from my children's friends. No lawyers, police, Revenue Canada or Corporations people contact me.

Thursday, 27 October 1988
My lawyer concludes Fred's examination for discovery. We order a copy, and he will let me know when it arrives.

Friday, 28 October 1988
In the mail today is another certificate. This one is typed and unsigned.

> CONGRATULATIONS
> are in order!
> YOU'VE COME A LONG WAY BABY!!
> IT TAKES A ONE-OF-A-KIND OF WOMAN
> TO RIP SOMEONE OFF FOR $500,000,
> KEEP TRYING TO SUCK HIS BLOOD,
> AND THEN TURN AROUND AND STEAL
> FOUR COINS FROM HIS COLLECTION YET TOO.
> THANK GOD THERE IS ONLY ONE OF YOU!
>
> JUST REMEMBER.........
> PAYBACKS ARE A BITCH.

The police agree this note could be seen as threatening, but since it is anonymous, they can do nothing, or so they say. I think the least they should do is try to pull fingerprints since Fred's are on file. They do not feel that is necessary. Apparently, we are going to wait for the payback.

The police operate and predict risk based on the actions of a reasonable man. I have long-term intimate knowledge regarding how Fred functions, and he is not rational. Police think they, as the professionals, know better. They refuse to consider that my expertise in how Fred operates has merit. Whereas police see an anonymous note, I perceive a loosely veiled death threat. The nuances between a woman and her abusive husband are complicated and difficult to explain. It is quicker for the police to treat me like an overreacting and unbalanced ex-wife than it would be for them to pay attention to my concerns.

It is the middle of the night and I am still awake. The house is clean. I have cooked more than we will eat in the next three days. Frenzied action keeps my thoughts at bay. It takes 158 swipes to wipe down the kitchen cupboard doors.

Friday, 4 November 1988
My suicidal thoughts scare me. I asked my doctor for a referral to a therapist covered by public funding. Today, I saw a psychiatrist and again told my story in a fifty-minute hour.

Monday, 14 November 1988
My lawyer successfully negotiated with Fred and Lawyer Buddy to sell our Victoria Street matrimonial home. Fred agreed to a listing price and a realtor. We had four offers that Fred refused for various reasons. We finally got one he deemed okay and Fred signed the offer. The sale will be going through at the end of January 1989 and I have given the Scottish renters notice.

One thing that happened during the house sale stood out. The realtor was Tessa, my friend who helped me get my first counsellor at the Task Force. When she met with Fred to get his signature, he used her audience to trash talk me. What shook her up was that, even when she knew he was lying, she found herself believing and agreeing with him.

In Tessa's words, "I felt like I was in the presence of evil."

Wednesday, 16 November 1988

Finally, a year and a half later, a CAS support group for non-offending mothers has begun. Today is the third session and I intend to keep going, mainly because it is good to know that I am not the only mother who is dealing with their child's sexual abuse.

Unfortunately, this group is not particularly helpful. With twenty-two attendees, there are far too many mothers for meaningful discussion. At the first meeting, the worker tells us that, as a child, she was molested. I give her a lot of credit for leading this group, but it is rapidly evident she identifies with our kids more than us.

During the first meeting, I eagerly asked questions about coping and shared some struggles I was experiencing. As we were leaving, a few of the other mothers pulled me aside and cautioned me to be more careful. I had no idea the group leader reports to my worker and that could get me in trouble. The other mothers tell me I am way too naive. These mothers are more astute than I, so I listen to them and now keep my questions to myself.

This week we have the opportunity to share our stories if we wish. At first, I thought this sharing was a good idea and would connect us. Once some of the mothers started, the stories swamped me. The most distressing was from a young mother whose boyfriend raped her baby girl.

Because of the significant role mothers play in keeping their children safe, a mother's group is necessary. I do have some thoughts about how it should be run. Obviously, the leader needs to take far more care so already distressed mothers are not re-traumatized, and it should be run by not one, but two experienced therapists. Due to the inherent authority and power of the CAS, they are the wrong agency to run this type of group. The educational aspect, such as statistics, is useful. But for me, it would be more helpful if we also addressed mother's feelings of anger, guilt, and shame, and how to help children in healthy ways.

I attend the same clinic where Fred was going for therapy when I see the psychiatrist. I get myself bent out of shape worrying I might run into him in the waiting room. I know Fred said he was done seeing his therapist, but there is not much he says that I believe. At discovery, Lawyer Buddy wanted reports from the children's counsellors. I did not have any to provide and would not have given them even if I had. He would demand a report if he became aware I saw this doctor. I cannot allow that to happen.

The psychiatrist agrees that avoiding Fred is a good idea. He checks when Fred's next appointment is so we can schedule around it. It turns out Fred's file was closed two weeks before he was sentenced to a term of probation. One of the probation conditions was, "to take counselling as directed." Obviously that has not happened, which means that he received no rehabilitation as part of probation.

I have not yet told the psychiatrist about how I count and of memory gaps so large I need my journal to "remember." He is unaware that while my children are in school, I spend a lot of time in what feels like a semi-coma, watching the spruce tree. The pine cones have almost all fallen off as winter is near. I guess I said enough, and he surprises me when he shows the Diagnostic and Statistical Manual III Revised (DSM III-R) description and symptoms of PTSD.[10] He asks if the symptoms fit. They do. The

---

[10] For DSM history and symptoms of Post Traumatic Stress Disorder (PTSD), see http://traumadissociation.com/ptsd/history-of-post-traumatic-stress-disorder.html#dsm-hist

diagnosis validates that how I experienced the trauma has a name, and it is not crazy.

One thing I know for sure is that I will not tell Bea about seeing a psychiatrist or the diagnosis he gave me. Every word I utter to her is carefully selected to hide the extent of my distress. I do not lie to CAS, but I do not share more than necessary. My motto has become, "Don't tell them everything, and don't let it show."

Day after day, the show must go on. I do my very best to be a good mother. I make dinner, get groceries, pay the bills, and do my utmost to give my kids the love and attention they so desperately need. I hold on and churn my way forward. I try to confine my madness to when the kids are not at home or asleep.

I use the answering machine to screen what are now mostly Mr Nobody calls. They are relentless. The other day we had thirty-two. Last week there were none one day, then twenty-seven and sixteen and nine and eighteen, and so on. The simple ringing of the phone sends me into a fluster. If I have to make a phone call, sometimes I can muster the grit to do so in an hour, other times it takes me days.

Avoiding people is a skill I have mastered. Alex and Lena are the only two I can handle because they continue to be supportive. I know neither of them passed my phone number along to Fred. I no longer trust anyone else. Lena and Alex are the only two who do not stare off into space in boredom when I talk. I will love both of them to the end of time for who they are.

The *dominee* is the most persistent of people still knocking at my door. When he does, it is easier to pretend that I am not home. With my car parked beside the house, it is obvious I am avoiding him.

When I think about Fred, I feel murderous. It is impossible to get relief. Sometimes, when the kids are at school, I turn up the music as loud as possible, then I scream and cry along with the songs. The intensity of my feelings scares me.

Monday, 28 November 1988

The court reporter finishes typing up the sworn testimonies of Fred's discovery hearing interview. My lawyer had asked Fred a total of 1,423 questions and the court reporter delivers two bound documents. In size and content, they read like a pulp fiction story.

Fred's testimony is lengthy because, for the most part, he is unable to answer with a simple yes or no. My lawyer saves the inquiries about Fred's abusive behaviour with Alida to the end. In answering these questions, Fred's responses stretch out, and I can see he is trying to lose my lawyer by driving him all over town. Fred has remained true to his belief that bullshit baffles brains.

1405Q. What did you tell the police at that time regarding the abuse of Alida?

A. Exactly what had happened. I had touched Alida's breasts at some times, and hey, if that's an offence, fine. They asked me if there was sexual intent and I said, no, none whatsoever, but I did have my reasons. You see, basically what we are dealing with here is that mine was reported, but you know, hey, at the kitchen table, one fine morning when Carlyn grabbed Kevin's you-know-what, his little peter, technically that was the same. It's sexual assault, you know, that's what we are dealing with here.

1406Q. Did the police ask you over what period of time that it happened?

A. I said, oh, I don't know. You would have to realize one thing, at that time, I was not as clear in my mind as I am at this point, and I had just lost a lot of weight, and in my condition, that doesn't sit too well. I was devastated by what had been going on and I had no idea at that time just how I had been manipulated. I do now. I have taken the proper therapy, counselling, and I learned just how much the plaintiff had manipulated me. I was in such a state that if Carlyn, or anybody with her, had come to me and said, darn it, Fred, why did you start WWII, I would have come up with some reason because I would have believed I started it. Okay, so there may be things in that, I haven't looked at that statement in so long, there may be things in there I don't agree with any more now. Now, one of the things would be the time frame because I am supposed to have touched her breasts, but the time frame I gave of two years, well, Alida did not have breasts at the start of that two years, you know, so I could not have done that.

1407Q. Do you remember if the police asked you how often it occurred?

A. They may have and I remember saying I don't know. I have no idea. Maybe once a month, once a week, I don't know, twice a week. I remember being totally…I don't know, you know. I'm not sure. It happened. What more do you want.

1408Q. Did they ask you where it occurred?

A. Yes, they [sic] said, in the house, it could have been downstairs, it could have been upstairs, it could have been in the car or the warehouse. I said I was the one always who tucked the kids in at night seven days a week, so very likely it would have happened then.

1409Q. Well, when you said you had your reasons for assaulting Alida, what were they?

A. Well, I don't want to get into a long, drawn-out thing you see, but basically what it was, okay, is that Alida, that's why it was her and not someone else, okay, yeah, she was a carbon copy of Carlyn as she was growing up. The same with her attitudes, too. Now Carlyn, in the house okay, when it was time to go to bed, if she did come, if she wasn't sitting with some joker in the kitchen laughing and drinking beer, would turn the lights out and turn around because, gee, I can't let you see my body when I'm undressing, okay. Alida was the same way. If she wore a T-shirt that even showed a little bit of outline, she'd be embarrassed all to heck. Yet I knew, and I know I was screwed up in my mind, okay, not that my reports show that, but my thinking was wrong. There was Carlyn, prim and proper as anything, and oh, gee whiz, you can't look at it, turn the lights out, and I knew she was having an affair after affair on the outside, and I associated that, in my mind, and I thought if my daughter grows up being this self-conscious about her body, okay, in my mind, I felt, hey, she is going to grow up being promiscuous as hell just like her mother, outside the home, okay, and my intent was, hey, you have breasts just like anybody else, so I mean, this so-called fondling would be the type of thing of me going, you know, that, a flip of a breast type of thing, coming up behind her, boo, guess who, you know. The word fondling is very misleading, it doesn't represent it properly because it wasn't a caressing type of thing. It was always in a joking nature.

1410Q. Was a pre-sentence report prepared?

A. I don't recall, like I don't know. I just, hey, I let my lawyer handle that. I told my criminal lawyer that okay, by the time we got to trial, I already knew because, you know, it gets put off and it is not that quick, but I already knew that there was a heck of a lot more and I was beginning to have serious doubts as to whether I had been given all the correct information as to how Alida was taking it, by your client, but it was my intention all along, that, hey, look, if that's what I did, fine, I'll plead guilty because I'm not going to put my daughter through a flipping trial, forget it. Anyway, it does not matter because the record is expunged after five years, so pleading guilty was no big deal. Now, if my criminal lawyer had said to me, you know, originally I couldn't have cared less, but by the time we got to trial, if my criminal lawyer *had said to me, well, you're going up the river for two years, I would have fought it because I still don't believe it was sexual assault, in the sense of sexual assault.*

1411Q. What were the terms of your probation?
A. How do you mean terms?

1412Q. Well, were you supposed to report on a regular basis?
A. Well, originally I went in, yeah, I reported to him after I got out of Court, which I, well, report to the Probation Office. I went to the Probation Office, and fine, yeah they told me they would get back to me to come in and I'd be assigned an officer. I was assigned an officer and made the initial visit. He asked me certain questions; he said I'm going to check this out. I made the second visit and he said, well, I believe it was in the second visit, it had something to do with under normal circumstances I would strictly be a, what do they call that? I don't know what they call it, but I'd be in the filing cabinet. I'd technically be on probation until next April but I wouldn't be required to report in. The only reason that he changed that was because Carlyn had called him a bunch of times and had been bitching to him on the phone, alleging all sorts of things I was supposed to be doing.

1413Q. What counselling did you undertake as a term of your probation?
A. Well, before court, right after Carlyn, yeah one fine day she came up to me. She said I molested Alida and damn near her whole family. I was so upset, and talked to my friend Herman, and he told me to talk, to get help from a lawyer, a good lawyer. I was told to take counselling as soon as possible, so I said, why not, what harm could it do. I had already taken counselling with the Task Force lady, I forget her name, but she turned on me and, yeah, I told her what Carlyn said I did and the bitch reported me, she called the CAS. There was no way I'd go back to her. So yeah, I went to the mental health clinic and saw

someone there. Judy, I think her name was, and she was okay. After a few times seeing her, she said I did okay. I made good progress and closed my file. I also took help from a psychiatrist and a psychologist and they thought I was not messed up so that was a big relief to me after Carlyn telling me so much B.S., saying I had abused Alida and her sisters and I was so stupid, and started believing it all. Your client was the one who messed me up. With all this help I took, the probation officer said I did not need to go for more, unless I thought I had a problem. I told him it is not me that has the problem. Now, your client, she is the one who needs all the help she can get, and it is not fair that for some reason she gets off scot-free even though she has abused Kevin and yeah, is telling all kinds of lies about me to everyone who will listen. The system really is screwed up that people like her do not have to pay for their slander and manipulation.*

When asked a question around personal finances during our marriage, Fred's answer included, *"Now you need to know I was building a business, and when I could I'd give her money and she was supposed to pay the bills and get groceries and whatever, take care of it all and get herself little something whenever she wanted. She was always bitching at me that I did not give her enough, but I did not ask, I never kept, you know, I'm no Gestapo chief."*

Wednesday, 30 November 1988
Fred takes out ads in the local papers to advertise a public liquidation sale of the remaining EuroMed Importing merchandise. He is holding the sale downtown, next door to Abingville Home Health Solutions, the store his father sold last year. I call my lawyer because the sale is in violation of the exclusive rights contract EuroMed Importing has with its customers. My lawyer says he will follow up with Lawyer Buddy. Fred is the one who drafted the contract that customers needed to sign before EuroMed Importing did business with them, so of course he is aware that the sale violates it.

Thursday, 1 December 1988
The Abingville storeowners do what I anticipate, and it is the right thing to do. They file a civil lawsuit against me. If I stop the sale, Fred will be furious; if I do not stop the sale, they will proceed to sue me. Lose—lose.

I revoke Fred's authority to sell EuroMed Importing merchandise at a public sale. According to my lawyer, Fred is mad. Really mad.

Thursday, 8 December 1988
With Fred mad, it is predictable he does something, and this time it is an affidavit-writing rampage. One is forty pages long. The next one is twenty-five. He has not filed a motion, so other than Carlyn-bashing, what he is up to is unclear. What I do know is that he is getting warmed up for a fight.

Friday, 9 December 1988
A furious Fred is a vicious man. Lena drops by and tells me to grab my camera because there is a big problem. She drives me over to the parking lot at Fred's store. He has rented an even bigger portable roadside sign than the Easter one. This one has flashing lights all around, with a message that can be seen by everyone driving by on this busy street or going into any of the nearby stores.

> BLESSED ARE THOSE
> WHO DRILL LITTLE HOLES
> IN BEDROOM FLOORS,
> FOR THEY SHALL SEE
> INTO THE KINGDOM OF CARLYN

Fred figuratively rips off my *panties* and puts me on public display. Fred, the born-again Christian with whom his black-suited flunkies think I should reconcile, takes the Beatitudes of Matthew

5 and twists them into perversity.[11] This is filthy, dirty, and nothing but pure black evil.

Lena parks between the front door of Fred's store and the sign. I jump out to quickly take photos, and then start ripping letters off the sign and toss them into car. Lena watches the store, and when she sees Fred come out, she lays on the horn. I manage to jump back into the car before Fred reaches me, and we careen away. We laugh hysterically, feeling like gangsters escaping from a bank robbery. Not Bonnie and Clyde, but Bonnie and Bonnie. In the blink of an eye, the hysteria transforms into sobbing.

This time I do not contact the police. Some things like the mocking poem he sent to Alida in response to her poem and this sign are just too bad to share with anyone. No good would come of being humiliated in another no win situation. Given my experiences to date, the police would probably do nothing. If a miracle happened and Fred were to be charged with something, I would be further demeaned in a courtroom with the evidence displayed before even more people. I can just imagine the courtroom spectators snickering and the gossip later. "Did you hear the one about the woman who had a pervert drill holes in her bedroom floor…and then her husband wrote…ha ha ha."

I would be mortified, and he would, if anything, only receive more meaningless probation or another useless restraining order.

With this experience, I now truly appreciate why women are reluctant to report.

No one is happy at my house this evening. I am a mess. Alex comes over to help out and relieve my stress. Alida is argumentative to the point where she becomes physical with me. Then she gets into a row with Alex. I wish he had not gotten into it with her. Alex thinks I let the kids away with too much mouthing off. I do. My reason

---

[11] King James Bible, Matthew 5:10. "Blessed are they which are persecuted for righteousness sake: for theirs is the kingdom of heaven."

is that they need to vent somewhere and it is at me. Alida does not want Alex to act like a parent, which is quite understandable. Kevin grows fed up with all of us and slams the door to his room.

Wednesday, 14 December 1988

I cannot cope with being figuratively put on public display with Fred's Beatitudes sign. Thoughts of complete escape are overwhelming. Dying is the only way out. Dying is such a strong urge, I find it difficult to resist. Nothingness, what bliss it would be. Sweet, quiet death. Peace. Rest. I know exactly how and where to use the knife so it will not be my children who find me.

I cannot stop my thoughts, so I do all I can to just hang on one more day, one more hour, one more minute. Survive one breath at a time if that is all I can do. Find something to grip onto and hold on, and what I hold most tightly to is the thought of my children.

Sunday, 18 December 1988

Today we visit the Kettles. Mom asks me who preached and what the sermon was about this morning. I take a deep breath and tell her we stopped attending church some time ago.

Dad hears me and offers his opinion. "Vel, dat means Fred is better den you are."

"Why is that, Dad?"

"Vell, Fred goes to church en you don't." That, father, is a low blow.

I turn to my mother for help. She says, "Your vader has a good point."

Christmas Eve, 1988

> I am a sad shroud of black
> in my soul's dark night.
> My own midwife

birthing a new self.
I hold on, breathe,
find a way out of hell,
While the enticing alternative remains
to slice back into the womb of safe nothingness.

Boxing Day, 1988

Our second Christmas alone is good and less good. I have less money, so gift buying is more stressful. The kids get no gifts from their father or his family. The Kettles give the children towels and they stop giving the adults any gifts this year. Stupid me. They gave money the last few years and I counted on it to pay the hydro bill. Alex has two children who live with their mother, and the Kettles do not allow Alex or his kids to come to Christmas dinner at their farmhouse. Alex's mother is generous and accepts us.

I finally ask Mom and Dad why, once they found out, they did not tell me about Fred abusing my sisters and the risk to Alida.

"De Christian counsellor we saw wit Grace told us not to."

I ask, "Then why didn't you talk to Fred like the counsellor suggested?"

"Vell, because ve aren't angry wit him. He did nutting to us. Ve did vat de Bible says: forgive and forget."

"In the Bible Jesus says that whoever hurts one of His little ones hurts Him. If Jesus was in your shoes, I think He would be furious. How can you not be even a little bit mad?"

"No. Jesus said, 'Vengeance is mine.' De Bible says it's not up to us to judge."

Sometimes I do not know when to quit. That I cannot shake off the immense guilt that my husband molested my daughter and little sisters is not for lack of trying. I have sought help from the therapist at Salem Counselling in Toronto, the Task Force counsellor, Women's Shelter group, pastoral support, social worker, two CAS workers, CAS mother's group, and now the psychiatrist, and no one has been able to help me find relief. Because their daughters were also molested, it strikes me that my parents may also be suffering with feelings of guilt. I try to connect with them as hurting parents.

"Mom and Dad, how do you manage the horrific guilt about what happened to your daughters?"

Mom was puzzled. "Vat do you mean, guilt?"

"Don't you feel guilty about what happened to your daughters and then to Alida?"

"Of course not, Carlyn. Ve did nutting wrong, so why should ve feel bad? It vasn't our fault. Ve prayed for Alida a lot."

That, then, is a difference between the Kettles and me. The Kettles knew and did not act, keeping silent behind the opiate of their religion. Their example provides a warning of what can happen when religious fanaticism overrules rational thinking.

I believe that child abuse makes Jesus cry. He cries for all the pain my husband inflicted on so many girls. I get comfort during my low times imagining that when I cry, Jesus weeps with me and I am not alone.

Dad has something else to tell me. "Dat Gus, he's a pretty good guy. He came over a veek ago and said he vas sorry about someting he did to you. He vent to see Dorothy too. Ve tink he's very sorry and ve're glad he came over." Gus knows my parents because everyone in the Dutch CRC community knows everyone else.

Dorothy said, "A few days before Christmas, there was a big gift basket of goodies and an anonymous envelope with a $100 bill at my back door. I am quite sure it came from Gus. He's such a nice guy." Dorothy and her husband separated earlier this year and she is now dating Gus. Apparently, the standards around dating that my parents hold me to do not apply to Dorothy. She always was their favourite.

Some amazing things also happened this holiday season. Bea dropped off donated Christmas gifts. I was incredibly thankful and touched. When I was closing down EuroMed Importing, a man from Revenue Canada Taxation in London came to do an audit, a usual business thing and not something Fred caused. He came to the house because that was where I had taken the paperwork he needed, and he asked me if I was managing financially. This complete stranger cared enough to ask. He called again later to check in on how we were doing and asked permission to phone the local Salvation Army to refer me for support.

A Salvation Army Family Services Officer got in touch. When he called, I did not require any material help, but being asked meant the world. Grateful for moral and spiritual support, I talked to him a few times and shared some of my struggles. His view is that God places no obligation on me to reconcile, but that my greater obligation is to protect my children and myself. He does not think of me as a harlot for seeing Alex. He brought us a Christmas food basket. It means a lot to receive caring support, and this from a church that I never even attended. From my own church where I am still a member, still "nutting."

My dear kids saved up pennies and dollars and bought me a painting of a winter scene in the woods. It reminded them of the Parry Sound property. The winter shades of grey and blue remind me of my lost dreams. After all the losses, the dream of a complete and happy family remains difficult to release.

One final contribution to our Christmas is astounding in its audacity. Fred discovered I was on welfare when he got a notice from the Support and Custody Enforcement Branch of the Ministry of the Attorney General. One could reasonably think a man might be embarrassed that his children are on social assistance and he is not paying support. Not Fred. He marched right up to have a little heart-to-heart with the welfare supervisor.

My welfare caseworker called the Friday before Christmas to let me know that because I lied and cheated the system, they will be terminating my benefits. I know I was completely honest with them when I applied. I complied with what they needed, and they made a decision. I resent them calling me a liar and a thief and pulling support based on whatever Fred said. Next week, I have a meeting with the caseworker and her supervisor.

```
27 December 1988
CAS Ongoing Recording,
Caseworker Bea
```

<u>Current Situation</u>

```
During this period, there have been no
changes in this family situation. Alida
and Kevin remain with their mother. Their
home situation appears stable. The children
have expressed no desire for another visit
with their father. The feelings of anger
toward their father fluctuate from time to
time. However, their desire for no contact
remains constant.

Mrs Smit feels overwhelmed and could
benefit from some occasional respite. Mrs
Smit's family lives at least a two-hour
drive from Abingville, and she would not
consider asking Fred's family to watch the
children for a weekend. Her bitterness has
```

not subsided. Due to the ongoing divorce proceedings, she has not been able to put her feelings to rest.

The children continue to side with their mother and they remain loyal to her cause. Although Mrs Smit recognizes that the children should be allowed to form their own attitudes and opinions regarding their father, the children are heavily influenced by their mother's bitterness and frustration.

Mrs Smit and the children are currently receiving funding from social services. Mr Smit has reported concerns that his children no longer enjoy the lifestyle which they were accustomed to when he lived with them. Mr Smit further alleges that Mrs Smit obtained benefits under false pretences. He is pursuing this matter with the authorities involved.

Mrs Smit would prefer CAS remain involved with her family so she can avoid contact with Mr Smit. The CAS position is that Mr Smit no longer presents a risk, based on assessment reports from his therapist, psychiatrist and psychologist. One of these professionals suggested that the marital relationship was, in part, responsible for Mr Smit's actions. The CAS investigation and ongoing intervention has found no evidence of Mrs Smit's collaboration in the abuse.

Mr Smit is in the process of submitting an

application in their family court matter for custody, and if unsuccessful, he will settle for unsupervised access with the children. This agency has no concerns with regard to this application. If he obtains these alterations to the current order, this file will be closed.

Reassessment

Ongoing legal proceedings have delayed the healing process. There remains a great deal of anger between Mr and Mrs Smit. The needs of the two children are being adequately and consistently met. The behaviour of both parents remains appropriate.

Mr Smit has undergone treatment and he is moving forward in family court to alter the current order whereby CAS is required to supervise access. He intends to request representation for the children from the Office of the Children's Lawyer. If he succeeds in his efforts, the CAS role will end and this agency will close the file.

Thursday, 29 December 1988

I meet with the welfare supervisor and explain all the financial stuff to him. He says my story is quite different than how Fred presented it. He peers at me over his glasses and says he might be able to do something for me.

It takes him a few minutes to rifle through his rulebook and conclude his staff made a mistake when I applied. I still qualify for support, but only under the condition that I repay benefits when my funds free up. He is unbelievably haughty and acts as if he is doing me a great personal favour. Because I cannot afford to tell the supervisor where to put his further benefits, I have no choice but to graciously accept his pretentious offer.

Thursday, 12 January 1989

While I was waiting for the meeting at the welfare office, I checked out job postings that were up on a bulletin board. There was a posting for a full-time pharmacy assistant at the same Shoppers Drug Mart where I worked when the kids were little. Many factors, in no particular order, went into putting together a resume and applying for that job: The condescending attitude of the welfare supervisor is demeaning, and being in this position long-term will suck self-esteem and self-respect right out of me. I had a break and more time off will not be helpful. If I stay stuck in a defeated state, Fred succeeds. I will not allow him to win. Finally, it is time to pull up my big girl panties and move forward.

Within two days of dropping off the resume, they call me for an interview and offer me the job. The pay will be enough to keep us going for the time being. I can hardly believe my good fortune.

I am unable to start work on the date Shoppers Drug Mart wants because I am subpoenaed as a witness to criminal court for Gus's charges. It is a useless day since the matter is plea-bargained. Gus pleads guilty to one charge of break and enter, claims remorse, said he began counselling, and receives, of course, one year of probation. Even the newspaper calls that a light sentence.

Not only am I starting a new job, but I sold a few things in order to afford one evening class at university. If I get an education, I will be able to better support my little family. The worst that can happen is that I might fail, which would tell me my dream is unattainable and I should let it go.

Monday, 16 January 1989

Fred must still be mad. He writes another affidavit and files four motions. He pulls out all stops and covers all his bases to use the courts to get back at me. Abuse-by-court filings is his new avenue for revenge.

> Motion 1. *That this matter be heard on an emergency basis to allow the father to resume the close relationship he enjoyed with the children prior to the marital separation in June of 1987.*
>
> Motion 2. *That the children of the marriage have independent representation in this matter from the Office of the Children's Lawyer.*
>
> Motion 3. *That the court order the completion of a psychological assessment on the mother to determine her parenting capacity, with her paying for said assessment.*
>
> Motion 4. *That the father be granted sole custody of the two children of the marriage with the mother's access to be supervised in order to prevent her from inflicting further emotional damage to the children by on-going parent alienation syndrome.*

In the supporting evidence, he regurgitates his standard complaints about me and adds a few new ones. He claims that I threatened to stop access if he did not settle the finances (a lie), that Bea told him I gave the kids too much information (she may have), and that the kids made negative comments during their visit (a lie, since he did most of the talking and Alida said nothing whatsoever).

He further believes I do not provide adequate care to the

children of the marriage because I am on welfare, and my income is about to be terminated due to my misrepresentation. He states that my manipulation is making visitation impossible, and that my negative attitude toward him makes it impossible for him to collaborate with me to ensure the children's best interests are paramount.

"Moreover," he wrote, *"Myself and my daughter Alida witnessed Mrs Smit sexually abuse my son when he was nine years old. A report was filed with CAS, and to date they have not adequately investigated this matter."*

That Fred wants custody has nothing to do with loving his children. Fred has never been much of a parent. That he never once changed a diaper was always a source of pride and a reason for him to brag. If I had to go out, he grudgingly "babysat" and would leave the babies soaked and dirty until I came home, unconcerned about their discomfort and rashes. At best, his parental involvement was more that of a carefree uncle playing with our children and even then, only at his convenience and pleasure. He went away for days or weeks at a time without concern for his family.

Our relationship had been a traditional one where I handled all the childcare and household chores. Things such as finances, medical appointments, meals, laundry, school issues, and homework were left up to me. He always said that those things were not really work, but what he did was. After he went bankrupt, he allowed me to get "a real job" outside our home, but only if I did not impose any inconvenience or extra responsibility on him.

I do not mean to say Fred did not care about his children at all, but it often appeared that way. When Alida was only two weeks old, she lost weight and needed hospitalization. I was sure I was a bad mother because I had not noticed the signs of my daughter's dehydration. The Friday she was admitted to the hospital, Fred visited just long enough to look at her. He said there was no point staying because she would never remember if he was there or not.

We lived on Victoria Street, a mere block from the hospital where our baby was struggling to put on weight. Alida's daddy said he was too busy to visit. He had to go "on the road for business." He had orders to fill, he had to work in the store, he had allergies, and he just had no time. Alida was in the hospital for a week. Other than the one brief visit from her father, I was the only person who went to see her.

The Sunday Alida was in the hospital, Fred slept until noon. Thereafter, he read and then watched TV until it was time for a nap on the couch. He not only refused to visit our baby, he ridiculed me for wanting to be with her. Fred thought I should stay home with him, and it still shames me that I juggled his neediness by only visiting my baby girl while he was sleeping. I thought that, besides being the worst mother, I might also be the loneliest mother on the face of the earth. I was much too humiliated to tell anyone.

A few days after Alida left the hospital, on a sunny Sunday in early July of 1975, Fred preened like a peacock as he carried our baby to the altar of our church for baptism. That day, I hated him. I also hated myself for going along with the charade.

Over the years, there were spells when he seemed interested in parenting Alida. Now I can see that his real interest was having a daughter to victimize. His participation intensified as Alida approached her teen years, but only as our daughter's advocate when she and I disagreed on privileges. It had made me angry when Fred swooped in and out of parenting and blatantly overrode my decisions, making himself the hero. Giving Alida wine on her birthday was one of countless examples. I can see now that what he had been doing was ongoing grooming and that somehow assured him she would remain quiet.

His lack of devotion to parenting was evident when Kevin was born. Fred went to Europe for a month, had a month of fun with his Dutch relatives when he brought them back for a vacation, and was absent for most of another two months setting up and opening his Windsor store. I had been essentially alone with two babies and zero support. Fred's interest in our son was always marginal and my guess is that the only reason he wants custody of Kevin now is to punish me and for the opportunity to turn my son against me.

For him, people are only as valuable as their usefulness. The kids are now exceptionally useful to him as pawns to get back at me.

Monday, 30 January 1989

Our matrimonial house sale closed and the money is deposited into a trust account. Fred thinks that he should be allowed to skim $20,000, what he says he stole, off the top before we split the proceeds. I decline and am counting on him being financially desperate before me. He always needs money for one scheme or another, and I am sure that will result in him capitulating long before I ever will.

Alex also sold his house, so we decide he will move in here. I really like it with him around and our kids agree with this plan. I am happy. I have yet to tell the Kettles who frown upon unwed couples living together; they call it living in sin. In their Christian view, it is better I live with a child abuser than my boyfriend who treats us well.

Thursday, 16 February 1989

Kevin and Alida received postcards from Paris, France. Alida's said:

> Too bad you are not in Paris with Melissa and me. When we come home, I hope you will be able to meet her and her daughters Ashley and Emily. They are all eager to meet you. Love Dad and Melissa.

My kids want to know who this Melissa is. I assume she is a girlfriend. We had plans for a family vacation in Paris and now he not only takes another woman, but he rubs his children's noses in it. This woman is more than welcome to him. With a bit of luck, he will want to get married and we can then be done with the divorce.

Two postcards. No breach, according to the police.

I am curious how a convicted criminal can travel the world. I thought his probation order said he had to remain in Ontario. I call the probation officer, and he explains the order only specifies Fred must "live in Ontario," so there is no violation. The more I learn about the justice system, the more disillusioned I become.

Tuesday, 7 March 1989

Initially, Alida was fine with Alex living here, but she is quickly becoming resistant to his presence. At this point, Alex is not even trying to parent, and he is never alone with my kids. Alida has increasingly been running roughshod over me. This is understandable since our lives have been out of control, and she is doing all she can to gain the upper hand. I know it is not good. However, Alex's behind-the-scenes support helps me be a better parent. I have noticed that as I get stronger, Alida gets angrier.

Alex and I discuss our dilemma at length, and we agree it is better that he moves out before things get worse. Our relationship is unchanged other than that his address is not here. It is remarkable to reason with a man and arrive at a solution that works for us all. I have to give up nothing to be with him. He does not love me less because I changed my mind, and I love him more for accepting this change. This kind of relationship is a liberating experience.

I take another inventory of things for which to be grateful. I have a reliable car, we have nice furniture, I know how to cook inexpensive meals from scratch, and I can sew to alter and remake clothes. We live in a safe and comfortable home. I discovered I do have brains (I passed my first university test). The half portion of the house sale proceeds will come my way eventually. Constantly reminding myself things could be a whole lot worse keeps me from nose-diving into a pit of self-pity.

I now work every Saturday and get one weekday off. That day is always busy with court appearances, appointments, and errands. A negative of working on Saturdays is that the kids are not doing so well. They are chronologically old enough to be alone for a whole day, but emotionally not so much.

Every week there is a crisis of some sort. Last week, I came home to find Kevin and Alida threatening each other with steak knives. The week before, they had friends over and broke some stuff. The week before that Kevin stole something at the mall and after work, I had to rescue him from security. Single parenting, especially of two kids who are reacting all over the place, is a never-ending bombardment of needs.

Thursday, 6 April 1989
During December, the Support and Custody Enforcement Branch of the Ministry of the Attorney General sent a notice indicating that a federal garnishee was placed on Fred to collect outstanding child support. That was what tweaked Fred onto me receiving welfare. I phone the agency today and am told to be patient, enforcement proceedings are in progress. I start looking for a second job to make our life less financially stressful and to cover tuition for two more university courses. Student loans are, unfortunately, not available for part-time studies.

Saturday, 8 April 1989
After a week of phone calls between lawyers, desperate to arrive at a

settlement, I agree to a meeting with Fred at the Tim Hortons near his store. We start calm, but before our coffee is cool enough to drink, Fred reverts to legal gobbledygook that triggers my mental confusion. Asking Fred to speak simply earns snide comments about how stupid I am.

We are still calm as he presents a proposal regarding the partially finished log house in Parry Sound. Fred believes he can earn us a small fortune by finishing the house and selling it. His proposal requires me to sign a very substantial loan and then hand over to him the money from the loan plus all the proceeds of the matrimonial house sale. He will manage it as long as he has no interference from me. I can see clearly where this is heading. The risk is all mine and he shares equally if there is profit. If there is a loss, which is how his schemes always turn out, I will be responsible for the debt.

I kind of lose it in a big way when, plus my risk, he explains that his whole proposal is further conditional on my withdrawal from the Support and Custody Enforcement agency, that I repay the outstanding support he owes the agency, and that I drop all claims for future child support. I begin yelling when I grab my purse and continue yelling over my shoulder as I storm toward the exit of the coffee shop. I make quite a scene.

Darn. I only met Alex's father once before and there he is, sitting with a lady friend, both of them staring at me as I rush past them. My smile is more of a grimace as I chirp, "Hello" and dash for the door.

Saturday, 15 April 1989

Fred has an original idea. He suggests that we should split the proceeds of the matrimonial house sale, with each of us getting half the funds in the trust account. By not giving Fred the upper hand, and for waiting him out, I significantly benefit. After paying my lawyer's account to date and repaying Alex's loan, I deposit the remainder into a savings account.

The money is enough for a 25 percent down payment on a modest home. Because mortgage payments would cost considerably less than rent, I search until I find a cute place in a neighbourhood acceptable to raise my children. Unfortunately, the bank will not give me a mortgage because my income is just a little bit too low. The bank manager will reconsider if I acquire a co-signer.

Since Alex has his own obligations, and mixing finances and friendships has potential for disaster that I would rather not risk, I only have the Kettles to ask to co-sign. It is an understatement to say they are not exactly poor. They have made substantial, well-publicized donations in their religious community. They gave Dorothy and her husband a stake for a new house on the Main Street of Oregon. After Fred went bankrupt, my father had no qualms about signing his name to start the new EuroMed Importing company when Fred asked for his help. I am not asking for money and want their names off the mortgage as soon as I qualify to carry it alone. The idea of increased finances and a stable home for my children helps me overcome pride. To be respectful, I drive to the Kettles farm to ask for their help in person.

Dad considers it for about two seconds and minces no words in rejecting both my request and me. "No. Ve von't even tink about co-signing vor you. Ve can't trust you to pay de mortgage and den ve vould have to trow you and de kids out on de street."

"Tanks vor nutting, Dad."

Monday, 17 April 1989
I get a registered letter from Fred that ignores all the negotiations with my lawyer last week, and he now wants to revert back to an oral agreement we supposedly made on April 1st. April Fools. There was no agreement then, or ever.

If I do not accept it by his deadline, he will hold me fully and personally responsible for the losses incurred. That is not news. I make a copy for my lawyer and take the original to the police station to file another complaint.

The police once again refuse to lay a breach charge for unlawful communication.

Thursday, 20 April 1989

At every court appearance to address Fred's motion for custody, Lawyer Buddy keeps yipping about me undergoing a parenting capacity assessment. I have not committed because, intuitively, it feels like a trap. I know that I am in trouble, tiptoeing too close to the line of insanity and that I am too fragile to put up a good front to risk an evaluation.

Today I have a rare day off with no appointments, so I spend it in London going down rabbit holes at a library on the Western University campus. I go looking for information about how professionals view non-offending mothers. What I find is alarming.

I learn that, as recently as 1975, a basic American psychiatry textbook estimated that the frequency of all forms of incest was one case per million children.[12] More recent professional articles quote statistics similar to what was in the CAS pamphlet: the risk of being sexually abused before age eighteen is one-in-four for girls, and between one-in-six and one-in-eight for boys. With 85 percent of perpetrators known to those who are victimized, and the abuse most often occurring in the child's home, that is a lot of incest hiding in a whole lot of homes.

What I also find in the academic journals is a considerable amount of mother-blaming. One article calls molesting an addiction, and mothers are co-addicts if they feel responsible for

---

[12] Incest in A.M. Freedman, H.I. Kaplan and B.J. Sadock, eds. Comprehensive Textbook of Psychiatry, 2nd ed. 1975. p. 1532. —Judith Lewis Herman, Father-Daughter Incest: With a New Afterward.

the abuse. She is also a co-addict if she blames the family problems on the offender. In other articles, mothers are called enablers, secondary victim, incest offender wife, silent partner, collusive mother, powerless mother, and the sexually or emotionally unavailable mother. I have yet to read anything that considers family violence factors, social, cultural, or religious contexts, or recognition that the perpetrator might have been bent that way prior to meeting the mother. The label that personally offends me most is, "enabling mothers." I could not have enabled Fred before we met, and I did not enable him when we were together because I did not know.

It is not new that fingers are pointed at mothers. It happened to mothers of people diagnosed with schizophrenia. While the causality debate of nurture versus nature raged on, those favouring nurture blamed mothers for being emotionally unavailable and they assigned the label "the schizophrenogenic mother." Autism has been blamed on "refrigerator mothers." For a time, male homosexuality was said to be caused by "smothering mothers," mothers who were thought to be over-attentive and thereby feminizing their sons. In the case of incest, scapegoating mothers is a gross injustice unless the mother put the child in the molester's bed, so to speak.

The more I know, the less confidence I have that professionals of any ilk would be willing and/or able to do an objective assessment. I fear that any psychologist assigned to assess my capacity as a mother might believe the rarity of incest or the negative labels their colleagues assign to mothers, without taking into consideration the mother's emotional distress caused by their children's molestation. Despite my own mental health issues, I am still a way better parent than Fred can ever be. I will not expose my emotional vulnerabilities and help Fred gain custody. Therefore, there will be no psychological or parental capacity assessment. Not happening.

Friday, 28 April 1989
The lawyers are back to negotiating another of Fred's proposals, where again the risk is all mine. It has been almost two years since we separated and I still allow him to push my buttons. I feel stupid about being overwhelmed and not understanding his proposals, counter proposals, and counter-counter proposals. Fred's deadline to settle his proposal as presented was today. The workday is over without us reaching an agreement.

Wednesday, 3 May 1989
While doing my weekly chore of putting curlers in Mom's hair, I explain to her the struggle of feeling angry about many things. Anger, in her opinion, is a sinful emotion and she tries to force my feelings out of reality. "Dis isn't you. You aren't an angry girl. God hates anger. You were always a good girl. Too sensitive, but never angry. No Carlyn, you really aren't angry."

"Yes Mom, I am really angry. I really am!"

When I ask her why she and Dad refuse to co-sign a mortgage for me, the conversation goes further south. She says they will not help because they disagree with me dating. I suggest that if that were true, there is no reason for Dad to be mean and say I am not trustworthy. Also, it follows that by co-signing, they would help me be independent. I offer Mom my word that as long as their names are on the loan, no man will live with us. She says I miss the point.

"What is the point, Mom?"

"You should not see a man at all. I know you can't go back wit Fred de way tings are now, but maybe later."

"Mom, there is no later. Fred and I are finished."

Friday, 5 May 1989
There is another flurry of faxes and phone calls between our two divorce lawyers, and phone calls between my lawyer and me. My

lawyer says these on-going efforts are necessary to demonstrate to the court that we tried to settle. I think he worries I will lose at trial because I walked away from EuroMed Importing. I still have faith that I will not end up with less than nothing, which is what Fred is still after. We begin with yet another of Fred's proposals and go back and forth with changes so many times this week, I have trouble keeping track of which is current.

It would have been easier to start the divorce poor than go through all this. Trust me, I am not overrating poverty, it would just be simpler. There is less to fight over when you have nothing. The upshot of the whole deal is that my legal fees climb higher and nothing is settled.

We end this round of negotiations with Fred's concluding correspondence.

"I don't want Carlyn involved PERIOD. I will not work with her."

At last. We agree on something.

Tuesday, 9 May 1989

I passed the university course, which is the first step toward a degree I hope to earn. I am thankful that I ploughed through the fear of failure and tackled the difficult.

I am also trying to slog through insecurity and not do things just to avoid conflict. Giving in and choosing to do things because they were easier that way got me to a place of condoning criminality and doing things about which I felt guilty. I am getting stronger in breaking my old patterns of behaviour and facing hard things. However, when it comes to church, I am totally and unequivocally stuck in a crevice so deep I cannot see a way out. On one side the idea of resigning raises all my insecurities, and on the other, the thought of remaining a member strangles me.

Monday, 22 May 1989

Therapy with one appointment every two or three weeks is not enough. When I deal with past stuff, there is no time to address current issues. I know I need to deal with the nightmares and intrusive thoughts to get out of this cesspool of emotions. I could use a therapy session at least twice a week to keep myself both upright and moving forward. The psychiatrist is doing his best and is not to blame that government funding limitations prohibit more frequent appointments. All the same, I am thankful for what he is able to provide.

Thursday, 1 June 1989

I wake up from a nightmare where Fred and I are dividing our assets. Fred cheerfully agrees to take an abortion machine in exchange for custody of our kids. Fred plugs the machine in and the nozzle whirs like a sewer auger. Then he jams the nozzle up inside me as far as possible and chops my insides to shreds.

Dreaming about Fred again is no surprise. Other than seeing his smug face in family court, he has been quiet, too quiet. His probation order has ended, and I cannot imagine that he is ready to let me go yet. That causes my usual anxiety. That, and the fact it is again June. Two years ago, I found out about Fred's sexual abuses and last year was the peeping Gus episode. I have a bad feeling trouble is brewing. I hope I am just superstitious and therefore wrong. I want to be wrong.

Wednesday, 7 June 1989

Fred was denied his motion for an emergency court hearing because the judge did not view his or the children's situation as time sensitive. The matter was finally heard, and for the past two months, we have attended family court weekly so that Fred can have his motions heard and ruled on.

At the first appearance, Lawyer Buddy was waving around some reports that had been prepared for Fred's 1988 criminal court matter. Fred allowed my lawyer to read them, but not me because he did not trust me. My lawyer said the reports were strong evidence for Fred not being a risk to my children, and because CAS refused to support me to maintain supervised access, he was certain that Fred would minimally succeed in obtaining unsupervised visits. If he represented me, his fees would skyrocket and I do not have that kind of money. His recommendation was that I represent myself in this matter, and he would provide phone support as needed. I carried on, knowing I would lose, yet doing the best I could.

Alida and Kevin received legal representation from the Office of the Children's Lawyer. When the lawyer met with me prior to talking to the kids, I tried to express my concerns. She cut me off and explained that my concerns were irrelevant. Her role was to advise the court of the children's wishes, not their best interests.

Kevin's wishes were to live with me and have visits only if and when he wants. Alida, on the other hand, was very upset that she needed to meet with a lawyer. She refused to talk privately and then, even when I was there to support her, she refused to speak at all. The lawyer finally asked her to nod yes or no, and was able to determine that Alida did not want access whatsoever, supervised or not.

Throughout this matter, I maintained I would not undergo psychological testing and Lawyer Buddy finally dropped it. Today, in a packed courtroom, he read aloud from Fred's reports that he presents no risk. When they refused me a copy, I asked the judge and she told them their evidence would not be considered in this motion unless they made it available to me. Lawyer Buddy grudgingly handed me three reports all written by professionals Fred saw in late 1987: a therapist for counselling and a psychiatrist and psychologist for assessments.

Now things make sense: why Fred thought that my seeing a

psychologist would work out well for him, why the criminal charge resulted in a common assault plea and meaningless probation, why CAS refused to support me to maintain supervised visits, and why today the court grants Fred unsupervised access with his children.

Fred began seeing a female therapist three weeks after he was charged with the sexual abuse of Alida. Based on the therapist's report, Fred told her that he only engaged in fondling behaviour by touching Alida above her waist a few times, and always over clothing. He admitted to nothing else and about nobody else. There was no mention of Fred's allegation of being sexually abused himself. It does not appear the therapist gathered a history from CAS or police to know that she was dealing with a long-time serial sex offender. She reported Fred made good progress in treatment.

I am shocked that she let him off the hook by saying that "the marital relationship" was a strong contributing factor. She bought Fred's story that he was the victim of a wife who was both frigid and promiscuous. I wonder if she ever considered that it was Fred's behaviour that ruined the marital relationship. Fred, the master manipulator, charmed her into believing his lies, and she obviously did not know enough about sex offender treatment to avoid being sucked in.

In my pursuit to learn all I could about sex offenders, I attended a seminar presented by a psychiatrist from Kingston Penitentiary. He is known as an expert in this field. He said that what a therapist could always be assured of was that their client would lie, making it critical to obtain a comprehensive history from collateral contacts when providing sex offender treatment. He was also adamant that no therapist of any age, sex, or experience level should ever do therapy solo with sex offenders.

During September of 1987, Fred saw a psychiatrist. The psychiatrist reported that over the course of *one* year, Fred had touched his daughter's breasts. It is extremely unfortunate, perhaps even malpractice, that this professional took Fred at his word without collaborating with other agencies, or professionals, or myself. Fred told the psychiatrist he had consensual relations with *one* of my younger sisters and that he was confused as to why she later blamed him for that. Fred also claimed he *never* had any extra-marital affairs. He did say he had been violent and thrown a chair and broke down a door when he caught his wife in bed with other *men*. The psychiatrist reported that Fred was not suffering from any form of mental illness or addiction.

The psychologist who assessed Fred in early November 1987 completed the third report. The referral came from the therapist, and all this psychologist knew about Fred's sex offending is what the therapist told him. He also did not speak with collaterals to get the full picture.

The report confirmed one thing I already knew: with a full-scale IQ of 143, Fred is a very smart man who functions in the superior range of intelligence. This score means he is a genius, more intelligent than 99.8 percent of people, and eligible for Mensa membership.

The psychologist's personality testing did not show signs of psychosis or neurosis. The only scale ever so slightly elevated was the Psychopathic Deviation Scale attributed to anger at his estranged wife. This form of testing is entirely based on self-reports, and in my opinion, Fred successfully faked normal.

When Lawyer Buddy read the reports aloud in a packed family courtroom, he used a louder voice for emphasis to relay what the psychologist wrote.

> Based on the assessment, it is my feeling that this man is not a danger to anyone regarding his sexual behaviour, or in any other way for that matter.

Fred was also successful in faking safe.

In reflecting on all of this, Fred's therapist, psychiatrist, psychologist, as well as criminal and family courts, lawyers, and child protection services have all taken an enormous, ill-informed gamble. If, or more likely when Fred re-offends, no professional will be blamed. It is those victimized, and their mothers, who will be forced to carry the burden of society's silence.

Tuesday, 13 June 1989
I would like to move out of Abingville, but if I do, Alida will have a royal conniption. She has been increasingly defiant. Bea meets with us for a closing visit and her only parenting recommendations are to give Alida options of other places where she can live and tell me that I should compromise. I am sure that neither Alida moving nor relaxing the rules are good ideas.

Alex stayed over Sunday night and has not contacted me since he left Monday morning, and now I worry he will never call again. It is normal for us not to talk for several days but that makes no difference. Today I am convinced he is done with me because I am such a mess.

Whether Alex is part of my life or not, there are things I want. I make a list of goals: I will love and have fun with my children and be the best mother possible, continue part-time university and earn a degree, see the psychiatrist as long as needed, stay alive, move out of Abingville, get a divorce, take a vacation with my children, quit smoking, get my weight over 100 pounds, and write a book to share my experience.

Wednesday, 14 June 1989
Men. Sometimes they all piss me off: Alex for not calling, Gus for being a peeper, Pa Kettle, Fred, Lawyer Buddy, Drunken Buddy,

Herman, John, and all the *dominees* and men in black suits. Too much of my life revolves around men. If I could choose sexual orientation, it would not be heterosexual.

Saturday, 17 June 1989
And things just got worse.

Lena comes over when I finish work and we are checking out my newly-planted flowerbeds beside the house when we see Fred's red Mustang. This time he does not do his habitual drive-by. He speeds into my driveway and screeches to a stop. Mr Hyde steps out of his car doing his Elvis saunter. I can tell by the tightness of his jaw that he has not come for tea. I ask Lena to please take the kids inside and keep them safe. I know she will also keep an eye on me, and I hope that Fred's awareness of her presence will provide me some protection.

I can see how upset he is and know this will not be good.

Fred is clearly distressed about his current financial troubles. *"My store is going bankrupt and it is your fault for trash talking me all over town. You told everyone what I did and now no one will shop at my store."*

When he exhausts that issue, he switches to rant about his coins. *"Carlyn, you need to give me the four coins that you stole from my collection. Go and get them for me right now. I'll wait."*

Aha. This sure sounds like the anonymous note threatening me about how "paybacks are a bitch." I cannot persuade him I never took his coins.

Next, with Godfather-like menace, he snarls. *"Your child support agency is garnishing my wage, and yeah, I can promise that you will never get a cent from me. I also promise that you will get a bullet through your head before this is all over."*

I had always known he would as soon kill me as pay child support. He told me that often enough. I slowly back into the house, slamming and locking the door behind me. Through the window, I watch him strut back to his car.

I see that the kids are absorbed in a computer game in the living room. With a nervous laugh I say, "Guess what, Lena. Fred just said I will be getting a bullet in my head."

Knowing Fred was not to be here, Lena had already phoned 911 for police assistance. Two female officers respond and they are charging Fred with uttering death threats and breach of family court order. I believe there is a correlation between female police officers and action. His probation ended two months ago, he repaid his debt to society, so they cannot charge him with breach of that order.

Lena also had to give a statement, and she will be required to attend criminal court (round three) with me. I do not like having my friend involved, but I sure appreciate her attitude. She is taking it in stride and I believe it will not change her level of support.

The death threat is, in a bizarre way, confirmation that my worry has been legitimate. I have known that allowing Fred to carry on, despite a restraining order, increased the risk to me. Fred has no regard for the law, and I wonder how I can feel assured today's criminal charges will somehow keep me safe when I know he will be angrier, which places me at greater risk.

Fred drives by a few more times this evening, so I know he is not in jail for the night. I can do nothing to stop the man if he means to kill me. That he talked about shooting suggests he may have access to firearms or knows someone who does. Locked doors and windows have never stopped him. The knife under my pillow would be useless against a gun. I consider getting a gun of my own, but it would be a liability because I could never shoot anyone, not even Fred.

28 June 1989
CAS Closing Recording, Caseworker Bea

Current Situation

This agency has been involved with this family since August 1987. At that time, Alida disclosed to her mother that her father Mr Smit had sexually molested her. Mrs Smit immediately separated from her husband when abuse was disclosed. Divorce proceedings have not yet been finalized. Mrs Smit is currently supporting her children by working as a pharmacy assistant at the Shoppers Drug Mart on King Street.

Mr Smit pled guilty to sexual assault of his daughter and received a probationary term because of this charge. Mr Smit also admitted to having molested his wife's four younger sisters, Dorothy, Grace, Irene and Helen, as well as his own sister Allison when they were in their teens.

In the past, Mr Smit has placed pressure upon this agency to ensure that he reconciles with his children. It was made clear to this individual that his own behaviour contaminated that relationship in the first place. He felt that, since he has admitted his mistake, life should go back to the way it was. Further, Mr Smit has been very impatient and blameful because the children were reluctant to resume regular contact with him.

In family court on September 10, 1987, Mrs Smit was successful in obtaining an order for supervised access, naming this agency as supervisors. This has been the primary role for CAS with this family. There has been one successful visit between father and children that occurred in one of the agency visiting rooms. The children used the visit as an opportunity to share feelings with their father, and it appeared to have gone well. However, since then, the children have resisted further contact, which Mr Smit blames on this agency and his ex-wife's negative influence on the children.

Mrs Smit is a highly motivated individual. Although she herself remains very bitter, with counselling from this worker, she has accepted the reality of her children possibly wanting contact with their father in the future.

Mr Smit has provided the CAS assessment reports that indicated he is not a risk of re-offending sexually or any other way. Over the past months Mr Smit returned to family court to alter the interim custody arrangement. He successfully petitioned the court for unsupervised access. He is now allowed to contact the children directly to arrange access visits with them and he will provide a copy of the court order to this agency when it becomes available.

Service completed.

This file may now be closed.

Sunday, 16 July 1989
Earlier yesterday, when I was tense about having company for my birthday, Alida and I argued. My kids need me to have tight control over my emotions, which is not always possible. Alida took off and stayed out until past curfew.

This year I tried for normalcy by having a birthday party. That's it. Never again. In the tradition of a Dutch party, we sat around the perimeter of my living room drinking coffee and eating cake. My friends gave me gifts of unsolicited parenting advise. To me, it felt more like sitting shiva or a wake than a celebration. Today, Lena tells me that her rough-around-the-edges husband thought my other friends were not particularly considerate of me.

Alida and I talk for a long time and we have come to some resolution. She thinks I am too strict and I think she wants the same privileges that I might give an older teen. To me, she is a young traumatized teenager pushing to get what she wants. I hear her out and agree to further compromise on curfews: 9:30 p.m. on school nights and 11:30 p.m. on weekends. I will make exceptions for special occasions if I approve of where she is going and with whom. There is peace in our home once again.

Thursday, 27 July 1989
Fourteen-year-old Alida and I got into an argument yesterday when I denied her permission to go on a date with a young man who looks to be ten years older than she is. She left the house anyway and did not return until 2:20 a.m.

Sunday, 30 July 1989
Alida went out Friday evening and did not return until this afternoon. She is hungry and stoned, so I feed her and let her sleep for a while. When she wakes, we chat. When I ask her what is going on, she first says she has no idea, and then admits she feels

badly about everything we have to go through. She believes it is all her fault. I ask what things she means. She lists off the phone calls when no one talks, all the drive-bys, that Kevin will now see Fred alone, that Fred threatened to kill me, and that I am always stressed. I let her know that I do not see any of those things being her fault. I suggest we go for counselling and she stomps off to her room, saying there is no way she will talk to anyone.

What strikes me is that, if Fred had been jailed for his crimes or if police had enforced the restraining order from the start, I would have stood a chance at helping Alida relieve the emotional and psychological burdens her father's abuse imposed. That the criminal justice system refused to control Fred with means at their disposal, and that he took advantage of their systemic reticence by wreaking havoc, exacerbates Alida's distress. I worry that it is impossible for Alida to heal without a village of collective support.

Friday, August 18, 1989

Alida comes and goes as she pleases. She will be home for a few days, and then for no apparent reason she will be gone again. I do not know if she is running away from home or toward friends and drugs. I search the streets of Abingville and phone everyone I can to find her.

Last week I located her and called the police for help. They picked her up and dropped her off. They left through the front door, she out the back.

Another time when I tracked her down, she was staying with the family of a girl she met in the CAS group. I spoke with the mother who talked to Alida about going home. She left there and then went couch surfing at the homes of friends who come without last names, so finding her became more difficult.

After much ado, today I get a lead on her location and go to the address myself. This place is on the wrong side of the tracks. Two tough looking young men who are clearly high answer the door. Once they are sure I am alone, they allow me inside. Alida refuses to come with me so I again call the police for help. Since she obviously does not want to go home, they will not look for her. However, if they happen to see her on the street, they will bring her home. In a nutshell, the police are not wasting time on a runner her age.

Friday, 25 August 1989
Alida continues to come and go. Right now, I have no idea where she is.

I have a week off. Alida knows we are going to Canada's Wonderland in Vaughn and then camping on our Parry Sound property. I had hoped she would come with us, but regardless, Kevin and I are going. We both need and deserve a vacation. In case she comes home while we are away, I leave a key in the hiding spot outside, a note on the table letting her know when we will be home, a $20 bill, and Lena's phone number in the event of an emergency.

Thursday, 31 August 1989
We had a great time at Wonderland. I am glad we went. We returned home earlier than planned because I felt guilty about leaving Alida alone in Abingville. Then I felt guilty that I cut Kevin's vacation short. I keep encountering situations where there is no good solution.

When Kevin and I return, the money is gone and so is the food I left in the fridge, so I know Alida has been home, which means she has been eating and is still in the area. I resume driving up and down the streets, searching for her. I call her old friends and they have not heard from her. I worry because Alida is quite naive despite what happened to her, and it scares me what she could be lured into.

Monday, 11 September 1989

Kevin and I have a new project on the go. He wants extra money and I need it, so together we started doing a paper route. Six days a week, we leave the house at 4:30 a.m. and arrive home just in time to get ready for school or work. The long days are worth it. Kevin gets spending money and the extra allows me to make ends meet without depleting my savings account. I am determined to hold on to my nest egg to someday buy my family our own little home.

Deciding whether to stay or resign from the CRC has been an ongoing internal argument. Even to myself, sitting on this fence is making me a pain in the ass. I have written and ripped up at least fifty resignation letters. I am over the worry that leaving the church will condemn me to hell. Staying is its own kind of netherworld. The reasons to resign have been obvious for a long time.

More obscure was my reason for not resigning sooner. I had hoped to influence the church into admitting to the existence of sexual abuse within the church family. I was ineffective as they ignored, hid, and shunned. They stubbornly clung to their perspective that I should reconcile with Fred despite his abuses. They chose not to support my family. My idea to change their attitude was grandiose, and I finally concede that I am entirely unable to shine a light in their darkness.

I write a final resignation letter, pop it into an envelope, and drop it into the *dominee's* mailbox at the parsonage.

Rather than worry about the Kettles finding out or trying to keep it a secret, I tell them right away.

Dad says, "Vat about de kids? How vil dey learn right vrom wrong now? You have to go to church."

Explaining from here to eternity will not help the Kettles understand. They are happy with their church and free to practice their religion as they see fit. I will not criticize them. It may be too much to ask, but I would like the same respect in return.

Saturday, 30 September 1989

Mom cannot convince me to see reason about my church resignation, so she bombards me with warnings on another front.

"Seeing Alex is a big mistake. You vil get hurt and de kids vil too."

"Vat does Alida tink of Alex? I don't tink she likes him."

On she goes, her arguments becoming increasingly malicious. "I can see dat you are making a big mistake, and it is my duty as your mudder to tell you. I don't vant to hear vrom you later dat you tink we should have told you, like vat you said about Fred doing to Alida. You don't know Alex and you don't know vat he vil do. He's a 'Canadian,' you know."

"Will you still love me if I continue to date Alex?"

She side-steps my question. "You know ve don't vant you to go back wit Fred de way tings are. Ve know a lot of tings have to happen before you and Fred get back together, but ve vant your marriage to verk."

I try to bring our conversation back to the issue at hand and ask again if her love is conditional on whom I date.

She continues with her parallel conversation, which I know means she is avoiding my question. "Vel, I said vat I tink. You should not see Alex and I know dat you are going to get hurt, and Alida, too. Dere. I said it, so you can't blame me."

With that, she escapes to the bathroom and locks herself in for fifteen minutes. I can hear sniffling and assume she is praying for her wayward daughter. She finally comes out of the bathroom and goes to the master bedroom. I hear her rummaging around.

Mom eventually comes back to the kitchen with a fistful of audiotapes. "Here, I have some sermons dat you should listen to. Dere is de one from your vedding too, de *dominee* vas so good den. Here dey are if you vant dem."

I take the one from the wedding (to destroy later) and hand the rest back to her.

Monday, 16 October 1989

Alida stole something in the mall shortly after Kevin. The deal I make with both kids is, as a first offence, I will not tell anyone about it. I am giving them an opportunity to learn from their mistake. They do not even know about each other.

Whereas Kevin walked away with a warning, Alida was charged. We have been to court several times and today she pleads guilty and receives a one-year probation order with nine conditions, three the same as Fred's. It is grossly unfair that my hurting daughter, for stealing an item worth $5.39, including tax, receives greater restrictions than the father who molested her for eight years.

Wednesday, 25 October 1989

The medical clinic's receptionist calls to give me an appointment because the doctor wants to have a chat. It is so strange the way things turn. After all my fears of dying at Fred's hands and thoughts of dying at my own, I now have a new worry to add to the list. My annual well woman test showed abnormal cells. I will learn the seriousness when I see a gynecologist. In the meantime, all I can do is keep a grip and breathe.

Saturday, 28 October 1989

The *dominee* concludes my church membership with finality I could never have anticipated. With the heave of a heavy sigh, he says he called to discuss my letter of resignation.

"You know Carlyn, it's just as well that you resigned."

"It is best," I say, "but what makes you think so?"

"Well, you may be aware that I've always had trouble being your minister."

"I had no idea," I said.

"You must know I have been sexually attracted to you. I've been very uncomfortable around you. Remember that time you were on the bleachers watching Alida's soccer game? I was shocked when

I came over to say hello and you offered me a coffee from your thermos. I should have said no. Sitting next to you was difficult."

"What! Are you kidding?"

"No. No, I'm not kidding. The temptation has been severe."

"You sorry sack of shit. You made me out to be a harlot, when all you wanted was to get lucky."

"You are being unfair," he whines.

"It's you who is unfair." I slam the phone receiver down. Good riddance to him and his church.

Sunday, 29 October 1989

I wake up in an outrageously terrible mood. It is not that I climb out of bed on the wrong side; I climb out of the wrong side of life. I am sufficiently beaten down by a society, church, culture, and family that treats me harshly. At this point, I believe it futile to tell anyone at the CRC my side of the story. No one has seriously gone to bat for me up to now, which makes me feel certain they will all side with their *dominee*.

Saturday, 11 November 1989

This past summer, Kevin landed himself a job in a convenience store down the road and he still works part time on weekends. Kevin continues to get up with me at 4:30 a.m. to do the paper route and he never utters a word of complaint. Even though I worry he is young for this responsibility, work seems to direct his energy in positive ways. He feels better about himself and is not getting into trouble at school anymore.

Fred buys cigarettes at the store where Kevin works, and they appear to be getting along reasonably well. Kevin had a couple of short unsupervised visits and there were no problems. Then Fred asked if he could take Kevin for a weekend. I only agreed to a day visit. When Fred calls to ask me to send along Kevin's birth certificate, I find out his plan is to take Kevin to Frankenmuth, in Michigan. Of course, Fred takes Kevin out of Canada and into the United States for their first full-day visit. That pushes my buttons. It is grim to be responsible for my kids' safety and have Kevin spend time with a man I do not trust.

Once Kevin is back at home, I question him. He feels I am grilling him (I am) and putting him in a bad position (ouch). We sort it out with an apology from me and promises from Kevin to let me know if anything uncomfortable happens during visits.

Last evening Alida made sure she knew what time Fred was due at the house to pick up Kevin, which was 9 a.m. She became very angry because I would be at work when he arrived. This morning, she is already gone by 7:30 a.m. when we return home from delivering papers. This evening, she calls at 11 p.m. to make sure Kevin is home and Fred is gone, and then arrives home about ten minutes later. She is doing all she can to avoid her father, which is understandable given what he put her through.

Monday, 20 November 1989

Parenting Alida is a challenge, and it is easy for us to get into disputes. To talk to her in an environment with less tension than home, I took her out for lunch yesterday. She was aware that we would be trying to figure out how to go forward, with less fighting and less running away. I asked what she thought she needed to stay home and she had no idea. At almost fifteen, she was as lost as she had been when we had the visit at Rotary Park, and as forlorn as those times in her bedroom when she was a little girl sitting on my lap and I was unable to console her.

Alida did want to work it out at home. She had no interest in a group home, foster care, her own apartment, or placement with family, all options Bea had presented to her during one of the last visits. By the end of our lunch, Alida had agreed to a one-week trial staying home. We compromised whereby I relaxed the rules a little more and she agreed to attend counselling with me.

Last night was pleasant. This morning, our house shook with her expansive repertoire of swear words, and I went to work upset and distracted. Tonight all is calm again. If her behaviour reflects her emotional turmoil, all I can feel is sympathy for her.

Wednesday, 13 December 1989
Life with Alida continues to spin up and down like a yoyo. Although she agreed, she is very unhappy that I arranged a counsellor for us. We have our first appointment and she barely says a word. When I rebook the next appointment, she insists she will not be coming back. All the same, I cling to hope. I know it will not be easy for her to talk and I expect her to balk. Maybe she will come around after the initial resistance, and if she does not, nothing has been lost.

Thursday, 14 December 1989
When I went to bed Alida was gone, but she was home this morning. Kevin said Alida threw stones at his window and he let her into the house in the middle of the night. I heard nothing.

She arrives home after school, goes straight to her room, and refuses to talk to me when I knock on her door. When I try to open the door, she has furniture jammed against it so I cannot get in. For an hour I sit outside her door trying to start a conversation. Alida does not say a word in response and turns up her music so loud she can no longer hear me.

The beat of her new favourite song, shakes the floor. The lyrics make me sad and it resonates with something in my soul. I am sure the words will always remind me of Alida shutting herself away, and my inability to find a way to reach her. Oh sweet child o' mine. [13]

---

[13] Guns N Roses, *Sweet Child O' Mine* from the album *Appetite for Destruction*, 1987.

Friday, 15 December 1989

Bea called this morning to say she reopened our file. Yesterday she received a report of parent/child conflict between Alida and me. I ask who called and she said callers are anonymous. Bea needs to see me today to discuss a plan.

We meet, and I feel tricked because her purpose is clearly to railroad me into consenting to a predetermined scheme. Alida refuses to work it out at home and now says she wants to get out of Abingville. Foster care is no longer an option because my family is willing to look after her. I say I am willing, too. I will happily move my family anywhere if this is about getting out of Abingville. All that gets me from Bea is "the look," a patronizing glare that insinuates I am being ridiculous.

I do not want Alida to go, but this is no longer my choice. It turns out that my parents purchased a one-way ticket for Alida to move to Moose Jaw, Saskatchewan. They have arranged for her to live with Irene. The Kettles have return tickets and are taking Alida next Wednesday. If I do not take her to the airport, Bea will arrange for a volunteer to do it.

Bea thinks this is a sound plan. Of course she thinks that. This plan allows her to ship the problem out of province and she can again close the file. What is routine for CAS is heart wrenching for my family.

Bea informs me that if I oppose the plan and stop Alida, CAS will take me to family court to force the issue. If that happens, they will also be required to serve Fred court papers. Bea says Fred can use it against me in the future. If I say no to Alida's move, Bea promises the court will overrule me, and I risk losing both of my kids. She got me. This is an overt and outrageous threat. She backs me into a corner where my only option is to give up one child in order to save the other. This resembles one of my concentration camp nightmares, but without the option of sacrificing myself to save them both.

This hurts so much because, all along, I made the mistake of thinking that the agency supported my family. I should have known better given they call themselves "Children's Aid."

I am in no position to oppose, and I do not agree to this stupid plan. My daughter is joining a childless couple in their mid-twenties who have no parenting experience. There is no reason to think they will be more successful than I am to care for my troubled teenage daughter.

This is grotesque. It makes no sense to tear Alida away from her family. Running is Alida's maladaptive coping strategy, and they just helped her to do it again. They have severed my opportunity to help my daughter and our family heal.

I phone my mother to appeal to her sense of motherhood. It is quickly evident I am paying for standing up and doing things they oppose. I left my child-abusing husband, I pulled the kids from Christian school, I left their church and their faith, I quit EuroMed Importing and they need to buy their merchandise elsewhere, I am getting divorced, and I am dating a "Canadian." In a family like mine, you cannot do so many things that they view as sinful and expect to get away with it. They make me pay, dearly, with my own flesh and blood.

My mother's response to my plea is, "I agree dat Alida should go away vrom you. Your sister loves her a lot and it vil be better for Alida dere den at your place. Dey vil take her to church and ve vil pay for dem to send her to de Christian School. You are divorcing. Irene has a husband to help. Alida does not like your new boyfriend, you know dat, but you still see him. I tried to tell you but you von't listen. Don't blame me. Dis is your own fault. You are a bad mudder."

Wednesday, 20 December 1989

When I help Alida pack, I stuff my hope for a healed family into her luggage. This is not for six months or one year. It is indefinite, a one-way-trip. In my heart, this feels as final as packing the belongings of a child who died.

For the sake of our future relationship, I will not abandon Alida to a volunteer driver. Difficult as it will be, I will take her to the airport myself. My kids say their goodbyes and Kevin is terribly sad. He begs Alida to reconsider, but she is determined to go. Kevin does not put up a fuss about going to school, so I keep to his normal routine. I am afraid that I will not do very well at the airport, and there is no value in further burdening him with my grief.

Alida and I lug her suitcases into the terminal, and the politest I can be toward the Kettles is to ignore them. I have never felt such hate and rage, such devastating betrayal. I want to rip Alida away from them, to hold her close, to keep my family intact. As soon as the three of them enter security, I dash out of the airport and cry harder than I ever have before. The ache in my broken heart is so extreme I can barely breathe.

I risked everything to save my children from abuse; losing my daughter is the price exacted.

```
27 December 1989
CAS Opening/Closing Recording,
Caseworker Bea
```

Current Situation

```
Mrs Smit's file was closed on June 28, 1989.
Agency policy is that closed files return
to the last worker when a complaint is
received within six months of closing. The
report of parent-teen conflict relating
to mother and daughter was received within
```

this time frame. Mrs Smit's mother made the report and indicated that the decision was made at a family meeting.

This is the third file opening for this family. The first was in July 1987 when Alida disclosed sexual abuse by her father. Mr Smit was charged, pled guilty, and has completed the probationary term. The second opening was from August 1987 through to June of this year, and it was due to an order made in family court that required this agency to supervise access, which it did. The file was closed when Mr Smit successfully petitioned the court for his access with the children to be unsupervised.

Since the June 1989 file closing, there have been seven reports relating to neglect or emotional harm made to this agency by Mr Smit. While each of these concerns was documented, none met the threshold for intervention. With regard to neglect, Mr Smit's concern was that the mother works and leaves the children unsupervised. He provided no specific evidence that his children were at risk of harm as a result. Because Kevin was not seeing his father as frequently as Mr Smit would like, and because Alida refused to speak to him when he phoned, most of his grievances related to his view that the children suffered from parent alienation syndrome stemming from Mrs Smit's negativity and manipulation.

The conflict between Mr and Mrs Smit regarding their financial settlement issues remains. Their divorce is pending and Mrs Smit remains bitter.

It is this worker's opinion that Alida was distressed due to her mother's bitterness. Alida successfully attended two sessions of the sexual assault survivor group at this agency, and it was believed at the conclusion that she overcame the effects of sexual abuse. Mrs Smit believes her daughter's turmoil and maladaptive coping strategies were brought on by years of sexual abuse. She also feels that Mr Smit's ongoing harassment triggers her daughter's emotional distress.

Mrs Smit was able to arrange family counselling for mother and daughter to work on their relationship, but this counselling was not effective. Alida called a maternal aunt for assistance and the extended family arranged for Alida to move to Saskatchewan and live with this aunt.

The lines of communication between this mother and daughter are slowly opening. It is unknown whether Alida will be returning in the near or distant future.

Assessment

The conflict between Alida and her mother has resolved. Alida has relocated to reside with a maternal aunt in Moose Jaw.

There are no further protection concerns and this file will be closed.

Monday, 15 January 1990
We got through Christmas somehow. I did my best to make it enjoyable for Kevin, but with our grief of Alida being gone and my anger being too intense to visit the Kettles, it was a dismal time. The less said about it, the better.

Today, after weeks of weather as gloomy and grim as my mood, the sun is shining. I have the day off and Kevin is in school, so Alex and I go for a drive to the beach in Port Stanley. We take a walk out on the ice and then head over to Tim Hortons for a hot chocolate. I had packed some snacks and pick out a ripe banana. It tastes strangely salty. Alex goes inside and when he returns to the car, I can hardly breathe. My tongue swells and my throat is closing. I know I need help and that I need it quickly.

Alex calls 911, and by the time the ambulance arrives, I have begun tearing off my clothes, trying to get some air. After the first needle, my heart feels as if it will explode. With lights flashing and ear-splitting sirens, they rush me to St. Thomas-Elgin General Hospital. Hovering above the gurney, I watch them tend to me. When they administer another needle, I slowly sink back into my body.

Tuesday, 16 January 1990
When I left the hospital, the doctor gave me pills to keep my throat from swelling. Alex sat watch beside my bed, being there for me every time I woke up throughout the night. I have never before had anyone care for me like that. Alex, a man of few words, demonstrated love by his actions.

I compare Alex's support with the time in 1979 when I was having a miscarriage and Fred opted to eat lunch at a strip club rather than come home for an hour to help me with two active toddlers. As I sat on the bathroom floor holding a fetus the size of a hummingbird, the kids watched Mr Dressup, and Fred was drooling over other women.

Yesterday I called in sick and got the impression my supervisor was growing annoyed. I saw my family doctor who referred me for allergy testing, thinking I may have developed a rare allergy to bananas. The doctor said that there is a correlation between trauma and allergies. He explained that stress weakens your immune system, and when your immune system is weak, you can develop allergic reactions. There is research that compromised immune systems are related to other health problems, even cancer.

Tuesday, 13 March 1990

Kevin needs $200 for his grade eight class trip and he thought his dad would give the money as an early birthday gift. A few days ago, Kevin called Fred and afterward he was quite hurt because his father could take a girlfriend on a trip to Paris, but would not help his own son.

Fred apparently reconsidered. By way of letter, he tells Kevin he will give him the money, kind of, but not before the payment needs to be made to the school, and not all at once. I pay for the trip and know better than to hold my breath waiting for Fred to come through.

> *Dear Kevin,*
>
> *Regarding your class trip, please let me know when and to whom I should make the second $100 payment at the end of the month. I have juggled things around so that I can make it. I will also be able to give you $50 toward the first payment next Friday, March 16th. The remaining $50 I'll pay in the following couple of weeks in two payments of $25 each. Please let me know who to give the money to, as I do not trust giving it to your mother. Sorry about the delay. I'm doing the best I can.*
>
> *Love,*
> *Dad*

Thursday, 10 May 1990

At the end of the school year, we are leaving Abingville to live with Alex on his hobby farm near Ailsa Craig. Kevin fully agrees; he likes the idea of a fresh start in a new community and looks forward to living closer to his uncle Bart. Fred never did give Kevin any money for the grade eight class trip and, at least for the time being, Kevin wants nothing to do with him.

After two years, I have a good idea who Alex is and know I can trust him. I was wrong before when I thought that women could not know for sure if their partners would harm their children. Lack of trust is an indication of something more happening in the relationship that needs exploring.

I know moving in with Alex might seem sudden after Alida left, and in all honesty, her leaving does have something to do with it. I knew Alida objected to Alex and was unlikely to accept him anytime soon, if ever. The only reason I stayed in Abingville as long as I did was that Alida opposed moving. If she had not moved away, I would have waited to live with Alex until she grew up.

Before I agreed to the move, I asked Alida if she would come home. After that, she avoided my weekly calls for a month, so I guess her answer is no. If my daughter changes her mind, there will always be room for her wherever I live.

Sunday, 20 May 1990

I finally spoke with Alida again last week. Today when I call Moose Jaw, I find out she has been gone for a few days. Irene does not know where she is. Now she tells me Alida has been bouncing in and out of their home ever since she got there. Irene and her husband are no more successful than I was to stop her running. I am disappointed, but not surprised, that Irene did not keep me updated.

Thursday, 21 June 1990

Lena and I are subpoenaed to attend criminal court as witnesses for Fred's two charges: "Intimidation contrary to section 423(a) C.C.C." and "Breach of Court Order contrary to section 127 C.C.C." The first is the charge for Fred's death threat and the second is a breach charge with respect to the family court restraining order.

This is Fred's first and only breach charge since the family court order was issued in 1987, but I cannot say it was for lack of trying. Since I got the restraining order, I have been to the police with complaints of Fred's phone calls, Mr Nobody phone calls, and tangible proof of breaches a minimum of twenty times. The first breach charge should have happened three years ago, yet here we are now with a death threat. Not only did police inaction leave me vulnerable, it has exposed my children to three years of unnecessary distress, too.

Court is a blur. Some black suit, I do not know who he is, asks if it is okay to settle the matter with a peace bond. When I question what that is, he explains that it is similar to a restraining order, but Fred will have to pledge $500 that he stands to lose if he breaches. With a peace bond the charges are withdrawn and nothing appears on a criminal record check. I know how utterly useless and dangerous a restraining order is, but this is supposedly different. Money, to Fred, has less value than revenge, so I am unsure how a peace bond is supposed to provide me any protection.

Since I have given up believing in criminal justice or protection, I shrug, and that is interpreted as my agreement. They drop the two charges.

Now the price for my head is $500.

Tuesday, 3 July 1990

Being an hour away from Abingville means that, for the first time in over two years, I can go to the grocery store without looking over my shoulder for the red Mustang tailing me. What a relief. The tension in my chest has eased and I can fill my lungs when I breathe.

Wednesday, 21 November 1990
After surgery, I still have not had an all-clear well woman exam. I see the doctor for another check-up. He asks how I am doing. I tell him that my psychiatrist retired and the PTSD is still bothersome. I struggle with my moods. He leaves the room for a phone call, and I see my chart where he gives me a diagnosis of bipolar disorder. I may not be as smart as this doctor, but I know myself and he is wrong.

When he returns to the examining room, I argue that the diagnosis is inaccurate. I ask him to remove it from my medical file. He refuses. I reject the diagnosis and leave the prescription for lithium on his desk.

Tuesday, 11 December 1990
Life is busy with twos. I have two children, one too far away. Our family now includes Alex's two kids who are living with us full time. Our house is too small. I am enrolled in two university courses. Driving to work at the Shoppers Drug Mart in Abingville was too far, and I was lucky to have the chance to relocate to the Shoppers in Strathroy. I may have bit off too much too soon. Alex's children are well behaved and of course I support them living with us.

My problem, which has nothing to do with them but affects them, is that I am still grieving, which makes it hard for me to be a good parent. While I do my best, my best is less than what all these kids deserve.

Alida says that while she refuses to live with Alex, she will return home if I move. I rent an apartment for us. Then she changes her mind. She will not move home after all. I cancel the place. I do not want to leave Alex, but I desperately miss my Alida. While my kids are still young, I will always choose them first.

Thursday, 27 December 1990

The Kettles invite us for Christmas dinner. All their biological grandchildren receive very generous gifts. They express their disapproval of my lifestyle by taking it out on Alex's kids, who each get a pair of socks and a chocolate initial.

We spend part of Christmas day with Alex's mother. While she is very fair about gifts, the tension there is thick. Alex argues with his mother who thinks his kids' clothes are not nice enough and with his sister about her dog eating off the supper table.

The Christmas celebration Alex and I have with the kids is great. We are forging new traditions. Last year, I made chocolate crepes for Christmas dessert and now the kids all think it is an annual ritual. Kids are like that, I guess. They are eager for their lives to be predictable and ready to take on new traditions without much ado.

Tuesday, 7 May 1991

The plan had been for Alida to fly home with my sisters and their husbands for the Kettles' fortieth wedding anniversary celebration. At the last minute, Alida called me to say she changed her mind. I wake up this morning convinced she said she was not coming to throw me off and that she will show up as a surprise. I drive to the London airport to pick her up, but when the Kenora and Moose Jaw contingents arrive, Alida does not disembark. The idea of not seeing her hurt so much that my mind did its denial trick again. I drive home feeling forlorn. I miss her so much.

Friday, 10 May 1991

The Kettles plan a dinner in London with just their biological children. Driving with Irene gives us opportunity to talk. Irene cannot keep Alida home and she did not come for this visit because she is again on the run. Irene had minimal success parenting my daughter. She admits moving Alida to Moose Jaw was a big mistake, but a sorry does not acknowledge the momentous loss for our heartbroken family. Sorry does not bring Alida home or keep her safe. My daughter is now on the run almost 1,700 miles (3,000 kilometres) away from home.

Sunday, 25 August 1991

Alida comes home by herself for a visit. She is aloof with Alex, but Kevin and I are thrilled to have her with us for a bit of time. She shows me a note that she got from her father.

> *It's been 4 years now, and I just regret very much that your total silence is based on so much misinformation and so many distorted facts. Maybe someday you'll want to find out what really happened, and why.*

I suspect he lied so many times that he now believes his own lies.

Tuesday, 10 September 1991

My brothers Bert and Bart come to my aid again and help Kevin and I move into a tiny apartment that I rent on a month-by-month basis. My brothers load my extra furniture onto a wagon and back the wagon into an empty shed on Bert's farm until I need it again.

Alex and I are not fighting, and he is not doing anything wrong. The issue is that I cannot get myself together. I am emotionally stuck and cannot find my way out. My hope is that a foundation of time and space will give me a base upon which I may heal. At this point, I am uncertain if there is a future for my relationship with Alex.

Saturday, 30 November 1991

I find us a little house, more like a cottage, for sale by the owner. It overlooks a treed ravine on a quiet dead-end road just outside of Ailsa Craig. The trade-off for being affordable is the mess that needs clearing. The inside is filthy and there are truckloads of junk in the yard. My brothers again help with the move. They unload my furniture from the wagon, and re-load it with junk. We will be having a big family bonfire at the back of one of their farms. My brothers are sure there when I need them. They show their non-judgemental love and support with meaningful gestures and genuine help.

All this time I saved the Victoria Street house sale proceeds as a nest egg. This is my down payment. With my savings, and my job at the drug store, the bank gives me a loan without hesitation. Now that I can afford a mortgage on my own, Dad offers to co-sign. I would sooner we live in a tent than accept his signature.

While Mom thinks the place is disgusting (and she is not entirely wrong), I am able to see beyond the grime and clutter. With some work and creativity, this is a perfect little home where my son and I will rebuild our resilience. There is a room for Alida if she wants to move home. I am thrilled, even with the brown kitchen and the out-of-date gold and red swirled wallpaper in the dining room. Mom clucks as she cleans the stove and nags at me to buy a new one. The bank account has no room for extras. The stove works and that is good enough by my standards, and my standards are good enough for me.

Sunday, 15 December 1991

Aside from no consistency and frequent lateness, what I hear about visits is uneventful. When Fred picks up Kevin, he often drives the extra distance to the Kettle's to pick up Julianna, too. How he weaselled his way into my younger sister's life is a mystery. What concerns me is, after all that their children and grandchildren have been through, that the Kettles allow Juliana to spend time with Fred. Fred being with Juliana has all my alarm bells going off, yet the Kettles are so well groomed and so unsophisticated that they cannot see the risks their youngest daughter faces.

Protective factors for Juliana are that she is a taller, outspoken, older teen, which are not attributes Fred favours in those he victimizes. In case that is not enough, I explicitly warn Juliana about the risks. She says she goes for the freebies, and if he tries anything, he will pay for it. Both Kevin and Juliana know that if things go wrong during a visit, I will come to pick them up with no questions asked.

Misguided hope seems to be my middle name. I had the idea that Fred and I might still co-operatively co-parent, and that by keeping my enemy close I could protect my son and youngest sister. I unbelievably and insanely allowed him to step inside the back door of my house a few times while he waited for Kevin. After I heard from Julianna that Fred told far-fetched stories about being in our house, when he started dropping by without prior notice, and when I found out Fred went upstairs to Kevin's bedroom when I was at work, I withdrew my welcome mat. He now waits in his car for Kevin, or at least, that is what he does when I am home.

I feel stupid about having allowed him in my home, but am thankful that I did not go so far as to allow him in my bed. When I attended the group at the women's shelter, I learned that on average a woman leaves an abusive partner seven times before she can break away for good. As implausible as it may seem to anyone who has not experienced intimate partner abuse, I understand this statistic. Since we separated, if I am being honest, I have felt myself waver when Fred twigged my sympathy. What has kept me focused on never seriously considering a return has been a shield of anger and animosity. Bitterness has served me well.

Thursday, 2 January 1992
Alida sends me a lovely Christmas card and yet another letter from her father. The man never quits. This letter is so bad. The worst yet.

> *Dear Alida,*
>
> *This has got to be the most difficult letter ever. I'd rather talk to you in person, but since that's not possible, here goes. I'll keep it short & without B.S.*
>
> *It's been 4 1/2 years now and finally things are moving to bring this whole divorce mess to a finish. Most importantly, I've been able to re-establish a relationship with Kevin, and as a result Kevin and also your aunt and friend Juliana are spending a lot of time with me in Abingville. That makes this the best Christmas ever for me, but there is still a very important part missing. You.*
>
> *Alida, if you want to stay mad for the rest of your life, well, that's your decision. But at least get your facts straight first. And before you think, oh sure, here comes the B.S., I'll tell you again you are more than welcome to look at the entire court file, cause it will back up everything I say.*
>
> *This has been a very messy & dirty divorce. There was a lot of money involved & the main intention was to destroy me & get it all. That can be proven. Although I wasn't going to let anyone steal me blind, someone knew that the only way to hurt me was through my kids. And it worked. No, I won't say I didn't do anything wrong because I did. But I've been lied about, lied to, stolen from & just generally harassed & slandered in the hopes that I'd roll over and die. And I had no idea just how much bullshit you kids had been told until I started talking to Juliana late this summer. Juliana started seeing through the lies & started asking questions. You have been with your mom or her family and now with Irene in Moose Jaw. Since they enjoyed dumping on me, I doubt you ever heard the truth.*
>
> *Alida, I touched you. But not for sexual purposes or intentions.*

It was always done in jest, with no threats or "don't tell anybody." I never tried, nor would I ever have tried to "make it" with you. The only sexual assault is the one that was planted in your mind. My stupidity was being sucked into pleading guilty to something I knew wasn't true. I thought it would spare you the stress of trial & was told it would be helping you. I had no idea that they'd turn around and say "see, he wouldn't plead guilty if it wasn't true." I'm not saying that what happened was right. It wasn't. But it was at worse an error in judgment on my part. Not sexual assault or anything even remotely close to that.

Our marriage ended the beginning of June '87. That's when I told your mom I was fed up & wanted a divorce. And right after that is when she & Gus made their plans. She needed an excuse to keep her smelling like a rose & I gave it to her. She knew that I joked with you and flipped your breast & she used it. And yeah, I was so wiped out physically & mentally & emotionally by that time from years of living with her manipulation, that I let her. Love is not only blind, it's also stupid.

I'm not going to say any more about that in this letter. If you want to know more, you'll have to talk to me.

As to all the other accusations (I guess I'm now supposed to have molested damn near the whole Ketel family), if there is any truth to it, charge me and we'll let a judge decide. Everyone who accused me of things will have to face me and this stuff will be straightened out in court before this is all over. I'm tired of being dumped on & there's two sides to every story.

Enough said. Bottom line is that you are my daughter, and I am your father. I love you. Always have and always will. Whether we ever again can go back to the relationship we had is up to you. You're not a kid anymore, you've got your own mind. You can wait 'til I'm dead & put flowers on my grave, or you can decide we should start talking now.

I miss you & always will while we're apart. I'd like things to change, but I can't do it alone. A lot of what really happened you can find out if you want. If you'd rather go through life thinking your father tried to put the make on you, well, I can't make you believe anything you don't want to, but you'd be very wrong.

Think about it. But even if you decide to hate me forever, I'll still keep loving you because, yeah, you're my daughter.

Love,
Dad

Monday, 6 January 1992

Up to now I have been plodding along with part-time university courses and using vacation time for studying. I am part way into the second year. I applied to the Family Allowance Program, colloquially called Mothers' Allowance, and they approved assistance so that I can start attending full-time.

To the intake worker, I fully disclosed my assets and finances. She said I am eligible for benefits. If I receive any child support, I will have to declare it. I am not required to repay them if I get funds in our divorce settlement, since that would be money earned in the past. Shoppers Drug Mart is a supportive employer and they will keep me on part-time.

If it were not for family benefits and student loans available to finance my goals, I would not be able to take this leap. I am super grateful and vow to pay it forward in the future when I will be in a position to do so. I am taking a big step toward the future I dreamt of.

I am excited that I will be more available for Kevin. Whereas in the past Kevin's struggles presented as behaviours, now he goes through gloomy spells where I worry about his mood. He denies being depressed or suicidal. What seems to get him through these times is his part-time job, being the school's computer whiz kid, friends, and his Uncle Bart. I feel that Kevin has a tenuous balance of stability and I hope he will be able to build on that between now and when he finishes high school

Tuesday, 3 March 1992

Fred invites Kevin who is fifteen, and Juliana, who is nineteen, to Guatemala for a week of vacation. They, of course, both say they are going. I speak with Fred, and he assures me he has booked a separate, adjoining room for Juliana, and that if I do not consent to this trip, he will fight for custody of Kevin. Of course he will.

I call the Kettles to ask them if they are crazy to allow their daughter to go, and it appears they are. They have no issue with Juliana taking this trip. After all, poor Juliana deserves a vacation, and they think it is generous of Fred to pay for it. They cannot understand why I might have concerns since I am allowing Kevin to go (touché) and Juliana thinks she will be safe.

Kevin is a responsible teen, and he agrees to keep his plane ticket, passport, and the phone number for the Canadian Embassy in Guatemala City with him at all times. It may seem stupid to say yes, yet at his age, saying no will start a battle I could lose. As long as I have custody, I have the authority to rescue Kevin if things go badly.

Sunday, 22 March 1992

When they return from the Guatemala trip, Fred drops off Juliana and Kevin at my place. They come in ravenous because Fred ran out of food money. While they eat, they burst with stories. I bite my tongue and listen. Kevin rifled through his father's wallet to fund meals and outings for him and Juliana as long as the travellers' cheques lasted. Fred spent most of their trip at the hotel bar with dancers draped over him. Fred tried to set Kevin up with a young woman, which Kevin refused.

The three of them had shared one room. Every night Fred would drink himself into a stupor and stumble into the room in the middle of the night. The first night he got into bed with Juliana and grabbed her under her t-shirt. She said she kneed him hard. He yelled at her and said it was accidental, which she did not believe. To keep herself safe, she spent the rest of the vacation sleeping on the floor between Kevin's bed and the wall.

Fred is now supposedly fluent in Spanish, and his latest business venture is being an agent who brings Guatemalan women into Canada to be strippers and escorts. His reason for the trip was to recruit sexy girls who want the "better life" he can offer them.

Juliana said he kept nagging at her to do a strip tease on the hotel bar stage. Bless her, similar to her sister Ellie, she finally told him to fuck off and he stopped. Juliana denies anything inappropriate happened other than his groping attempt, but she is disgusted and done with him. What they describe could have been dangerous, and I am grateful the kids made it home safely.

Friday, 1 May 1992

We spend the entire day in Abingville for our pre-trial hearing. The judge sends us out of his courtroom mid-afternoon with instructions to settle everything. We return to the courtroom late in the afternoon no further ahead. The judge is mad. He sends us out again, demanding we settle, or we will be forced spend the weekend at the courthouse with him. I hope the judge follows through and this nightmare ends.

Fred persists in wanting more money than there is and he does not come up with anything that I can remotely agree to. He rejects all my suggestions. It is late evening and quite dark outside when the judge sees us for the last time. He literally throws up his hands in frustration that we made no progress whatsoever. He raises his voice and yells at us to go ahead and have a costly trial where nobody will win. I am disappointed that the judge gives up so easily.

Mother's Day 1992
I am sitting in the sun watching Kevin's dog Puppy chasing something, a bug maybe. She jumps up and down, runs in circles, and digs at the ground for the longest time. I wish I could video her because she reminds me of me, chasing windmills in my mind. I always thought my biggest problem was that I do not have enough self-control. I kept trying harder and harder to do everything perfectly.

Watching Puppy play makes me realize that it is not that I have too little self-control, but that I try too hard. It is time I work on letting go. I feel ready to release my past in order to create a space where I can step into my future.

A NEW BEGINNING

What we call the beginning is often the end.
And to make an end is to make a beginning.
The end is where we start from.[14]

Wednesday, 15 July 1992
Alida sends the nicest birthday card with the loveliest message.

> "I think your job as Mom was a lot more than some can handle. You have done a great job. Even through the bad times these past five years, you have always been there. I love you so much. Thanks for being so great."

Even if this is the only reward I will ever get, it will all have been worth it.

I call her to thank her for her kind words and we talk for quite a while. I tell her I am sorry and still feel guilty for what happened to her. Alida says I have nothing to feel bad about because I believed her and acted, and that has made all the difference to her.

---

[14] T.S. Eliot, *Little Gidding*, Four Quartets (Gardner Books, main edition, April 30, 2001) Originally published 1943.

I also tell her I often think that if I had left her father sooner, maybe the abuse she suffered would have been less. She is adamant that if I had left sooner, she and Kevin would have been at a greater risk. If they had been alone with him, he could have, and she feels he would have, done much worse than what he did before we separated.

Monday, 31 August 1992
Mom tells me a secret. Dad just remembered that when he was five years old, his mother had been in the hospital for a surgery and their housekeeper sexually abused him. That, according to Mom, is all he remembers.

I understand vague memories. I have one that is hazy fragments, insufficient to say that I was molested, but too much to say I was not. The summer I was fifteen, my Opa arranged with the Kettles for me to help him on the farm for the summer. With Oma in the hospital for another surgery, I was in the middle of nowhere, alone with my Opa.

One day we had been working in the barn with the baby chickens when I ran into the house to use the bathroom. When I finished there was straw and mucus in the toilet. I went to the living room to watch an episode of *General Hospital* and then claimed I did not feel well and went to bed before dinner to avoid Opa. By the next morning, I had pushed the memory out of my consciousness and we carried on as usual. In a vague, dissociated way, I have always remembered the bathroom trip and feeling distress that day, but that is where the memory starts and stops.

Friday, 11 September 1992
Alida is home for two weeks and this has been an awesome visit. It is probably the best time together that we have had in our lives. She is a sweet young woman; a daughter of whom any mother would be proud.

Alida is engaged to a man a few years older, and they have plans to marry in Moose Jaw next summer. She has lived with him for a while and is certain he is a good man. She reminds me that I was the one who taught her not to put up with a man's crap and she assures me she never will. My daughter is much wiser than I was at the same age. I think Alida will be okay.

Wednesday, 30 September 1992

Wondering if I had been mistaken in believing the Kettles would have insisted I marry Fred if they had known he date raped me, I finally ask them. They both confirm they most certainly would have. Sex is sex.

I asked, "If it happened today, what would you say?"

They say that of course they would still demand marriage because once you have sex with someone, you must marry them.

Being forced into marriage does not mean I was dragged by my hair down the aisle. I did not fight my fate. It happened to me without a word being spoken. I was aware of the expectations and my eighteen-year-old self was not strong or brave enough to refuse.

The woman I am today is finally able to forgive her younger self for marrying Fred.

Wednesday, 7 October 1992

Our divorce trial takes three days. Before going into the courtroom, we did some negotiating. I put up a token fuss, and then readily gave up all past and future child support. I doubt Fred will pay any more than he has up to now, which is still only $100 since July 1987. The Support and Custody Enforcement program has been involved for four years and they initiated wage garnishment, bank garnishment, federal funds garnishment and filed a writ to collect support and arrears. However, to date, by moving ownership of his businesses among various people and manipulating the books, Fred has evaded their efforts. If Fred is required to pay support going forward, it will only make him try harder to persuade Kevin to take his side and live with him. Forgoing support is my way to safeguard Kevin from Fred's coercion, and me from Fred's anger.

I am on the witness stand for two entire days. Fred has his turn and I just about choke when he spends an hour testifying, in excruciating detail, how I do not take care of my son's needs. The entirety of evidence is the ratty and unseasonable clothing Kevin wears for visits.

At recess, I tell my lawyer how Kevin strategically dresses in old clothes, coats and shoes, going so far as to collect worn-out clothing from his friends to wear to access visits. Juliana was doing it too when she visited and it worked for them every single time. The kids called their game *The Freddy Recycling Program*, and they made it a competition to see who could get Fred to spend the most money on them. Fred was blind to the kids' manipulation and preferred to believe I was failing as a mother and sister. He saw himself as the knight who swooped in to make things right.

My lawyer has a chuckle about the kids' swindle, and we decide not to clarify to the court. We trust the judge will see that Fred has not been paying child support and buying his son what he believes the boy needs is what any good parent would do.

At the trial, my lawyer's position is that, since Fred is equally liable for depletion of the assets, we should each get half of the current value. Lawyer Buddy argues that I should give Fred half the value at the time we separated. With one thing and another, the value of the remaining assets drastically reduced to where the difference is several hundred thousand of dollars. This happened because the log structure rotted, and Fred never produced any money from supposedly disposing of EuroMed's assets. I think he took most of it for his own use, and it was just not a struggle I could bear to fight.

The judge's decision is every bit as good as I had hoped. Fred has won many battles along the way, but I have been mostly successful in fighting the war for my children's safety. Today I win again. The judge rules for my position and does a Solomon act by splitting all our remaining assets half and half.

The Parry Sound waterfront property deed is now in both our names. That means I still have to deal with Fred to dispose of it.

Fred gets thirty days to appeal.

I am no sooner home when one of his creditors contacts me to ask how soon Fred's money will be available. Apparently, he gave Fred a substantial loan and has concerns about repayment. I cannot speak to Fred's finances, but as past actions are indicative of future behaviour, it would be surprising if the funds are ever repaid.

Friday, 6 November 1992
It is precisely the thirtieth day after the trial and my lawyer receives Fred's Notice of Appeal. Violence comes to mind.

Monday, 30 November 1992
Once a week, I see a counsellor at the Sexual Assault Centre. Talking shakes loose old memories and feelings. Now that Kevin is too old to be apprehended by CAS, I finally feel free to speak about my counting habit, which seems to be getting worse again, and about losing big blocks of time. Nightmares and night terrors continue to haunt me. When I read my notes to study, I cannot remember being in class, so it often seems as if I do all my schoolwork twice. Sometimes I lose days. Therapy helps to fill in the gaps.

Saturday, 27 March 1993
This semester I took an Abnormal Psychology course. We had to do a term paper on one of the mental disorders in the DSM

III-R, the same guide to mental disorders the psychiatrist showed me. There are many disorders, but the one I was most interested in learning more about was antisocial personality disorder, also known as psychopath or sociopath.

The traits that persons with this diagnosis have are behaviour conflicts with social norms, disregarding or violating the rights of others, inability to distinguish between right and wrong, and no remorse or empathy. They tend to be overrepresented in criminal populations. On the surface, they can be charming, warm, and engaging. People with this disorder may also have a cruel and violent side. Those who experience the charming side (Dr Jekyll) think that those who describe the cruel side (Mr Hyde) are out to lunch.

I am not qualified to diagnose, but the features of those with antisocial personality disorder are remarkably descriptive of someone I know.

Friday, 18 June 1993
At my university, five courses an academic year is considered full-time. With overload status and summer school, I finished eight courses this calendar year, kept Dean's list status, worked part-time, was a parent to a teen, maintained our home, and attended weekly counselling. I managed all this in spite of problems with losing big chunks of time, flashbacks, night terrors and not sleeping well. My progress pleases me. I am going to be okay.

Sunday, 15 August 1993
Being in Moose Jaw to be with Alida for her wedding is a bittersweet time. The sweetness is that her husband is a kind and gentle man, and their deep love is obvious. The wedding is lovely, and the bride is stunning.

Alida neither invited her father nor wants him at the wedding, but worries he will show up. Alida's husband and his friends assure her that if Mr Fred appears, he will either leave in a body cast or a body bag. Alida feels safe, for which I am thankful.

The bitterness is my burden to carry alone. At the ceremony, I feel very sad about Alida not having a father to walk her down the aisle. My beautiful daughter deserved so much better than she had, and my guilt makes a vivid appearance. As she walks toward an adult life in Moose Jaw, I have to set free the hope that she will come back home.

Tuesday, 21 September 1993
I think Kevin is going to be okay. At school he is on the honour roll and involved in extra-curricular activities. He has two part-time jobs, spends a fair bit of time with his friends, and is a helpful, well-behaved young man. What positively influenced Kevin was when his uncle, my brother Bart, took my son under his wing. Bart and his family invite Kevin to join them on special outings and occasions. When he needs some fatherly advice, Kevin turns to Bart for guidance. I cannot adequately express my gratitude to my brother for what he does for my son.

Fall classes are in full swing again and I find I am able to manage our finances well enough to ensure we have all we need.

Today I saw my family doctor and, after scares and treatments, I finally got an all-clear on my well woman check-up. There is no longer any indication of precancerous cells.

Tuesday, 23 November 1993
Aside from filing the Notice of Appeal, Fred has done nothing more about it. We bring a motion to the court to dismiss it for delay. The judge dismisses the appeal and, hallelujah, grants a Divorce Judgment Order. It has taken me six years and three months of slogging through Family Court to go from separation to divorce.

Now I only have some property issues to settle. Fred refuses to sell the Parry Sound lot, so I plan to stop paying the property taxes. Eventually the taxman will ensure this comes to a head. Via their lawyer, we prod my in-laws' to resolve their lawsuit, but get no response.

New Years' Day, 1994
Kevin and I had a liberating Christmas day. We broke from tradition with no tree, decorations, gifts, or turkey dinner. Instead, we had a pizza party. Celebrating Christmas in a way that felt right to us was freeing.

We have not seen much of the Kettles lately, but Kevin and I attended their annual Boxing Day family dinner. To avoid the adults, I spent most of the time playing games with my nieces and nephews.

This past year, Dorothy got a job and moved her kids to Plaster Bay, New Brunswick, and we have hardly spoken since. The chasm between us started when she would only "kind of" tell me what had happened with Fred, and it widened when I found out she dated Gus.

Dorothy's two daughters are spending the Christmas holidays with their grandparents. When I ask Nakita about their travel, she says, "Aunt Carlyn, can you help us? We don't like Gus and are scared of him. Why does he have to drive us home?"

I had not known that Dorothy was still hanging out with Gus, not that it is my business. I do consider it my business that my niece asks my help to feel safe.

Classes will not start for another week, giving me time to do something to help the girls. I phone Dorothy with an offer that I come for a visit and drive her daughters home. Dorothy will not hear of it. She believes her daughters are not fearful, but just manipulative and interfering with her relationship. After all our family had been through, I beg her to listen to her children's feelings. Dorothy ends the discussion with, "My decision is that Gus will drive them home, and that is that."

I return to the Kettle farm to plead with them on behalf of the girls. Mom and Dad think I am unreasonable for asking them to take a stand. Just because I take issue with Gus does not mean they do; in fact, they like him. They know he drilled holes in my floor and they know their granddaughters are scared of him, but they will do nothing. If there were a snowstorm during their fourteen-hour trip home, the girls could be stranded in a hotel with the man, and for some reason the Kettles are okay with that possibility.

"No, ve are not going to interfere. It's up to Dorothy. She tinks it's fine so ve agree someone has to put a stop to de girls vrom making it difficult vor Dorothy to have friends."

It makes no sense to the Kettles that I am not saying for sure Gus will hurt the girls, but that the girls' expression of fear should be sufficient for the adults to listen. The Kettles have not learned a thing about creating an environment where kids have the freedom to exercise their intuitive faculties. I am mad, mostly at myself for being helpless and lacking the capacity to disrupt their oblivion.

In a final effort to shake them up, I blurt, "This answers a lot of questions for me. When I was little you didn't listen to me, either."

Amid the silence, Dad paces and rearranges dirt in the flowerpots.

"You don't care that your daughters and granddaughter were sexually abused, and you will do nothing to stop it from happening again. This is just wrong."

Mom cleans the house from top to bottom with Dutch vigour once a week. One is more likely to find gold nuggets than dust bunnies behind her couch, yet Dad goes down on his knees with his back to me and pushes his head behind the couch, acting as if he sees something lurking there.

Mom says, "If you are going to talk about abuse, den you have to tell us who did it to you."

Dad dives deeper behind the couch until only his feet show.

"I will, when I am ready."

They both walk me to the door and stand there waving and calling out, "Goodbye honey, ve love you! Come back vor an udder visit with your mudder and vader soon."

Saturday, 30 July 1994

If Dorothy and I had any hope for our relationship improving, today we blew that apart. She is visiting and we meet in town for lunch. When I get there, we sit in silence for a few moments until she asks, "So, how are you? How's school and what have you been up to?"

I cut right to the chase. "Dorothy, before we begin, I want an apology for last Christmas."

She gives me a saccharine smile. "There is nothing for me to apologize for. You overreacted."

"Let me know when you are prepared to say sorry. I have nothing to say to you until then."

Our lunch is over before the server takes our food orders.

How can I convince my sister that a child's intuition is a precious skill for a parent to nurture? Does my sister know how to access the knowing she was born with? Because we grew up in the same family, it is fair to surmise that my parents' suppression of my inner wisdom also quashed hers. Unfortunately, our parents were unable to teach us what they did not know, and we cannot teach our children what we do not know. It is tragic that it took me so long to learn, and I can only hope that I did so in time to teach my children that their intuition is a gift worth nurturing and (I may have said this before) that their safety is a fundamental right.

I have given a lot of thought to the attributes of intuition or what I call creep radar. What was the stimulus that stirred me from living a detached existence where I accepted too much and did not fight for what, deep inside, I knew was true? Learning my husband had abused my sisters and daughter was not the catalyst of my awakening, but the consequence of a process I had already begun.

One evening, in the fall of 1986, I took a risk and lied to Fred when I told him I was going to a Tupperware party. Instead, I attended a seminar about loneliness sponsored by one of the Reformed churches in Abingville. Up to then, all my efforts to improve my situation focused on my marriage. Going to this event was my first attempt to change myself.

The speaker challenged our Calvinist view that good Christians only have positive attributes. God accepts us as we are. Nowhere in the Bible does it say that we are always to be bubbly and happy, and if we hide behind a façade that everything is positive, we remain unknown and alienated from others. The speaker encouraged us to be honest about all aspects of who we are, thereby giving ourselves the opportunity to foster genuine connection. While the speaker put his message in a religious context, I believe that the lesson is true for anyone who feels isolated. For me at the time, the talk gave me a roadmap to open the door of the lonely cage in which I was trapped.

After the talk, we gathered for social time in the church basement. I found myself standing beside an acquaintance, a man who attended our CRC and taught at the Christian school my children attended. With a coffee in hand, we chatted about the seminar.

Then I dove headfirst into a sincere effort to be genuine, and said, "I, too, am often lonely."

"I don't believe it. You and Fred have it all. Your family always looks happy together. You can't be lonely." At that moment, I felt even more isolated.

All this man did was accept the superficial, fake version of our family that I worked so hard to maintain. My oh-so-bright smile successfully camouflaged the awful secrets of my marriage and my crippling feelings of disconnection and guilt. I realized I was living a lie and, therefore, I was the creator of my own misfortune. What this interaction provided me was a nudge that launched me toward immense change. In psychology, it is called "the butterfly effect," where small changes in thinking can alter the course of one's life over time.

The nudge led me to honestly look at my life. That in turn helped me to listen to my inner knowing, my intuition, and from there I started paying attention to dreams. Then a snowball effect occurred where I came to appreciate that I was not safe (understanding the meaning of the concentration camp dreams) and my children were not safe either (the nasty bedroom dream). Ultimately, I came to the place where a nightmare (the nuclear war dream) prepared me to open my eyes to what I needed to see, and having the strength to make the critical decision to leave Fred. That changed our lives. As they say, the rest is history.

Monday, 15 August 1994
When Kevin graduated high school, he moved to Moose Jaw to begin his adult life and to spend time with his sister. My son is a stable young man who is finding his way. I am a very proud mudder.

Wednesday, 15 March 1995
The proposal for my PhD thesis is worked out. Using a feminist approach, I will interview non-offending mothers (n=60) between

two and ten years after disclosure of their child's sexual abuse. It will be a quantitative study exploring the relationship between the mother's support systems (according to a spectrum of helpful, neutral, or harmful) in their efficacy to mitigate maternal trauma responses to their children's sexual abuse. I will recruit mothers to interview by asking all the agencies and organization we were involved with to refer participants. Mothers participating will be invited to join a twelve-week support group that will be co-facilitated by a colleague who will study the efficacy of the group.

I am in the middle of the literature review examining what is known about how mothers respond to their children's molestation. A summary of what I learn is that typically, non-offending mothers' reactions and issues include anger, guilt, fear of damage done to their children, fear of consequences from the offender, blame by extended family and friends, PTSD symptoms, clinical depression, intrusive thoughts, generalized fears, sleep and eating disturbances, increased hospitalizations, and suicide attempts. Adverse experiences such as domestic violence or sexual abuse are known to significantly increase risk of cancer in both mothers and children.

After going through the court process, 80 percent of non-offending mothers would not report the sexual abuse of their child if it occurred again, and 75 percent of mothers reported spousal abuse. Of all non-offending mothers, 41 percent reported their own sexual abuse as children, and they found their child's abuse was particularly traumatic and intense as they relived their own painful emotions.

Learning this information gives me the same feeling I had when I read the pamphlet at the CAS so many years ago. It is still a relief that I am not abnormal. In preparing for my thesis, I was aware that choosing this topic was of personal interest and therapeutic. Initially, I worried this over-identification might be a problem, but in paying close attention to what my classmates were studying, I realized most of us chose topics based on our own experiences. I will discuss it with my faculty supervisor to make sure I do not trip over my own blind spots. By learning and growing, those things in life that touch us deeply become our passions, and those often include a measure of pain. Facing our greatest sorrow can become our greatest gift.

Friday, 24 March 1995
When I discovered my husband had been molesting girls in our families, a flood of practitioners, organizations, and agencies became involved. They all, for better or worse, came to be part of my family's village. I put together this list for my thesis and it surprises me that I was able to cope with all these people. No wonder I felt as overwhelmed as I did in negotiating between all of them at the same time I was parenting and managing my own reactions.

- Task Force for Domestic Violence, pilot project
- Children's Aid Society (CAS)
- City of Abingville Police
- Abingville Women's Centre
- Office of the Children's Lawyer
- Criminal court lawyers
- Family court lawyers
- Civil court lawyers
- Criminal court judges
- Crown Attorney for each criminal court case
- Civil court
- Family court
- Youth court
- Adult probation
- Youth probation

- Support and Custody Enforcement Branch of the Ministry of the Attorney General
- Welfare/Social Assistance/Ontario Works
- Family Allowance which, along with other social programs, was later folded into the Child Tax Benefit.
- Ontario Student Assistance Program (OSAP)
- Youth Counselling Services
- Mental Health Clinic
- Private practice therapists
- Sexual Assault Services
- Additional school supports for the children
- Chiropractor
- Medical doctors, including paediatrician, allergist, and gynecologist
- Psychiatrists
- Psychologist
- Churches & Clergy

It is impossible to calculate the personal financial losses and costs I paid out of pocket to carry myself and my children through the trauma of incest and domestic violence. In addition to our personal expenditures, there were massive costs incurred by the agencies and organizations involved. In our situation, the total cost must be multiplied by the number of those Fred victimized.

> There comes a point where we need to stop
> just pulling people out of the river.
> We need to go upstream and find out why they're falling in.[15]

Despite all the services and costs, there is no evidence that the risk this one man presented declined. It is more likely the risk of his re-offending increased. There is no simple solution, but it will

---

[15] Desmond Tutu.

take collective effort to find ways whereby our resources for sexual abuse and domestic violence are not only for mopping up after the damage has been done, or for pulling people out of the river. As a village, we need to each find our place where we can stand upstream and stop women and children from falling into the river.

Wednesday, 15 November 1995

I finished my coursework, completed the interviews with non-offending mothers, and wrote my thesis. My dissertation has been defended and the last step before becoming a fully qualified psychologist is to do a one-year internship. The child protection agency where my family received services has amalgamated with the children's counselling agency, and I am very fortunate their staff psychologist has agreed to be my field supervisor.

In part, I chose this organization to help me understand the rules and forces that caused child welfare to treat us as they had, both positive and negative. To ensure there will be no future surprises for the agency or myself, I make sure that during the entry interview, they are aware I was a previous client. I want to know up front if it matters. It turns out that my having relevant lived experience is actually a plus, not a negative. My file will remain locked in the executive director's office for confidentiality throughout the duration of my time with the agency.

I now have a desk in the same office building in Abingville where my family received services. The scummy ugly orange furniture is still in the waiting room, the table that Alida hid under is still in the corner of the visiting room, and Maggie is still in the same office at the end of the hall where she interviewed my kids.

Tuesday, 9 January 1996

Seven years ago, I officially left the church, but the church has not left me. I continue to feel every bit as hurt by the congregation and the *dominee* as I had been. I want to forgive the church, the Kettles, and of course Fred, but it is still impossible. Token statements of forgiveness are useless; they sound magnanimous, but the anger bubbles up again within minutes to burst my good intentions.

I have begged God to take away the hard feelings and God remains silent on this topic. Forcing myself to forgive makes me feel worse. There is no room for forgiveness within me, and in all honesty, I doubt if there ever will be.

Wednesday, 13 March 1996
A few weeks ago, I made an appointment to discuss with the Kettles how I felt about their treatment of me. I guess I had to beat my head against that wall one last time.

They deny ever harming me, including the bare bum spankings and the application of Vicks during puberty. The Kettles believe my secular therapist put ideas in my head and gave me False Memory Syndrome. Mom is bewildered that she is included in the discussion and asks what any of this has to do with her. The Kettles feel they are above reproach in how they parented me and how they helped my family, and that includes taking my daughter from me.

I am in the same place I always was and can clearly see for the first time that despite the Kettles' best efforts, they were not available to me in the way I needed them.

Friday, 14 June 1996
One of my mother's brothers, not one of the funny uncle-duo, drops by for a visit. I pour him a coffee, and before he takes a sip, it is evident that his objective is to have me forgive the Kettles and repair our relationship. "Honour your father and mother." That may have been true when I was a child, but now that I am an adult, I believe that I must first honour myself and my children. My poor uncle gets nowhere with me.

Before my intensely religious uncle leaves, he asks whether I mind if he reads the Bible and prays with me. Not too sure about his intentions, I say I do mind. I will not let myself get cornered into a situation like what had happened with the *dominee* ever again. My uncle is dismayed that I strayed so far from my CRC roots. He is entitled to think I am lost. I know that I am not.

Friday, 21 June 1996
Life is the most normal I have ever enjoyed. My relationship with my children is good. They are grown up and moving along their own paths.

I know that my personal experiences have a lot to do with how I approach my clinical work. More than a few times, clients have told me I am different because I understand. They have no idea how much I really do understand.

Maintaining emotional stability is an ongoing effort, and my success varies. Last night I had a vivid nightmare. In it, Fred again had the abortion machine going, chewing up my insides. This time I recognize that this recurrent nightmare is actually about his rape of me twenty-five years ago in my rented room.

Intellectually, I know that I was not to blame for being date raped. However, deep in my heart where guilt festers, I have always felt that the rape was my fault because I did not say "no" at the exact moment Fred penetrated me. Today is the first time I can put aside the guilt when I remember that we had been dating for two and a half years by then. I had said "no" over and over on every date, which would have been hundreds if not thousands of times. That evening, prior to the rape, I had said "no" repeatedly for two and a half hours, while he kept after me to have sex. He knew I wanted to marry as a virgin, that is why he chose an aggressive method to get what he wanted. There is no way that Fred could have believed for a second that my silence at the moment of the rape implied consent.

By putting aside the guilt, I feel even more anger toward Fred than usual for all the violations he perpetrated. I want to scream so everyone knows what my children and I survived, but there are many forces compelling me to only whisper. On a protective level, it is taboo for mothers to talk about their sisters' or daughters' abuse because when they talk, it exposes the experiences of the girls. That mothers are burdened to remain silent is only a problem because in our hierarchical society, blame is downloaded on to the victimized, who most often are female. It is difficult for mothers to protest in solidarity with their sisters and daughters as long as talking about being victimized carries even a sliver of social disgrace. If all shame was firmly attributed to the offenders, as a mother, I could claim the right to express to the world about how angry I really am, and why.

I have had people ask me how I could let Fred live. In the question, I hear insinuations that I did not care enough for my children to kill the man who harmed them. It sounds to me they are saying I failed as a mother.

Ironically, I have not murdered Fred because my trust in the criminal justice system remains non-existent. Nine years ago, I had no reason to trust that the law would excuse a murdering wife. More recently, Karla Homolka appears to have used the battered woman syndrome defence successfully, but her bargaining power was information about Paul Bernardo. I have nothing of value to bargain with.

An even more important motive for not murdering Fred was because, over and over, I made the decision that being a mother was a much more important task than exacting revenge. All the same, I am as angry today as I was then. At work, I dress in business casual attire that includes a façade of tranquillity. Underneath, the anger continues to fester.

I have biked thousands of miles hoping for the wind to blow away my rage. I have ranted and raved in the woods, screamed along to loud music, worked out, meditated, prayed, lamented, cried, cried some more, smashed an old lawn mower to bits with a baseball bat, burned Bibles, and gone for more hours of counselling than would be considered decent. Still, the anger roils unabated.

Because journaling has been therapeutic in the past, I pick up my pen and the words pour out as if they had been lying dormant, just waiting for an opportunity to be heard. What comes out is a violent revenge fantasy. This is a last-ditch effort to heal the rage. It expresses the ugly truth of my pent-up feelings.

(Sensitive content warning) I will start my revenge by shooting him through the knees to stop him in his tracks and then chop off his groping hands. I will punish him by scooping out his leering eyes and cut his wicked tongue out of his mouth. He will get a bath in lye with a washcloth of sandpaper until every pore burns. To make sure he is clean inside and out, using his own medical equipment I will give him a 3H bleach enema: high, hot, and a helluva lot.

Then I will administer a dose of truth serum and interrogate him, recording every confession and sharing it with each person he harmed to give them validation. Mr Talker will talk to his heart's content, and every time he makes it someone else's fault, I will poke him with an electric cattle prod until he learns to be responsible for himself.

The final step in the fantasy is to taunt him with plans for a titillating party. The invitation list will be the 3,287 men he is most in awe of, the roughest and toughest prison inmates who detest child molesters. There will be one man for each day since I first learned what he had done.

"Oh Fred. It will be the most awesome swinging encounter you ever experienced. I am doing it all for you.

You are going to be the star of the party, the main attraction. Oh, it will be to die for, just imagine how it will feel when they..., and then when they do..."

I will leave before the party starts because swinging never has been my thing.

Sunday, 4 August 1996
Dorothy's daughters spend the summer at the Kettle dairy farm. Nakita asks if I had anything to do with her grandparents driving her and her sister back to Plaster Bay after their Christmas visit. I never knew the Kettles did that. I guess I raised enough of a ruckus about the transportation arrangements that they felt cornered into responding.

"Thank you, Aunt Carlyn, I always knew you were behind it. You were the only one who listened to us."

How sad is that? I might not have done much, but it pleases me that Nakita experienced someone listening and responding to her fears.

Tuesday, 10 September 1996
Thirty years ago, in our small Christian elementary school, six girls graduated from grade eight. Yesterday, one of these girls was murdered by her husband. He killed her in their home on the main street of Oregon, next door to the house Dorothy and her husband had built.

This man was suave and charmed many, including the Kettles, and he too thought he was above the law. After he brutally murdered her, the coward tried to make it look like an accident. He did not outsmart the law, but now with their mother in the grave and their father in custody, my classmate's children are orphaned.

Monday, 30 September 1996
It was time to sever my last ties to Fred and his parents. My lawyer contacted my in-law's lawyer again to see where that lawsuit stood. Again, we got no reaction, so we filed a motion to dismiss. We got a court date where neither Fred, his parents, or their lawyer showed up, and the judge dismissed the case. That was one matter wrapped up.

There was the log house and property still to deal with. I asked my lawyer to facilitate the sale of the log house property, even if it meant bringing another motion to court. After his typical objections, a new "friend" of Fred's bought it. It does not matter a hoot to me if the devil himself now owns the property in Parry Sound. I am finally free of the last financial link to Fred.

After paying my lawyer the last of his legal fees, I have enough money left over to pay off my student loans. I leave my past with no outstanding legal issues, no debt, and an education no one can take away. My lawyer smiles when he says he is sorry to close my case, since he had been counting on me for his annuity. No doubt. He also says it was the most acrimonious divorce he ever heard about. That is a distinction I would rather not have experienced, but it validates the absurdity of how difficult it was to leave Fred.

I, too, am sorry to say goodbye. I mean it when I tell him he was the best, and I made it through only because he had my back every step of the way. I assure him that he deserved every dollar he earned. I was well-represented and am satisfied with how I conducted myself. My gentle and steady lawyer levelled out my extremes, understood my moral ground, and helped me end my marriage with my integrity intact.

Sunday, 1 December 1996
I thought I was slipping backward when I wrote the revenge fantasy. In retrospect, it was cathartic. Putting my feelings onto paper

created distance and decreased their intensity. For many years, I struggled with daily thoughts of self-harm and suicidal ideation. It was a long battle between my will to live and the lure of death. The last time I had self-destructive thoughts were the moments before I wrote the fantasy.

Boxing Day, 1996

Alida, her husband, and Kevin all come home to spend Christmas with me. We had a wonderful time. Kevin borrowed my car today to visit his father and his new family. When he comes home, he gives us an update.

Kevin met Angel and he says she seems nice. Kevin learned that Angel and her former husband lived on a chicken farm. Because they could not have children, they became foster parents with a plan to adopt. When her husband died in a traumatic farm accident, Angel sold the farm, moved into town, and kept right on fostering. Fred and Angel married two years ago. Right now, in their home, they have a two-year-old boy with Down Syndrome, his baby sister, and eight-year-old twin girls that Angel has fostered since they were little. Last spring, Fred and Angel adopted the twins. My kids want to know how this might be possible, so I tell them:

> Just to be clear, because of my personal connection with your dad, when I was doing my psychology internship at CAS, I removed myself from anything to do with this foster family. Now that I am in private practice, I have no connection whatsoever with him or his new family. Therefore, what I say is based only on what I know from our divorce and an educated guess as to what could have happened later.
>
> In 1987, after being criminally charged, a psychologist reported he was a very smart man at no risk to reoffend.

Your father used the report to get his sexual assault charge plea bargained to a common assault with a one-year term of probation.

I am pretty sure he used the same report to convince CAS he was safe for unsupervised visits, and again in family court where the judge granted him unsupervised access to both of you. Alida, you refused to see him; the last visit you had with him was in April 1988 when you spent the whole time sitting under a table. When he was still on probation, he already talked about plans to get his criminal record expunged. These things I know for sure.

Please understand that I am now venturing into conjecture. If your father followed through, his criminal record could have been expunged as early as 1994. When he moved in with Angel, he minimally would have needed to apply to CAS for permission to live in Angel's house. It sounds like he applied for foster parent status. The worker would have processed his application under Angel's file, and with an expunged criminal conviction of simple assault, and a few years of clean living (or not being caught), CAS would have approved his application to foster. I am not aware how far a CAS worker would or could go searching in our family records from 1987, but even if they did, they would have found the psychologist report that he was not a risk. He would have appeared all-around clean to foster little children.

With two girls eating up space in an already overcrowded foster system and a family willing to give them a forever home, it is entirely possible that Angel and Fred, as good foster parents, would have had the adoption approved quickly. Within child welfare legislation, the CAS adoption worker would have covered all her bases. What could go wrong?

My kids roll their eyes. They know.

New Year's Day, 1997

A new year has arrived and the strangest thing happened. I wake up this morning thinking, "I'm so glad I am who I am, and if it wasn't for having the experiences I had, I wouldn't be me. At this moment, I am not angry at anyone, and I think that I have quite forgiven the whole lot of them."

The thought startles me and I question it all day. It still sticks. That forgiveness happened so quickly is quite a surprise. For the first time, I have forgiven Fred and my family. I have let go of the need to get even and have given up waiting for karma. I do not expect to continue to feel this good from now on, but at least I have a glimpse of what it feels like with the shackles of anger removed.

A barrier to forgiving Fred has been the worry that it would appear I was excusing the harm he caused others. Now I realize any forgiveness I can offer only relates to what he did to me as his girlfriend, wife, the mother of his children, and the oldest of my sisters. I cannot forgive on anyone else's behalf. My forgiveness does not discount their experiences.

Ten years ago, I would have said that I had a great childhood. Now I see that some parts were good and some were not. As I came to grips with what was not good, I was angry. Now that my anger is spent I can see that, in spite of the pain my parents caused me, they did the best they could with what they were given.

Through the eyes of the woman I have become, I can see that my parents lived their own challenges and struggles, making them who they are. My mother grew up in a home where religious fanaticism gave them conviction that they knew right from wrong, and a sense of comfort that they were always right. That certainty is not easy to give up. My father grew up with a sick mother, a bully of a father, and the trauma of sexual abuse that he carried silently for fifty years.

They grew up in a culture that devalued daughters. Both survived the losses and terror of WWII as young teens in occupied Holland, and yet they were parents full of hope when they immigrated to Canada. Their focus was to work hard and make a good life for their growing family. Within five years of starting over in a new country, their baby Frances died. Since there is no recovery from the death of a child, this loss is part of them. This is the tinderbox of vulnerabilities that I was born into and Fred took great advantage of.

If I put myself in my parent's shoes, perhaps it was inevitable that they could not absorb more pain when they learned a man they trusted had harmed their daughters and granddaughter. I can somewhat understand why they made the choices they did and I forgive them. Understanding is not agreeing, and forgiving is not forgetting. I will never forget and never want to because I am thankful for surviving and learning. It satisfies me that, although I also did not give my children all they needed, I too gave them the very best that I could. I hope that when it is my children's time to look back on their lives through their adult eyes, they will be able to forgive me for the ways I was not the mother they needed.

Wednesday, 26 February 1997
Angel phoned me at the office to ask if I would meet her for lunch, which we did today. She was able to find me because she had heard from Kevin that I was in private practice.

Angel has a sad story. I always thought that if Fred had not married me, someone else would have lived that life instead of me, and another woman and her children would have been victimized. Talking to Angel confirmed that. It was as if I was talking to a younger version of myself and her story and mine blended into one.

Angel met Fred shortly after her husband died. Fred was so charming and she fell for his charisma, at least for a while. When they met, she was twenty years younger than Fred and looked up to him. He was so sure of himself and so smart. He always had money to spend on them. She thought he was a catch.

Fairly early in their relationship, he had taken Angel and the twins on a trip to Disney World in Florida. The girls were still in foster care at that time and CAS approved the vacation. They thought it was so nice of Fred to take the girls at his expense. While they were in a motel in Orlando, with the twins who were then five years old in the bed beside them, he raped her the same way he had me. When he finished, she went to shower and he followed her into the bathroom with his camera and took nude photos. To protect the girls, she had remained silent during the rape and the aftermath.

The following day, he carried on with their vacation as if the rape never happened and was super nice to her. Angel said she had not invited him to live with her, but he somehow got CAS permission, changed his address, and the next thing she knew he weaselled his way into their home. When the girls became available for adoption, Fred convinced her that her chances of being given the twins were better if she was married, so she agreed.

After they adopted the girls, it did not take him long to resume his nastiness. He threatened to show CAS, her minister, and her parents the nude pictures he had taken unless she had a threesome with him and Lawyer Buddy. She did. It was awful. Now he says it was her idea and uses it to control her. She is sick of his blame, name-calling, manipulation, porn, his hounding for swinging encounters, and all his peccadilloes. His behaviour has persisted indistinguishable from what I experienced with him.

Back in September, when she told him she wanted a divorce, he threatened to kill her. It never dawned on her to call the police. She will not do so now because she finally got him out of the house on New Year's Day and she does not want to piss him off.

She applied for interim custody of the twins and so did Fred, of course. The judge ordered interim joint custody. Fred was also successful in his motion that Angel has to submit to a parental capacity assessment. Apparently, he learned from his experience with me how to use the courts to his advantage. Fred has the twins now. He was to return them on Sunday but is refusing, claiming he cannot because one time, in their kitchen, he saw Angel sexually abuse the little boy with Down Syndrome.

Fred repeatedly told Angel that I made false allegations of him sexually abusing Alida and damn near my whole family. He claimed he got a common assault conviction for defending himself when I stole his car and attacked him. It seems that ever since they met, he often complained of how awful I was and how I had shafted him. She had thought I was a real bitch. Now she wants to know what actually happened.

After I tell Angel enough so she gets the idea, she starts to worry about the twins. Fred refers to both as "*Princess*," as if they are one girl, each without her own identity. He gives them flowers on their birthday, Fred has special secrets with them, and the girls told Angel he got a new camera to take pictures of them when they are having a bubble bath or in bed. This is horrifying. He is using the same modus operandi, with deviation into now producing child porn. There is every reason to worry about those children. Angel agrees to tell CAS what she knows.

Appreciating better than anyone what Angel is up against, I offer to show up for her. After work, I meet Angel at her lawyer's office, give the relevant historical information, and swear an affidavit to explain to the judge in their family court proceedings what I, as Fred's ex-wife, know about Fred's history of sexual offending.

The Count:
- eight confirmed (my sisters Grace, Helen and Irene, my daughter Alida, Fred's sister Allison, Fred's cousin Jeannie, me/Carlyn, and Angel),
- two attempted (my sisters Ellie and Juliana), and
- eleven suspected (the teenage store employee, Fred's former girlfriend, our customer's daughter, my niece Nakita, Fred's Dutch cousin, my sister Dorothy, Drunken Buddy's three daughters, and Fred and Angel's twin daughters)

Thursday, 1 May 1997
Angel gets in touch to update me after their final family court appearance. She is devastated. Fred had managed to get an order for the Office of the Children's lawyer representation for the twins, and the girls told the lawyer they wanted to live with their Daddy because he is always so much fun. Angel said Fred had met with the psychologist who did her parenting capacity assessment and he lied about many things, including her mental health. He used true information about when she was grieving her husband's death and spun it to his own end. In family court, he also used his recycled assessment reports. They again served him well.

Fred was awarded sole custody of the twins. So many years later, and the consequence of society's silence, lackadaisical or even incompetent professionals, and an inept criminal justice system has handed Fred two girls to bring home and do with as he pleases. Their mother did her best to protect her daughters, but she was overruled. If it takes a village to raise a child, it takes a village to protect one.

For Angel, things got worse. Fred gave CAS a copy of the parenting capacity assessment report. Based on that report, CAS placed Angel on hold from fostering until the psychologist gives her a positive re-evaluation. Angel lost custody of her twins to Fred, CAS took away the little fellow who has Down Syndrome and his baby sister, and her livelihood is suspended.

I feel so bad for Angel because, to the extent one woman can understand another's circumstances, I know what she is suffering. However, I am certain we will not maintain contact in the future. It is too difficult for both of us. For me, it is better to steer clear of Fred. For Angel, it is better she has no contact with me because it will anger Fred, and he will make her pay by denying access. Now Angel, the CAS, and the courts will have to do their part to ensure the safety of Angel's daughters.

I have been fully aware of the risks I took by becoming involved. It may appear that I totally lost my marbles. Maybe I did, but I think not because my heart feels content.

Friday, 16 May 1997
From CAS, I requested the opportunity to review my file. There are a few things remaining unresolved for me, and my CAS involvement is one of them. I receive a date and time to read the redacted file. They will not provide me copies. It is quite uncomfortable to sit in a small office for several hours with a CAS supervisor. In the hierarchy of the agency organizational chart, when I was doing my internship, my name had been above hers.

My solution to being denied copies is to bring a tape recorder. I abide by their condition of only reading the file, although clearly not in the way they intended. From my involvement at the agency, I know what a file contains. What they show me is only a meagre fraction. I am not allowed to read any case notes. All I get to see are recordings, and even then, more than half are blacked out. I will never know what secrets about me remain hidden from me.

What strikes me is the discrepancies between what I knew and what workers knew or believed they knew. There are many reasons for that. One is because it is impossible for a worker to understand all the nuances of a family's history in a few visits; the best they can do is an approximation. A second reason is that any worker comes with their own biases. In Bea's case, she had a thing about anger and bitterness, and she evaluated my parenting through the lens of those biases. A third reason is that CAS workers get information from various sources, and not all perspectives are complete or accurate. The final reason that my CAS file differed from my reality was, that although I never lied by commission, I sure did my best to hide by omission. The CAS has the power of God, and in order to protect my family from that power harming us, I tried to keep the worst of what was happening from them.

While sitting in the office reading, I do not want to show any emotion for fear the supervisor will interrupt the tape recording. A few times I have a hitch in my voice and tears quietly roll down my cheeks. I learn that in addition to confessing that he abused Alida, Fred had admitted to much more.

In the July 1987 closing recording, I read, "The police intend to further investigate the matter regarding Mr Smit's involvement with other family members as well as this other person in the community." I have no idea who this person is. In the redacted file there is no evidence of follow up. I hope there was and that the "person in the community," like my sisters and Allison, was not marooned to deal with it alone.

Reading the June 1989 closing recording is a total shock. I learn that, "Mr Smit also admitted to having molested his wife's four younger sisters, Dorothy, Grace, Helen, and Irene, as well as his own sister Allison when they were in their teens." All along I was not sure that Dorothy was molested and it turns out I did her a disservice.

The Count:
- ten confirmed (my sisters Grace, Helen and Irene, my daughter Alida, Fred's sister Allison, Fred's cousin Jeannie,

me/Carlyn, Angel, a person in the community prior to 1987, and my sister Dorothy),
- two attempted (my sisters Ellie and Juliana), and
- ten suspected (the teenage store employee, Fred's former girlfriend, our customer's daughter, my niece Nakita, Fred's cousin in Holland, Drunken Buddy's three daughters, and Fred and Angel's twin daughters)

A decade ago, Allison told me Fred had raped her when she was a little girl. Her emotional struggles are ongoing, exacerbated by her family accusing her of fabrication. I contact Allison and let her know that today I found proof of her assault. This is phenomenal confirmation that overwhelms Allison in the best way possible. It would have made a world of difference to her if the police or CAS would have broken their silence and given her this validation a decade earlier. It would have helped her, and perhaps her family' denial would have shattered if they had known that Fred confessed. All the same, I feel thankful that I have the gift of proof for her, and hope it helps in her healing journey.

When the police interrogated Fred and he was going through his very brief truth-telling phase, he confessed to molesting Alida and six more girls. How could it be that police did no further follow up with the six girls and that they issued only one charge relating to Alida? Police may have their reasons (perhaps it was a means of plea bargaining, due to a cost/benefit analysis, or it was just easier that way), but their inaction has the appearance of those in positions of authority condoning sexual abuse, thereby allowing the perpetrator to go on and inflict further harm. Police and crown attorneys not only have the power to enforce laws, they have discretion whether the laws are even applied. The sexual abuse problem is not absence of law, but an absence of institutional determination to keep women and children safe.

Thursday, 22 May 1997

Another unresolved issue is the CRC. I cannot move forward as long as I still feel chains of guilt that I should have stayed loyal to my marriage. I know it stems from my upbringing and from the treatment by the CRC and their *dominee*. If I leave it unresolved, the shame will doom my future.

Since the resignation letter, I wrote dozens of journal entries about how angry I remain and as many speeches that I imagine giving from their pulpit. I have prayed hundreds of prayers that I be given the strength to forgive this institution and the *dominee*. Since none of it helped, it is time for something more concrete.

Because the *dominee* moved away, I make an appointment with the current Abingville CRC minister. He has never heard my name before, nor I his, but it turns out our relatives are relatives, a common occurrence in the Dutch CRC community. His wife is a second cousin to Bert and Bart's wives. I arrive at the parsonage office to drop off the pain and shame of the congregation's silence and their minister's mistreatment. I go to repair myself, not the relationship with the CRC.

This minister listens carefully as I give him a rundown of my story as it relates to his church. He admits that individual congregations, and the overarching body of the CRC, do not know how to deal with sexual abuse and they do so very poorly. I am shocked that he has the courage to say the *dominee* was out of line, and that he and the congregation abused my children and me. I was unable to use that word, thinking it was too harsh. Abuse.

"Sexual and spiritual abuse, both" he says.

When I am ready to leave, he asks if he may pray.

I think about it and relent, "Only on the condition that if I don't like what you are saying, I can say stop and you will."

It is unlikely anyone asked that of him before, but he is a good sport. His prayer is fine and the meaning for me is not in the words, but in confirmation that I will never again endure manipulation in the name of God.

My tears lead him to believe I still need help and he suggests therapy. I say nothing about how much therapy I have already had. Being in his office is therapeutic enough for the time being. When I leave the parsonage office for the last time, I feel lighter and stronger. Shedding the shame that I never should have dragged around in the first place is another huge step forward.

I did not skip home in delight. It has been a day of tears. What tragedy that all those CRC people, most of them decent folks, treated us in such an uncaring manner. It was a big loss for my children and me. Although I do believe in something that I alternately call God, Light, Higher Power or the Universe, I doubt I will ever again join organized religion. I cannot say never, just that it seems quite unlikely.

Saturday, 14 June 1997
We have a family wedding and our two "funny uncles" are there. I keep an eye on their movements and make sure to hover nearby when they skulk off down the hall toward the women's restroom. Today, if I can help it, no unsuspecting girl will be subjected to our uncles' harassment. The men are clearly not about to bother me or anyone else within my sight. They know I took a stand against Fred and that I also would hold them accountable, so now the risk for them has become too great. I am no longer a scared little mouse.

Come to think of it, it has been a long time since I have had any unwanted male attention. My intuition is strong and I back out of situations the moment I start feeling uneasy. Looking back at all of the sexually inappropriate or abusive situations I have endured, each of them was avoidable. In my situation, it would have taken me having a voice and a village that fostered safety. Fred would have stopped the date rape if I had dared to scream. I would never have been isolated with Opa in the middle of nowhere if my parents had listened to me voice objections about going there in the first place. Lawyer Buddy would have left me alone if he thought I would report him. What happened to me as a child would have been avoidable if I had caregivers who listened and responded appropriately.

The common denominator for all the incidents that I experienced is that first I did not have, and later I did not know I had, the right to demand safety. Anyone wanting to prey on the timid girl that I was could spot that vulnerability a mile away. Please do not misunderstand that I think I was to blame for anything that happened to me. It was never my fault and it is never the fault of a girl who is molested.

Most of my siblings are also at this family wedding. My brothers are still ready to quietly support me whenever I need their help. The outcome of my relationships with my sisters is less fortunate. Fred's arrival in our midst was a match in the tinderbox created by my parents' history, and the resulting fire burned my family to a shell of what it had once been. From my perspective, there are many factors complicating my relationship with my sisters, including the havoc wreaked by Fred's abuse, the Kettles' complicit silence, and my sisters' conspiracy with my parents to remove Alida from my care.

I do not know what issues my sisters have with me at this point, but suspect that one factor is that, in me, they still see the spouse of their abuser, a sister they thought knew of and condoned their molestation. A second issue is that they are angry I accused my parents of mistreatment. A third reason is that I kept my distance from the family for a few years to focus on my healing, and this, quite understandably, hurt and angered them. Of course, these are my thoughts and their views may be entirely different.

We never had professional help and now with time and distance, mending our relationships has grown unlikely. I can only hope that someday my sisters will read my diary, recognize that I did not know, and that when I found out, I loved them enough to take a stand. I have been angry with them for not telling me, yet I always understood that they could not have acted any different, no more than I could have. We all came out of the same broken family, and in each other we see the reflection of our scars. I hope someday, somehow, the echo of our history of survival will resonate between us and the dormant seed of love I feel for them will have an opportunity to blossom.

Back when I was on a mission to find all of those Fred victimized, I asked Dorothy if her daughter Nakita might have been molested. Nakita was at the wedding and pulled me aside to have a chat in the restroom. She wanted me to know that Uncle Fred had molested her during those drives between her home and ours. No one asked her and she told no one. For her, this abuse started a spiral of other life challenges. When I tell Nakita I have evidence in my journals starting in 1987 that I had suspected, it provides her comfort that her Aunt Carlyn believes her.

The Count:
- eleven confirmed (my sisters Grace, Helen and Irene, my daughter Alida, Fred's sister Allison, Fred's cousin Jeannie, me/Carlyn, Angel, a person in the community prior to 1987, my sister Dorothy, and my niece Nakita),
- two attempted (my sisters Ellie and Juliana), and
- nine suspected (the teenage store employee, Fred's former girlfriend, our customer's daughter, Fred's Dutch cousin, Drunken Buddy's three daughters, and Fred and Angel's twin daughters)

With eleven girls victimized by Fred, as alarming as it is, he is nothing more than an average, run of the mill perpetrator. I realize the suspected column of my count may appear excessive, and yet it is realistic given that some offenders are known to have as many as seventy victims. When I placed each name there, I did so based on titbits of information and a whole lot of intuition, none of which is proof. To those named in that column, I want you to know that if my suspicions had validity, like with Jeannie, Dorothy, and Nakita, I have sincere empathy for you and am strong enough to listen to your story if you wish to tell me.

Friday, 20 June 1997
Tomorrow it will be a decade since the fateful day that I told my sister about one nightmare and she in turn told me about a situation that I could never have imagined. That was the time I came to a crossroads, a critical point, where everything came down to making one monumental decision that affected my family going forward. My choices were equally awful. I could either carry on as we were or ignite an explosion that I knew would have far-reaching consequences.

The path I took extracted heavy costs from all of us in terms of faith, family, friends, and finances. All the same, had I known then what I know now, I would choose my children's safety all over again. For better or worse, Alida and Kevin lived the ramifications of my decision and walked every step of this journey with me. My children are the true heroes in my story.

Saturday, 21 June 1997
The sun is shining and I have set aside today to celebrate that a decade ago I was able to get my children and myself to safety. Because I am in an introspective mood, I decide to take a drive to Oregon to visit the graves of those who have gone before. On the

way, I buy flowers for them and a coffee for me. I get white roses for innocence, a red rose for life blood, and white tulips.

My first stop is the angel headstone where underneath my baby sister Frances lies. I gently place the bouquet of white roses for her, and also in memory of my children gone too soon: my unborn baby and Alida who left home too young. I will always mourn our lost time together. While on the one hand I am able to look to the past, on the other I see the future with a great deal of hope. Alida just found out that she is pregnant with a baby girl, and I hope that having done my part will make this child's family a safe place.

Next I go to the grave of my murdered classmate and leave her the single red rose. We were born the same year, and she would have turned forty-four-years-old last week. I sit with her a while and think about all those who have died because of domestic violence: the years they probably lived in fear, and all the richness of life they missed.

I do not mean it as trite when I think, "There but for the grace of God go I." These words come to mind as respectful recognition, prayerful gratitude, of how blessed I am to have made it through alive.

The white tulips are for Opa's gravesite in memory of the of the flowers he and my Ketel ancestors grew in Holland, and more importantly as a gift of forgiveness for how he harmed me. I reach over to lay down the flowers and am surprised to see that Oma's death date is engraved on the tombstone. She died in 1995 and because I had distanced myself from the Ketel family for my own healing, no one informed me. I know Oma understands why I did not pay my last respects at her funeral. I will do it here today in my own way and trust she will hear me.

In the early 1990s, I notice the beginning stages of senility are kind to Oma. With dementia, Oma's protective walls come down and she is able to return my hugs for the first time in my life. With nothing much left to lose, she shares with me a few family secrets and allows her fears a small voice. One secret is that her mother had been from France, something that could explain why my darker complexion and slight stature is often mistaken for French rather than Dutch. Not being a blue-eyed blond, I stand out as different in our Dutch community. I remain unsure why having French blood in our veins is a secret. Another story, I am sure.

Oma tells me that she had also been sexually abused. I ask by who, and she says, "It was Opa. But nobody knows. You understand, ya, because of Fred?"

I assure Oma that I do understand, and ask her if there was anyone else. She nods again. "Who? Was it someone before you married Opa?"

Fear clouds Oma's eyes and her lips draw into a tight line. She gives one final slight nod. That is as much of the long-held secret that she can tell.

Learning this little bit of my Oma's history drives home the multigenerational nature of incest and sexual abuse within my family. That Oma also experienced it means that, in my family, sexual abuse began before I was born and the reverberations of it will go on in my family of origin, the family I married into, and my own children's lives until I am but a vague memory. It has gone on for four generations, starting with Oma, then my father, me and my sisters, and my daughter and niece. We can only heal what we know, so it is my hope that this knowledge will allow those younger than I to mend what still lies broken.

Telling me so much is all Oma can tolerate. When she is stressed, her dementia causes an obsession with time. She jumps up, oblivious of the wristwatch on her arm, to search through kitchen drawers, in the oven, and under the coffee pot to find it. I comfort Oma that there is still lots of time and she finds a moment of peace.

During some of her moments of lucidity, Oma gives me her best advice.

"Stay away vrom men like Fred, ya."

"You don't let men like dat hurt de kids."

"Keep fighting Carlyn, you keep fighting and you tell dem."

My grandmother and I hold hands in womanly understanding that transcends words. It is a holy moment as we draw comfort and strength from our shared legacy. I am blessed to have had that brief time with the Oma I never knew.

Oma's flitting confidences last no more than a few weeks until she again lapses into quietness. When she resumes her stoic silence, I hope her dementia allows her to blissfully forget her past, and not that her long-held shame regains a grip on her voice.

During the era Oma lived, silence was demanded, and she suffered for it. Her life, her emotional remoteness for most of the years I knew her, and her many illnesses were testament to the cost of silence. I was given much more than she ever had. Nowadays, women have a voice, although often only a feeble one, to protest abuse. I realize why she could not have been more of an Oma than she was, but in the end, she gives me more than I believe possible. My Oma adds her voice to mine and that gives me strength.

When I look into the sky on a dark night and see the brightest star twinkle, I think of Oma. She is cheering me on, urging me to speak of things she never could. Sometimes, when I am tempted to give up, I can hear her voice.

"Keep going, Carlyn. Tell. And make dem stop."

ACKNOWLEDGEMENTS

Completing a book, like raising a child, takes a community effort. I am grateful to my village who helped make my vision reality. Specific thanks to:

- Steve Oughtred for researching, sensitivity feedback, consistent encouragement, and for reading every single draft
- My children, who through support or opposition, steered me to an appreciation that a writer has the freedom to reveal their deepest truths in fiction
- Early and beta readers Maggie Rath (RIP), Lennie deMaat, Kelly Peterkin, Cindy Watson (author of *The Art of Feminine Negotiation* & *Out of Darkness*), David Patterson (author of *Square Wheels* & *Forthright but Furtive*), and to Linda Simpson and friends for holding the first unofficial book club meeting
- Kaitlyn Sutey, kaitlynjnsutey@gmail.com for editing
- Darlene Dafoe for the final proof reading
- Muskoka Authors Association www.muskokaauthors.ca, for extraordinary support

- The Saturday morning writers group in Bracebridge for helpful critique
- Nancy Beal (author of T*he Endurable Alex Tilley*) for the retreat at her lovely cottage
- Michael Duboff, Edwards Creative Law, www.edwardslaw.ca for legal direction and advise a few times along the way
- Ellie Sipila, Move to the Write, for cover design and production. www.movetothewrite.com

I would fail dismally if I were to try to name all others who supported and inspired me to tell this story. Your generosity has been immense and my gratitude knows no bounds. I may not be naming you, but I see you and thank each of you for being part of this incredible journey.

Printed in the USA
CPSIA information can be obtained
at www.ICGtesting.com
LVHW051115221124
797233LV00002B/158
9 781069 017505